D1799954

Cultural Studies and Transdisciplinarity in Education

Volume 15

Series Editors

Aaron Koh, Faculty of Education, The Chinese University of Hong Kong, Shatin, Hong Kong

Victoria Carrington, School of Education, University of Tasmania, Launceston, TAS, Australia

We live in a time where the complex nature and implications of social, political and cultural issues for individuals and groups is increasingly clear. While this may lead some to focus on smaller and smaller units of analysis in the hope that by understanding the parts we may begin to understand the whole, this book series is premised on the strongly held view that researchers, practitioners and policy makers interested in education will increasingly need to integrate knowledge gained from a range of disciplinary and theoretical sources in order to frame and address these complex issues. A transdisciplinary approach takes account the uncertainty of knowledge and the complexity of social and cultural issues relevant to education. It acknowledges that there will be unresolved tensions and that these should be seen as productive. With this in mind, the reflexive and critical nature of cultural studies and its focus on the processes and currents that construct our daily lives has made it a central point of reference for many working in the contemporary social sciences and education. This book series seeks to foreground transdisciplinary and cultural studies influenced scholarship with a view to building conversations, ideas and sustainable networks of knowledge that may prove crucial to the ongoing development and relevance of the field of educational studies. The series will place a premium on manuscripts that critically engage with key educational issues from a position that draws from cultural studies or demonstrates a transdisciplinary approach. This can take the form of reports of new empirical research, critical discussions and/or theoretical pieces. In addition, the series editors are particularly keen to accept work that takes as its focus issues that draw from the wider Asia Pacific region but that may have relevance more globally, however all proposals that reflect the diversity of contemporary educational research will be considered.

Series Editors:

Aaron Koh (The Chinese University of Hong Kong)
Victoria Carrington (University of Tasmania)

Editorial Board:

Angel Lin (Simon Fraser University, Canada), Angelia Poon (National Institute of Education, Singapore), Anna Hickey-Moody (RMIT, Australia),Barbara Comber (University of South Australia, Australia), Catherine Beavis (Deakin University, Australia), Cameron McCarthy (University of Illinois, Urbana-Champaign, USA), Chen Kuan-Hsing (National Chiao Tung University, Taiwan), C. J. W.-L. Wee (Nanyang Technological University, Singapore), Daniel Goh (National University of Singapore, Singapore), Jackie Marsh (University of Sheffield, UK), Jane Kenway (Monash University, Australia), Jennifer A Sandlin (Arizona State University, Tempe, USA), Jennifer Rowsell (University of Bristol, UK), Jo-Anne Dillabough, (University of Cambridge, UK), Megan Watkins (University of Western Sydney, Australia), Mary Lou Rasmussen (Australia National University, Australia), Terence Chong (Institute of Southeast Asian Studies, Singapore)

Book proposals for this series may be submitted to Associate Editor: Lay Peng Ang E-mail: laypeng.ang@springer.com

More information about this series at https://link.springer.com/bookseries/11200

Claire Lee • Chris Bailey
Cathy Burnett • Jennifer Rowsell
Editors

Unsettling Literacies

Directions for literacy research in precarious times

 Springer

Editors
Claire Lee (iD)
Children and Young People Network
Oxford Brookes University
Oxford, UK

Chris Bailey (iD)
Sheffield Institute of Education
Sheffield Hallam University
Sheffield, UK

Cathy Burnett (iD)
Sheffield Institute of Education
Sheffield Hallam University
Sheffield, UK

Jennifer Rowsell (iD)
School of Education
University of Bristol
Bristol, UK

ISSN 2345-7708   ISSN 2345-7716   (electronic)
Cultural Studies and Transdisciplinarity in Education
ISBN 978-981-16-6943-9   ISBN 978-981-16-6944-6   (eBook)
https://doi.org/10.1007/978-981-16-6944-6

© The Editor(s) (if applicable) and The Author(s), under exclusive license to Springer Nature Singapore Pte Ltd. 2022
This work is subject to copyright. All rights are solely and exclusively licensed by the Publisher, whether the whole or part of the material is concerned, specifically the rights of translation, reprinting, reuse of illustrations, recitation, broadcasting, reproduction on microfilms or in any other physical way, and transmission or information storage and retrieval, electronic adaptation, computer software, or by similar or dissimilar methodology now known or hereafter developed.
The use of general descriptive names, registered names, trademarks, service marks, etc. in this publication does not imply, even in the absence of a specific statement, that such names are exempt from the relevant protective laws and regulations and therefore free for general use.
The publisher, the authors and the editors are safe to assume that the advice and information in this book are believed to be true and accurate at the date of publication. Neither the publisher nor the authors or the editors give a warranty, expressed or implied, with respect to the material contained herein or for any errors or omissions that may have been made. The publisher remains neutral with regard to jurisdictional claims in published maps and institutional affiliations.

This Springer imprint is published by the registered company Springer Nature Singapore Pte Ltd.
The registered company address is: 152 Beach Road, #21-01/04 Gateway East, Singapore 189721, Singapore

Foreword

We are living in uncertain and turbulent times. For many of us, our very foundation has unraveled underneath us. We are struggling to achieve and understand what a post-global pandemic looks like. We are fighting for the humanity and lives of Black and Brown people. We are regrouping from political mayhem that has forced us to pay attention to how we internally and externally respond to what we believe and know to be true within ourselves. As a nation, we question the racial, economical, societal, mental, and educational parts of ourselves, that at times, seek to divide us.

Truth be told, we are burnt out. We have been subjected to the colonization and racism within society that has attempted to oppress us for years. We are faced with extant forces that affect our psyche while adulting through traumatic, horrific, anxious, and vulnerable times in familial, work, and social relationships. There is nothing normal about these spheres we find ourselves in today. To say that we need to go back to the normalcy of 2019 is a fallacy of truth – of opposing positions – to go back to what we have always known and hide behind what we are afraid to face. And we are still shifting. Everything about our lives is different and beautiful, complex and unique, and we need to recognize these visceral thoughts and feelings in our bodies, spirit, and soul.

What would it look like to face these uncertain times and how are they problematized in education, literacies, practices, praxis, and policy? In this book, *Unsettling Literacies: Directions for Literacy Research in Precarious Times*, Lee, Bailey, Burnett, and Rowsell address the truths and notions of how we might attempt to cope with literacy research during these uncertain times. They ask, "what [does] uncertainty mean for literacy research?" and I extend this question to include: *What roles do literacies play in lives of individuals during uncertain times*?

Each author in this volume speaks to how across many facets of their lives, as educators, researchers, and citizens, they choose to interpret literacies in ways that are unsettling – that cause them to embrace and deflect their perceptions of power structures and privilege in literacy research. To take an "archaeology of the self" (Sealy-Ruiz, 2020) means to dig deep within the self, to see how and why, and in what ways issues of literacies, racism, class, practices, power, teaching, sexual orientation, and music live and are disrupted inside of one's self.

While literacies are multiple, fluid, and complex, they move across narratives and practices to positively and negatively affect how we research, listen, move, and think. If 2020 and beyond has done anything for our individual lives, it has caused us to become more self-aware – aware of our situations, and how we are faced with uncertain and unsettling life moments – because life is cyclical in nature. Before the global pandemic, there was *Larnee*, my dissertation participant and research partner (Lewis, 2009). She described the unsettling and tumultuous times in her life of using digital literacies/tools to communicate, disseminate information, read, and write, learn, have fun, cope, and perceive literacy with her sons. As a survivor of a life-threatening skin disease and physical and sexual abuse, she shared how she engaged, slept with, and embraced digital tools as a coping mechanism. She used these tools as a way of making sense of and reconstructing her past and present histories and online and offline identities in multimodal spaces and everyday practices in her home (Lewis, 2011). In my research, she and her family's digital literacy practices did not diminish her experiences, but instead gave grace, humanity, and power to their lives. As a result, she demonstrated resilience, agency, and determination, showing the good in her life and practices.

Unsettling Literacies is calling for a realistic reckoning of recognizing literacy research vis-à-vis times, events, and things to come. This book will help us to rethink how we view and dismantle literacies, how we require new ways that literacies have spoken to us, and how we have failed literacies and certain literacy experiences around us. To understand *Unsettling Literacies*, one must recognize what is unsettling, the why, and what we plan to do with the unsettlingness within us before we enter into physically distanced, but socially safe classrooms, communities, and cultures.

Stuckey (1991) reminds us how the violence of literacy perpetuates injustice and is a system of oppression that works against certain societies and individuals who may not have the power to fight against these injustices and biases. Therefore, while reading this book, we should ask ourselves: *How will today's changing literacies remain meaningful to our research partners and research communities during unsettling times? How should we reclaim literacy research while centering on activism, community, and love during precarious times* (Haddix, 2019)? *In what ways do we take on a "knowledgeable agents of the digital" stance in digital literacy research that acknowledges the powerful, agentive, and candid realities and experiences with digital and non-digital texts that are reaffirming and salient* (Lewis Ellison, 2018, p. 88)? *How do we embrace uncomfortable and vulnerable literacies of Black pain, grief, and trauma in how Black and Brown bodies are read, not read, oppressed, and silenced in a white racist society* (Lewis Ellison & Qiu, 2022)? *How can we as researchers and educators embrace and dig deep into the "archaeologies of the self" before we begin research and praxis* (Sealy-Ruiz, 2020)?

These questions are uncomfortable, raw, and sensitive, but we are living in uncomfortable, raw, and sensitive times. We must hold ourselves accountable to the work we do, the actions we take, and the words we speak. We can no longer research in a juncture in which these entities are disconnected. We must recognize that in these precarious, unsettling times, in our literacies, and in our practices, "not everything that is faced can be changed, but nothing can be changed until it is faced" (Baldwin, 1968/2016).

Associate Professor, Department of Language   Tisha Lewis Ellison
and Literacy Education at
The University of Georgia in Athens, GA

References

Baldwin, J. (1968/2016). *I am not your Negro*. Film.

Haddix, M. (2019). Summary of the 68th annual conference of the literacy research association, November 28–December 1, 2018. *Literacy Research: Theory, Method, and Practice, 68*(1), 11–15.

Lewis, T. (2009). *Family literacy and digital literacies: A redefined approach to examining social practices of an African American family*. Unpublished dissertation. University at Albany, State University of New York.

Lewis, T. (2011). Family digital literacies: A case of awareness, agency, and apprenticeship of one African American family. In P. J. Dunston, L. B. Gambrell, K. Headley, S. K. Fullerton, P. M. Stecker, V. R. Gillis, & C. C. Bates (Eds.), *60th literacy research association yearbook* (pp. 432–446). Literacy Research Association.

Lewis Ellison, T. (2018). Integrating and humanizing knowledgeable agents of the digital and Black Feminist Thought in digital literacy research. In K. Mills, A. Stornaiuolo, A. Smith, & J. Z. Pandya (Eds.), *Handbook of digital writing and literacies research*. Routledge.

Lewis Ellison, T., & Qiu, T. (2022). From exclusion to empowerment: A knowledgeable agents of the digital approach to understanding the STEM and racial literacies of a Black adolescent girl. *International Journal of Qualitative Studies in Education*.

Sealey-Ruiz, Y. (2020). Archeology of the self: Toward sustaining racial literacy. University of Maryland, Baltimore County, Department of Education, Equity and Excellence 2020 Lecture. Retrieved from https://education.umbc.edu/events/2020-january-23/

Stuckey, E. J. (1991). *The violence of literacy*. Boynton/Cook.

Acknowledgements

We would like to acknowledge the tremendous support of Dr Aaron Koh for his involvement at all stages of the editorial process. Professor Bill Green reviewed the entire collection, and we are grateful for his time and reflections on the book. We owe a debt of thanks to Peter Lee for his creative and dynamic illustrations that serve as segues for each part. We are grateful to all of our contributors for their hard work and intellectual energy that they put into their chapters. We acknowledge the time that Dr Tisha Lewis Ellison took to craft her foreword. Thank you too to Jennifer Turner for her editorial support, and to Lay Peng Ang at Springer for moving the book through so smoothly.

Abstract

Unsettling Literacies is a book that provides inspiration and direction to the field of literacy studies as pressing global concerns are prompting literacy researchers to re-examine what and how they research in times of precarity. This edited volume explores conceptual and methodological challenges associated with researching literacies in a rapidly changing, interconnected world characterised by political unrest, the rise of nationalism, big data, climate change and environmental degradation, threats to personal security and health, rampant social injustice, and a post-truth society. In such a world, literacy researchers must wrestle with complex procedural and pragmatic concerns as texts move far and fast, practices quickly spring up and fade away again, literacies span hybrid on/offline sites, and reaching and working with research participants entails practical difficulties. For many literacy researchers, the experience of COVID-19 brought such pressures into sharp relief, as the challenge of 'staying safe' intersected with attempts to research in ways that matter in the world, and this raised questions with much wider resonance for researching literacies in an age of precarity. Face-to-face research was impossible, for reasons of personal safety and security or physical distance. However, these difficult times have also surfaced new communicative practices and opened out spaces for exploration and activism, prompting re-examination of relationships between research, literacy, and social justice. Drawing on the reflections of a truly international group of leading literacy researchers and important new voices – generated both from experience of working through a global pandemic and from sustained engagements with social injustice over many years – this book presents re-imagined methods and theoretical imperatives. Authors in the collection move across varied and consequential events to explore new ways to think and research literacy and to unsettle what we know and accept as fundamental to literacy research, opening ourselves up for change. Through doing so, they both unsettle how literacies are conceived and hence researched in the context of a rapidly changing and precarious world, and explore ways in which literacies themselves can work to unsettle normative views and practices. Such perspectives are needed for literacy researchers to navigate the focus and conduct of literacy research now and into an uncertain future.

Contents

List of Figures

List of Tables

List of Appendix

About the Contributors

Funké Aladejebi is an Assistant Professor in the Department of History at the University of Toronto. Dr Aladejebi researches African Canadian history and holds a PhD in Canadian History from York University. Her articles on Black Canadian history and feminist pedagogies have appeared in *Education Matters*, *Ontario History*, and the *Southern Journal of Canadian Studies*.

Chris Bailey is Senior Lecturer in Education at Sheffield Hallam University. His work explores play; literacies; affective lived experience of space and place; sensory and embodied meaning-making; and multimodal, participatory methods in research and communication. Chris is autistic and is interested in trying to work out what this means for how he understands and represents the world. He won the UK Literacy Association Student Research award in 2018 and the UKLA / Wiley 'Literacy' Article of the Year Award in 2017.

Pete Bennett is Senior Lecturer in Post Compulsory Education at the University of Wolverhampton. He is co-author and co-editor of a number of books including *Barthes' Mythologies Today: Readings of Contemporary Culture* (Routledge 2013) and *Popular Culture and the Austerity Myth: Hard Times Today* (Routledge 2016) and of film and media textbooks for Routledge. He is also co-editor of the research series, Routledge Research in Media Literacy and Education.

Jana Boschee Ellefson is a PhD student at the Werklund School of Education at the University of Calgary. Her research interests are directed toward aesthetic and playful literacies beyond primary grades. Exploring posthumanist and Indigenous philosophies, Jana considers the possibilities held in generative and creative literacies. She is currently an instructor at the University of Lethbridge – teaching, exploring spaces, and writing alongside pre-service teachers in the Faculty of Education.

Casey Burkholder is an Associate Professor at the University of New Brunswick's Faculty of Education. Her research programme centres on exploring participatory visual research approaches with youth to explore their ways of knowing and experiencing school and social structures. This work seeks to work with youth activists to agitate for social change through participatory visual research approaches.

Cathy Burnett is Professor of Literacy and Education at Sheffield Institute of Education, Sheffield Hallam University, UK, where she leads the Language and Literacy Education Research Group. Her research has focused predominantly on the relationship between new technologies and literacies within and beyond educational contexts from a sociomaterial perspective. She has published widely on these themes and her recent books include *New Media in the Classroom: Rethinking Primary Literacy* and *Undoing the Digital: Literacy and Sociomaterialism* (both with Guy Merchant). She also has an interest in knowledge and data practices and her most recent work explores how research methods act on the phenomena they attempt to investigate. From July 2019 until July 2021 she was President of the United Kingdom Literacy Association.

Catherine Compton-Lilly holds the John C. Hungerpiller Chair at the University of South Carolina. She engages in longitudinal research projects. Her interests include examining how time operates as a contextual factor in children's lives as they progress through school and construct their identities as students and readers. In an ongoing study, Dr Compton-Lilly is following children from immigrant families from primary school through high school.

Karla Ferreira da Costa is an international PhD student in the Faculty of Education at the University of Manitoba. She is also Professor of English as an additional language and practicum at the Federal University of Mato Grosso do Sul – UFMS in Brazil. Her research interests focus on teacher learning, teaching English as an additional language, critical literacies and decolonial perspectives in education.

Beryl Exley is an experienced classroom teacher and teacher educator and is now Professor, English Curriculum and Literacies Education, and Deputy Head of School (Learning and Teaching) in the School of Education and Professional Studies at Griffith University, Australia. Beryl completed a PhD on teachers' knowledge bases for literacy teaching. Beryl's research is supported by an Australian Research Council Discovery Project Grant 190100518 'Quality Teaching Work and Reducing Educational Inequalities' (awarded to Singh, Exley, Heimans, & Ivinson 2019–2023). Beryl has held volunteer positions on the Australian Literacy Educators' Association National Council from 2005 to 2019 and from 2017 to 2019 served as National President.

Abigail Hackett is a Research Fellow at the Education and Social Research Institute, Manchester Metropolitan University. She is interested in the role of place, materiality, and bodies in young children's lives. She researches mostly in community spaces, in collaboration with children and families, employing ethnographic and post-qualitative methods. Abi currently holds a British Academy Postdoctoral Fellowship to investigate the literacy and language practices of children aged between 12 and 36 months in community spaces. Her new book *More-Than-Human Literacies in Early Childhood* was published in Spring 2021.

Sara Hawley works at UCL's London Knowledge Lab, teaching MA and BA Digital Media students. Her research covers literacy in the digital age, learner agency and digital divides, looking at new ways to theorise the debate about technology in schools so that it reflects issues of equity and social justice. Sara's PhD, *The Sociomateriality of Literacy, a Study of the Relationship between Institutions, Identity and the Internet in a Primary Classroom,* analysed the digital literacy practices of 8–9-year-olds using Third Space as a theoretical lens. Sara previously worked in schools as a teacher and Assistant Headteacher.

Michelle A. Honeyford is an Associate Professor of Language and Literacy in the Faculty of Education at the University of Manitoba. Her research focuses on transcultural, multimodal, and critical literacies; writing pedagogy, identity, and place; and anti-oppressive language arts curriculum and practice. She is passionate about her work with the Manitoba Writing Project, the Research in Renewing Literacies project, and CanU, an innovative and interest-driven afterschool programme collaboratively designed with teacher candidates for middle and high school students.

Kelly C. Johnston, PhD, is an Assistant Professor of Literacy in the Department of Curriculum & Instruction at Baylor University. Her areas of specialisation include sociocultural, critical, and affective approaches to literacy research and practice across interdisciplinary contexts. Her recent research examines how children and youth engage with literacies in expansive ways and how these findings inform more equitable and humanizing opportunities related to teaching, learning, and students' lives. https://orcid.org/0000-0002-9287-8237.

Claire Lee is an Early Career Research Fellow supporting the Children and Young People Network at Oxford Brookes University, UK. Previously she was a primary-school teacher with specialisms in literacy and music. She completed her PhD in 2020, investigating the learning lives of children from armed forces families, in the School of Education, University of Bristol. Her interests include understanding how children develop a sense of self in educational settings, as well as pedagogy, children's literacies, power, and classroom relationships. She uses art-based and participatory ethnographic methods in her research, which is committed to creating spaces for dialogue with children.

Amélie Lemieux, PhD, is an Assistant Professor of Literacies at Mount Saint Vincent University, in Halifax, Nova Scotia. Working at the intersections of literacies, the arts, and technology, her research addresses and seeks to re/define adolescent engagement in digital contexts using arts-informed perspectives and posthuman inquiry. A TEDx speaker, she has received a Lieutenant-Governor's Medal for academic excellence (Quebec) as well as federal and provincial funding to conduct her research. https://orcid.org/0000-0002-0701-4638.

Kim Lenters is Associate Professor and Canada Research Chair in language and literacy education at the University of Calgary where her research focuses on the material worlds of children's literacy development. Most recently, Kim's work has engaged with the affordances of comedy in children's classroom literacy learning and has been published in the *Reading Teacher* (2018), *Literacy* (2018), and *Research in the Teaching of English* (2019). She is also the co-editor of the volume, *Affect and Embodiment in Critical Literacy: Assembling Theory and Practice* (2020). In her spare moments, Kim is learning to make comics and enjoys exploring Calgary's river paths and hiking in the Rocky Mountains.

Tisha Lewis Ellison is an Associate Professor in the Department of Language and Literacy Education at the University of Georgia. Her research explores the intersections of family literacy, multimodality, and digital and STEM literacy practices among African American and Latinx families and adolescents. Her research studies are advancing the field of families' digital literacies and STEM literacies across lifespans, in homes and community settings, in ways that inform parents, adolescents, and teachers by (a) contributing to the field of family literacy by including an awareness of families' and adolescents' digital literacy practices and parents' counter-narratives; (b) integrating digital literacies and multimodality in learning environments across race and class; and (c) examining the role of feminism in digital literacies.

Julian McDougall is Professor of Media and Education, Head of the Centre for Excellence in Media Practice and Principal Fellow of the Higher Education Academy. He runs the Professional Doctorate (EdD) in Creative and Media Education at Bournemouth University and convenes the annual International Media Education Summit. He is author of a range of over 100 books, articles, chapters, and research reports and has provided research for external funders, charities and non-profit organisations. Julian took a National Diploma and Polytechnic degree, but has benefited in his career from the advantages and privileges afforded to a white male in higher education.

Bethany Monea is a PhD candidate in the Reading, Writing, and Literacy Program at the University of Pennsylvania Graduate School of Education. Her scholarship centres youth writing and media-making practices, critical digital literacies, and participatory multimodal methodologies. Her current research examines how first-generation Latinx students' literacy practices are networked across high school, college, and community contexts. Her work has been funded by the Sachs Program for Arts Innovation, the American Educational Research Association, and a

GAPSA-Provost Fellowship for Interdisciplinary Innovation. She has published in *Kairos: A Journal of Rhetoric, Technology, and Pedagogy, Perspectives on Urban Education*, and *Computers and Composition*. https://orcid.org/0000-0002-1164-9951.

John Potter is Professor of Media in Education at the University College London Institute of Education, based in the UCL Knowledge Lab. His research, teaching and publications are in the fields of: media education, new literacies, theories of curation and agency in social media, the changing nature of teaching and learning in response to the pervasive use in wider culture of media technologies. He has worked in literacy and media in education throughout his working life as a primary school teacher in East London, a local authority education advisor, a teacher-educator, and, most recently, as an academic and researcher.

Jennifer Rowsell is Professor of Literacies and Social Innovation at the University of Bristol's School of Education in the UK. Her research interests include multi-modal, makerspace and arts-based research with young people; digital literacies research; digital divide work; and applying posthumanist and affect approaches to literacy research. She has worked and conducted research in Australia, Canada, the UK, and the USA. Her most recent co-authored books are *Living Literacies: Rethinking literacy research and practice through the everyday* (MIT Press) with Dr Kate Pahl (Manchester Metropolitan University) with Diane Collier, Steve Pool, Zanib Rasool, and Terry Trzecak and *Maker Literacies and Maker Identities in the Digital Age: Learning and playing through modes and media* (Routledge) with Cheryl McLean (Rutgers University). She is a co-editor of the *Routledge Expanding Literacies in Education* book series with Carmen Medina (Indiana University) and she is a co-editor of *Digital Culture and Education*.

Fiona Scott, PhD, is a specialist in young children's digital lives, literacies, and play. She has paid particular attention to the roles which parents/carers and other family members play in this engagement, including within diverse socioeconomic contexts. Her recent research includes researching: children, technology and play (with the LEGO Foundation); young children's use of AR and VR technology; young children's engagement and learning with an AR coding app; play and creativity in preschoolers' use of apps; and young children's engagement with television and related media in the digital age (with CBeebies). https://orcid.org/0000-0002-8689-2905.

Jennifer Thompson is a Postdoctoral Fellow with Myriagone, the McConnell-University of Montreal Chair in Youth Knowledge Mobilization at the University of Montreal, Canada. Her research interests include participatory visual methodologies, research ethics, water and water infrastructure, and gender and intersectionality. Jen has a background across engineering, education, and international development, and has conducted fieldwork in Cameroon, Canada, Ethiopia, Kenya, Mozambique, Sierra Leone, and the UK.

Shelley Warkentin is currently the Divisional Principal for the Seven Oaks School Division in Winnipeg, Manitoba. She was previously the K to 12 English Language Arts and Literacy Consultant for Manitoba Education. Shelley's areas of inquiry, research and development have focused on rethinking curriculum, teacher practice, language and literacies, and critical pedagogy.

Bronwyn T. Williams is Professor of English and Director of the University Writing Center at the University of Louisville. He writes and teaches on issues of literacy, identity, digital media, sustainability, and community engagement. His most recent book is *Literacy Practices and Perceptions of Agency: Composing Identities*. Previous books include *New Media Literacies and Participatory Popular Culture Across Borders*; *Shimmering Literacies: Popular Culture and Reading and Writing Online*; and *Identity Papers: Literacy and Power in Higher Education*.

Linda-Dianne Willis is Program Director, Bachelor of Education, and Senior Lecturer in the School of Education and Professional Studies at Griffith University, Australia. Linda is an educator and researcher, having taught in primary, middle years, and tertiary settings. Linda completed a PhD on parent-teacher engagement. She teaches curriculum courses and researches parent engagement, multiliteracies, inquiry curriculum, and dialogic pedagogies. Linda has led major research projects in parent-school-community engagement for government, Catholic, and independent school sectors. She is the National Publications Director of the Australian Literacy Educators' Association. Linda is lead author on the book, *Principal leadership for parent engagement in disadvantaged schools*.

Introduction: Unsettling Literacies

We've known for a while that ash dieback disease was likely to decimate the ash woodland just near to our house. It arrived in Derbyshire, England in 2015, carried to the UK they think on imported trees. At first there were notices on fences and footpaths – urging people to clean their boots to stop spreading the disease. These notices didn't last long in our damp climate and soon tore, dissolved, and fell away. In the years that followed, we thought we saw some signs that ash dieback was with us – crumpled leaves on a few trees here and there, although it could just have been the warm weather or the onset of autumn. But this year, 2020, when leaves burst from branches in May then June – hawthorn then blackthorn then sycamore then beech – the ash just never woke up. A few saplings grew leaves that crumpled and fell. But most of the ash trees remained bare and still, corpses amidst the eruption of spring. The ash trees that were our neighbours were just quietly, collectively dying.

This story of 2020 ran parallel to the emerging COVID-19 pandemic. A quieter disease but also deadly, wiping out whole populations with devastating implications for the ecosystems to which these trees belonged. It's anticipated that between 70% and 90% of the UK's estimated 80 million ash trees will die over the next 20–30 years. And yet, apart from a few short articles in newspapers and TV programmes, ash dieback has featured little in the narrative of 2020. As COVID-19 made the jump to humans it shot into the public consciousness accompanied by tectonic shifts in working patterns, social contact, economic and mental wellbeing, and a devastating death toll. 'Nature' (that all-encompassing term used to refer to everything from grand landscapes to individual species) did feature, but always in relation to what it does for people: the salve for troubled minds, the green escape from lockdown, or an emergent force in human lives – 'Perhaps COVID-19 is nature's way of telling us something?' was a common refrain. All of this objectifies 'nature' as something that is either at our disposal – for consumption or wellbeing – or something to be observed or entered. This objectification prevents us from seeing our own intricate relations with other living and non-living things, and also from recognising that 'nature' has a value and right to exist that extends beyond the aims, ambitions, and preconceptions of human beings.

Of course, there are many other narratives of precarity to be told of 2020, of pressing episodes in human and more-than-human lives. Some of these have circulated widely, like the murder of George Floyd and the climate emergency, while others have been largely squeezed from the headlines by COVID-19 – Ebola, widening inequalities, unsustainable farming practices, oppression, migration, war. And then of course there are more private experiences that weave through societal, economic, environmental, and political developments – of relationships, ill health, work, and debt. While 2020, for privileged individuals in the global north, has been a year of uncertainty like no other, for much of the world there have been other concerns, gradations of concerns from severities and urgencies about life and survival to concerns that challenge interactions, values, convictions, and morality.

So, this book is a book about uncertainty. It's a book that holds at its centre the idea that uncertainty is nothing new, and that it manifests in multiple ways, often exacerbated as different dimensions of experience intersect. And it's a book that asks what uncertainty means for literacy research, and for how literacy plays through uncertain lives.

While this book is not focused only on COVID-19, it is significant that it was written in 2020–2021 when our authors' working and personal lives were thrown into disarray by stay-at-home orders. Reflections prompted by this experience underpin the stories told in many chapters of this book. Bronwyn T. Williams tells a story of suddenly moving his research of higher education students' writing lives online and the qualitative, felt differences between sitting beside an individual as she or he recounts writing experiences as opposed to speaking and sharing through a screen. His chapter animates the gains and losses of virtual research. Other contributors approach uncertainty from more personal stances, such as Chris Bailey's account of receiving an autism diagnosis during the pandemic and the ensuing shifts that took place in his research and his ways of framing conceptual trajectories. Still other contributors such as Jana Boschee Ellefson, Kim Lenters and Bethany Monea look closely at everyday objects as apertures into other worlds, experiences, and issues. While this book is not a book about COVID-19, the experience of COVID-19 has, we believe, surfaced perspectives that may not have emerged otherwise, perspectives that shuffle us into different positions, and that allow different meeting places between researchers and literacies which illuminate aspects of practice that might otherwise have gone unnoticed or unexplored. As Strathern (2020, p. 35) argues,

> As the anthropologist's own world changes, he or she may in certain respects get closer to, rather than farther from, the subject of study. Thus, the present ecological crisis, which precipitates imaginings of the end of the world, suddenly casts the first extinction of the Amazon in new light. As far as the indigenous populations of the Americas are concerned, it has been said, the end of the world has already happened.

The world then is perceived as in peril when things happen to us that disrupt habitual ways of living, and this can shift our perspectives on other events. The climate emergency has been an emergency for decades. And disease has always ravaged populations. But following recent extreme weather events, and because we've endured COVID-19, we're perhaps more sensitised to precarity more broadly. Nonetheless, as Abigail Hackett eloquently expresses it in her chapter, 'thinking with the shifting and precarious experience of living during the COVID-19 pandemic, now is a good time to consider young children's literacy practices in relation to living well in the future'. With tragedy, mayhem and precarity to the fore, there have also been wisdom and discoveries about the rich possibilities for future thinking.

The stories we tell ourselves are selective, always eliding so much more than they tell. It is important therefore to take notice of the stories that we tell ourselves and others and how we bring these stories into the world – what we include and what we leave out. This reflexiveness runs through many of the chapters in this book, such as Cathy Compton-Lilly's chapter, which explores the stories of two men's literacy lives over two decades and what becomes visible and invisible with time. Her chapter throws into relief her own research reflexivity and a resolution she has made to *be* research as she moves forward with her career and her longitudinal research with both men. Over the course of COVID-19, legacies have been revealed such as histories of racism and rampant social injustices. Such legacies and social injustices are threaded throughout the book, as in Casey Burkholder, Funké Aladejebi, and Jennifer Thompson's chapter that considers systemic oppressions in Fredericton. Their research harnesses the power of the arts and film-making to excavate and push back on heteronormative and racist discourses and movements through DIY and multiliteracies visual participatory research methods.

In the light of all of this, it would seem that a key challenge for literacy studies is to multiply the stories we tell, but also to connect them. This raises questions for how we see literacy, for how we engage with research, and for the kinds of practices we document and enable. How do we tell compelling nuanced stories of individuals' literacies, but also recognise the relatedness of lives? How do we research literacies as emergent, mobile, and contingent? And how might literacy research act positively in the world – how can we conceive and practice literacies research as activist research? The chapters which follow speak to these questions in different ways. In doing so, they unsettle a number of related ideas that circulate in the landscape for literacy education, ideas that persist in upholding some unhelpful certainties: (1) that directions for literacy education are incontrovertible; (2) that precarity is best seen at scale; and (3) that big times call for large scale literacy interventions. In what follows we consider each of these in turn, sketching some alternative orientations that arise from the chapters in this book – ways of thinking, researching, and doing literacy that make a case for acknowledging and working with the mobility, contingency, and relatedness of literacy.

Unsettling Certainty in Ways Forward for Literacy Education

The first of the certainties that we want to unsettle – that directions for literacy education are incontrovertible – relies on the idea that literacy education is aimed at an irrefutable 'good'. Such clarity of direction is rarely straightforward in practice. Law and Mol (2002) problematise the notion of the irrefutable 'good' in their analysis of a response to a train accident. They argue that the criticism directed at certain actors (the signalmen, the track maintenance team, and so on) for not following procedures is essentially underpinned by a utopian viewpoint. It's based on the idea that there is a singular 'good' to aspire to, and that 'goodness' is possible:

> Particular actors are being accused and called upon to justify themselves and account for their actions. And we will argue that this is a Utopian mode of engaging with 'the good'. This is because, with the loss of the irony implied in the origins of the term 'utopia', utopian modes for dealing with the good came to suggest that perfection is possible: that the absence of good is not necessary. Thus they evoke the possibility of a tension-free zone: a place or a situation where there are no clashes between what one might call, in the plural, different goods. (Law & Mol, 2002, pp. 84–85)

For Law and Mol, this singular perspective elides the complexity of competing pressures and discursively works to uphold the unproblematic possibility of getting things 'right', without recognising that the very process of doing 'good' in certain ways can lead to things that are problematic from other perspectives.

We see something similar in educational policy, with similar effects. We might, for example, trace a singular utopian view in the 'evidence-based practice' movement – the well-funded moves to draw on 'what works' to shape literacy provision in schools (e.g. https://ies.ed.gov/ncee/wwc/). The 'hard evidence' provided by randomised controlled trials and other quasi experimental studies essentially works to define a 'good' – a way of working 'proven' to be most 'effective' for children – written into policies and frameworks and subsequently monitored and upheld by inspection agencies and high stakes assessments. However, taking up such approaches may interfere with other 'good's (Biesta, 2010) – a strong emphasis on phonics, for example, may undermine the literacy identities that young children bring to school; and the considerable time spent ensuring that young children have a firm grasp of the metalanguage of grammar (as happens in England) may reduce the time available for children to develop their own voice.

An alternative is to sidestep the idea of literacy 'goods' and approach literacy research with an open mind, exploring the cultural, social, and material significance of literacies to people's lives. This is the track that literacy studies have been on for the last 40 years or so and this work has brought us to where we are now. Going into varied contexts to document so many different ways that literacy is taken up and what counts as literacy has given us a platform now to truly open the potentials and possibilities of literacy. This book provides rich examples of this. Hawley and Potter's chapter, for example, includes an account of how children co-produced research across spaces, digital and analogue. The children made videos of their playground, produced drawings and maps, took photographs of playspaces, and interviewed each other – driven by their own thoughts, feelings, and convictions and most of all, strongly informed by their voices and their agencies. This not only gave children control over what they shared but also enabled the researchers to 'unknow' and 'reknow' children's play. Law and Mol's critique of the utopian view is helpful perhaps in explaining why well-meaning attempts to improve literacy education so often fall short. The utopian view requires a stability (as evidenced in literacy tests, targets, and schemes) that is at odds with the diversity and multiplicity of literacies documented by studies such as this one.

Unsettling the Need to Look at Scale

This brings us to the second certainty we want to unsettle – that precarity is best observed at scale. In pandemic times, precarity has been writ large in the graphs and tables that account for tens of thousands of cases and deaths from COVID-19, in headline grabbing tales of failed testing procedures, rapid vaccination and international disputes. And, at the time of writing, a similarly quantitative analysis of children's performance on standardised tests is being used to define an educational 'gap' created by 'lost learning' following months away from school (Rose et al., 2021). The datafication of schooling in countries such as England has been the subject of much critique over recent years, for the narrowing of educational provision and for its effects on teacher professionalism and pupil wellbeing (Bradbury & Roberts-Holmes, 2017; Lewis & Holloway, 2019). A problem that's particularly relevant to our argument though is that such applications of data present precarity as solvable: act on the data, refine the system, and all will be well. But knotted into these easy logics of health, education, policy, and capitalism is a more pervasive sense of unease, fragility, and unpredictability that creeps through everyday life. Engaging with precarity requires more than large scale analysis.

Kathleen Stewart's work has much to offer here. Stewart's interest is in how precarity takes shape in the moment, in how a shift in feel, a sensing of 'something' accrues, builds and somehow takes hold. She sees precarity as 'one register of the singularity of emergent phenomena – their plurality, movement, imperfection, immanence, incommensurateness, the way that they accrete, accrue and wear out' (Stewart, 2012, p. 518). Following Stewart, a concern with precarity then is a concern with what emerges as things combine or overlayer or diverge, with what takes shape or dissipates. It means engaging with 'emergent forms' rather than those that are easily identified, categorised and explained. Rather than solving or theorising what has happened (as the 'data' does), this involves an ongoing sensitivity to how things are shifting, to how 'something that throws itself together in a moment as an event or a sensation: a something both animate and inhabitable' (Stewart, 2007, p. 1). As she writes,

> the terms neoliberalism, advanced capitalism, and globalization that index this emergent present, and the five or seven or ten characteristics used to summarize and define it in short-hand, do not themselves begin to describe the situation we find ourselves in. The notion of a totalized system, of which everything is always already somehow a part is not helpful (to say the least) in the effort to approach a weighted and reeling present. This is not to say that the forces these systems try to name are not real and literally pressing. On the contrary, I am trying to bring them into view as a scene of immanent force, rather than leave them looking like dead effects imposed on an innocent world. (Stewart, 2007, p. 1)

For Stewart, one way of encountering precarity is through writing, not the kind of writing that orders or distils or proposes, but rather a 'writing culture lodged in emergence, generativity, and potentiality' – writing that attunes to what's happening, that assembles impressions and feelings, intensities and momentary occurrences in ways that evoke precarity, and does so in ways that are not totalising or permanent. In *Precarity's Forms*, Stewart (2012) tells tales of everyday lives – of her father's death, her mother's life, the road running through the town, a river pool frequented by locals on a summer's day. Her stories don't explain, but edge up to, or 'near' a feeling or sense of something that assembles through – or perhaps *as* – precarity. This notion of 'nearing' echoes some of the ways in which authors in this book talk about their work. Kelly C. Johnston, Amélie Lemieux, and Fiona Scott's chapter gives readers a generative way of sharing data through diffractive readings – treating data as spaces to share, think, and be. Researchers working closely together, trusting each other, and collectively crafting a methodology of the *otherwise*. They demonstrate the possibilities generated through wrestling, sharing, pushing against, relating to, and untangling assemblages within human and more-than-human research.

Unsettling the Need to Solve Problems Through Grand Gestures

This notion of 'nearing' also provides a stance from which to unsettle our third (related) certainty – that big times call for big responses, for grand gestures delivered at breakneck speed. In literacy this often means roll outs of standardised literacy interventions, interventions consisting of easily codified, easily implemented strategies designed for a quick catch up, as we have seen in responses to missed time in school and the need to address the so-called 'Covid gap' (e.g. https://national-tutoring.org.uk/). If however, as literacy studies research suggests, literacy is too complex to be addressed in this way – too social, too deeply entangled with place, space and identity, embodiment and materiality – then we need a subtler response, a response that does not aspire to a single unified 'good' but to recognise the complex entanglements of different 'goods' that run through practice as experienced, to acknowledge the value and significance of those things that escape easy description, quantification and rational justification.

In contrast Donna Haraway speaks of a thick present in which it is productive and even advisable to stir up trouble to unsettle brackish and perilous waters in order to rebuild (Haraway, 2016). Haraway argues, 'in urgent times, many of us are tempted to address trouble in terms of making an imagined future safe … of clearing away the present and past in order to make futures for coming generations' (p. 2). How prescient her words are now in 2021, as we grapple with what comes *after* a pandemic; after Derek Chauvin's trial; after Biden rights the wrongs of Trump; and the list goes on. These disturbances can be, no, are emergent and furtive ground for 'eschewing futurism' (Haraway, 2016, p. 8) and for dwelling with uncertainty and precarity to draw out ways forward.

Part of our Unsettling Literacies project therefore is to explore what happens – in these uncertain times – if we dodge the taken-for-granted and the singular logic of the 'good' (or indeed the 'bad') and try to tangle with potentiality in our work for a more equitable, more empowering literacy education. Our aim here, and that of many of our contributing authors, is not to make blanket recommendations for literacy education but to stay 'in the middle of things' (Stewart, 2012, p. 128). Hackett, for example, nudges readers to be in-the-world with all of its chaos and closely examine the unfolding mix of things, movements, atmospheres, and bodies. Her suggestions are relevant not just to literacy researchers but to literacy educators, too.

Unsettling Literacies

Together the chapters in this book suggest different pathways for unsettling literacies, for troubling how we conceive literacy and how we engage with literacies as researchers, and for illuminating new textual practices that mediate our relationships with one another. The book is divided into three parts with interconnected graphics as a segue into each one.

In Shiftings, the chapters stay with the trouble of COVID-19 and other urgencies to unsettle conceptualisations, methods, frameworks, and reflexivities by questioning our relationships with what and who we research. Compton-Lilly for example longs to *be* in her research and transparent about her whiteness as she tells the stories of young men she has known for some time. This resonates with Hawley and Potter's use of Ingold's work to reflect on the notion of 'dwelling' in research. Drawing on observations about children's tacit, sensory-laden co-research practices and reflections on embodied experiences of becoming a teacher-researcher, they foreground the need to see our understanding of the world as not so much about making views "*of* the world but of taking up a view *in* it'" (Ingold, 2000, p. 43). Monea's digitally mediated engagements with Latinx teenagers' ever-changing relations with humans and more-than humans, and Williams' embodied and sensory reactions to a sudden migration to online spaces and online research methods, remind us that literacies research always occurs in shifting assemblages of people, things, texts.

The next part, Openings, spotlights working within the constraints of online research, precarity, and urgencies to open up cracks for new possibilities, new veins of ideas and inquiries. Lemieux, Johnston, and Scott induct readers into collaborative and diffractive readings to forge connections and relational moments. Bailey opens out new ways of thinking through telling stories of three texts that intersected in different ways with a diagnosis of autism, arguing that work in the neurodiversity paradigm can offer generative possibilities for literacy studies in challenging normative ways of understanding difference. Boschee Ellefson and Lenters engage in a series of noticings of children's play and of pop-up productions such as chalk pavement drawings and painted stones that open up, buoy, and sustain them during lockdown and pandemic lives. They see these practices as a form of activism, generated by an urge to be seen and heard, and note how they emerged in conversation with each other, as new forms were taken up by others, generating new spaces and marking out new points of connection. They also, however, chart the challenges they faced in gaining ethical approval to document these emerging literacies, a process which effectively closed down spaces that opened out – for the purposes of research in any case – and rendered them less visible. Willis and Exley similarly trouble the notion of order in educational research and practice through their account of the challenges they faced when engaging in design-based research. They demonstrate how work to develop literacy in education requires an agility to respond to emerging challenges and possibilities thrown up by unpredictable encounters.

The third and final part, Disruptings, uncovers research and perspectives on unsettlings in practice – chapters that make no gesture to fix things or soften the impact but rather to dive deep into precarity and urgencies. Hackett, in an argument for acknowledging 'inter-dependency between human meaning making and the more than human world', powerfully ushers readers into literacies-yet-to-come and an acceptance that we are existing in a world out of control that children sense, negotiate, and disrupt in relational, distributed ways. The emergence of meaning making, as Hackett explores, is not explicable solely in terms of intention or progress towards competence, but needs to be understood in terms of provisionality, potentiality, fluidity. Honeyford, Warkentin and Costa pierce through curricular writing and thinking that feels unknown, unpredictable, and untameable, yet at the same time is a process that is filled with forces, tensions, and flows. Burkholder, Aladejebi, and Thompson disrupt gender and sexuality norms through participatory visual methods with LGBTQ youth. The part concludes with McDougall, Bennett, and Potter on a walk through Hoggart's seminal work on cultural studies and disruptions of 'good' working class culture and the ways that mass media rendered them passive and static. They push us to think about how literacies are on the move right now, unhinged, unfettered, and yes, unsettled, in ways that might invite promise and possibilities as much as they do disquietude and instability.

Back to Ash Dieback

Nine months – and two more lockdowns – later, tree felling has begun. They're cutting down the trees that overhang footpaths and roads, concerned that branches from the dying trees will damage people or property, but leaving much of the wood for organisms to feast on as it decays. Huge limbs litter the dale, massive trunks span the stream. At the entrance to the dale someone has written on one of the stumps, punning in neat capitals in black felt pen – 'EYESAW DALE'.

And it is really. A scene of devastation on a popular dog-walking route. And yet it must be more than this. It must mean more than an unsightly mess. Further along the dale, sitting in a pile of wood chippings a chair has appeared. Hewn from the felled timber and fixed to the ground. This isn't one of those official sculptures that feature here and there in the dales. Apparently one of the neighbours made it – they wanted to mark the deaths in some way, out of respect or to trees that have been lost. To bear witness perhaps to what's happened. On the chair are carved the words, Ash Requiem. Often when we walk past, someone is standing in front of the chair, taking photographs. So much so that I regularly google 'ash requiem' and 'tideswell dale', expecting it to gain a new life on social media. Oddly, it doesn't.

Things move on. They shift, open out, disrupt. And literacies play a part in this. Sometimes this is through stamping meanings onto the world, paying testament to the sense we make and the sense we assume others will make too. Like the pop-up productions that Elfers and Lenters observed in Calgary during 'stay-at-home' periods, 'EYESAW DALE' and 'Ash Requiem' are encountered as complete texts. We can only infer the feelings, processes, and objects and people that brought them into being. Nevertheless, they invite responses. Perhaps Eyesaw Dale closes down, defining the felled trees only in terms of their impact on human perception. Perhaps Ash Requiem opens out, leaving space for contemplation, for what this requiem might be, whom or what it is for, and who or what will be touched by it. More likely perhaps, both – alongside all the other human and more-than-humans in and beyond the dale – are potential participants in literacies yet-to-come.

If we are to better articulate and challenge inequitable ways of doing, being and thinking, we need to notice where and when things open out in other ways, and to cultivate spaces where we can do and think in ways that work against the common tide. In addition to grand gestures then, this may involve small, slow work that works to unsettle and unravel tightly tied assumptions about what lives can be, and about what literacy is and what it does. The chapters of this book, in different ways, provide generative starting points for doing just that. Together they suggest different pathways for unsettling literacies, for troubling the way we conceive literacy, for how we engage with literacies as researchers, for questioning taken-for-granted protocols for engaging in research, and for interrogating the way in which textual practices mediate relationships between the human and more than human world.

Sheffield, UK   Cathy Burnett

Bristol, UK   Jennifer Rowsell

References

Biesta, G. (2010). Why 'What Works' still won't work: From evidence-based education to value-based education. *Studies in the Philosophy of Education, 29*, 491–503.

Bradbury, A., & Roberts-Holmes, G. (2017). *The datafication of primary and early years education*. Routledge.

Haraway, D. (2016). *Staying with the trouble: Making kin in the chthulucene*. Duke University Press.

Ingold, T. (2000). *The perception of the environment: Essays on livelihood, dwelling and skill*. Routledge.

Law, J. & Mol, A. (2002). Local entanglements or utopian moves: An inquiry into train accidents. *The Sociological Review, 50*(1), 82–105.

Lewis, S., & Holloway, J. (2019). Datafying the teaching 'profession': Remaking the professional teacher in the image of data. *Cambridge Journal of Education, 49*(1), 35–51.

Rose, S., Twist, L., Lord, P., Rutt, S., Badr, K., Hope, C., & Styles, B. (2021). *Impact of school closures and subsequent support strategies on attainment and socio-emotional wellbeing in Key Stage 1: Interim Paper 1*. NFER.

Stewart, K. (2007). *Ordinary affect*. Dukes University Press.

Stewart, K. (2012). Precarity's forms. *Cultural Anthropology, 27*(3), 518–525.

Strathern, M. (2020). New and old worlds: A perspective from social anthropology. *European Review, 29*(1), 1–11.

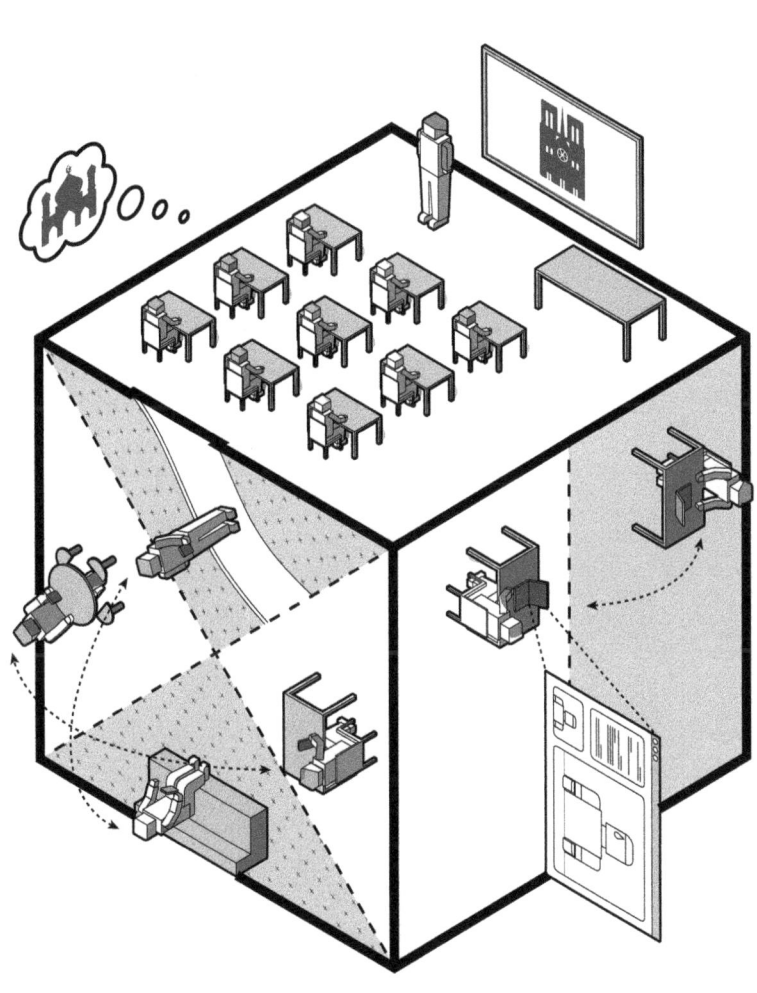

Chapter 1
Trajectories of Being and Becoming: Relationships Across Time That Keep Us Humble

Catherine Compton-Lilly

Abstract In this chapter, Catherine Compton-Lilly unsettles and explores her shifting trajectory of being and becoming a researcher. Specifically, she revisits the cases of Peter and Adam, two students who participated in longitudinal case studies that span her 24-year academic career. After briefly describing the methodology for each longitudinal study, she revisits three critical dimensions of each child's trajectory that she has written about in the past. She then examines the reflexive stances that she brought to her longitudinal projects, highlighting the ontological – her being and becoming a literacy scholar (Parkin, 2016). Compton-Lilly ends by considering how race has affected this work. Along the way, she explores previously under-recognized and generally unspoken dimensions of research as she unsettles her own position as a researcher and considers the intellectual biases, experiences, and presuppositions that limited and directed how she made sense of students' experiences.

Keywords Longitudinal · Reflexivity · Research · Researchers · Academic fields

While it is easy to think about precarity in relation to global shifts and international disasters, I explore the unsettling of who we are as literacy researchers. Writing during the fall of 2020, at the forefront of my mind are the COVID-19 pandemic, systemic racism, and climate change. As I draft these words, a radio reports on election outcomes in Pennsylvania, Arizona, and Georgia – 5 days after our historic presidential election. These unsettling times have shattered American comfort and complacency.

Twenty-five years ago, Elder (1995) argued for a situated notion of development that attends not only to social aspects of experiences but also to historical events that define generations (Elder, 2018). As I consider this volume's call to attend to a

C. Compton-Lilly (✉)
John C. Hungerpiller Professor, University of South Carolina, Oxford, UK
e-mail: comptonlilly@sc.edu

© The Author(s), under exclusive license to Springer Nature Singapore Pte Ltd. 2022
C. Lee et al. (eds.), *Unsettling Literacies*, Cultural Studies and Transdisciplinarity in Education 15, https://doi.org/10.1007/978-981-16-6944-6_1

"rapidly changing, interconnected world characterised by political unrest, the rise of nationalism, big data, climate change and environmental degradation, threats to personal security and health, rampant social injustice," I propose that we reconsider our roles, how we teach, how we research, and how we have become literacy scholars.

Specifically, I explore trajectories of being and becoming for two youth and for myself. I revisit the case of Peter, an African American student in my first grade class during the 1996–1997 school year. I then present the emerging case of Adam, a Muslim American student whose family immigrated to the United States from Morocco. As I write, Adam is participating in his 12th year of my longitudinal study. Taken together, these two cases span my entire academic career (25 years) – from dissertation to my current position as an endowed full professor.

My goal in this chapter is to unsettle myself, which is essential for examining the certitude of the claims I have made and the representations I have created, in order to understand how racism, poverty, and privilege intersect and unfold in my research. Specifically, I reflect on what I have witnessed, the inequitable experiences of children of color as they move though US schools, and how long-term trajectories are crafted and curated within spaces that allow and restrict particular ways of being. I consider my own positionality relative to my participants and the sense I have made of other people's worlds. I do not do this as an academic exercise but as an invitation for literacy researchers to "unsettle" our field and rethink, reconsider, rework, and renegotiate the literacy opportunities provided to all children.

Drawing on Bourdieu's theory of reflexivity (see Grenfell, 2018), I ask "not how to *do*" research, but "how *to be* it." Bourdieu (1993) argued that researchers must reveal the rules, the game, and the habitus of the field in which we operate. He lamented the failure of academics to recognize and attend to the full scope and significance of their relationships with participants and with academic fields.

While Bourdieu was concerned about inequities related to social class and the varied amounts and forms of capital that people brought to educational spaces, I argue for an additional layer of reflexivity that reflects our North American legacy of racism and inequitable opportunity. Thus, in the closing section of this chapter, I draw on antiracist theories (Dumas & ross, 2016; Johnson et al., 2019; Love, 2019) to intentionally recognize the significance of my white skin, my white heritage, and my white experiences. Whiteness is a real and formidable dimension that has informed my experiences as a North American, as a woman, as a teacher, and as a scholar. Growing up in the United States during the 1960s, teaching in an under-resourced school in a high-poverty urban community, living through 9/11, surviving a global pandemic, and witnessing the emergence of the Black Lives Matter movement have defined my historical moment. In short, my understandings of the world are not separate from the histories within which I reside (Elder, 1995), the language I use, the communities I participate in, and the truths that resonate. Both Bourdieu's sociology and antiracist perspectives require researchers to move beyond simple explanations – deficit parents, pathological communities, and deficient teachers – to reveal silenced and hidden positionalities, perspectives, and experiences.

While I aspire to comment on the longitudinal trajectories of two students, the constraints of a book chapter require that I choose particular dimensions of their experiences. Thus, I have identified three critical dimensions of each child's trajectory: one from elementary, middle school, and high school. After describing the methodology for the longitudinal studies, I present these critical dimensions and explore the reflexive stances that I brought to my longitudinal projects, highlighting the ontological – my being and becoming a literacy scholar (Parkin, 2016). I end by considering how race has affected my work. Along the way, I explore previously underrecognized and generally unspoken dimensions of the longitudinal research process as I "unsettle" my own position as a researcher and consider the intellectual biases, experiences, and presuppositions that limit and direct how I have made sense of Peter's and Adam's experiences.

1.1 Two Longitudinal Studies

I met Peter and his mother, Ms. Horner, when I taught at Rosa Parks Elementary School – a large urban school where 97% of the students qualified for free or reduced-price lunch. Most of the children walked to school from the housing projects that surrounded our school. While the local media often depicted the neighborhood as violent and drug-ridden, I was impressed by the dedicated families. Our school was on the State's list of failing schools.

It was in this context that I began my doctoral dissertation. My goal was to document the literacy practices of my students and their families. Ten families participated in what I planned as a 1-year study. Eventually, I was able to revisit eight of my former students in grades 5, 8, and 11. During each phase of the project, I interviewed children and parents and collected reading assessments and writing samples.

As the initial 10-year study ended, I conceptualized and began an intentionally longitudinal study. Having moved to a new city in the Upper Midwest, I considered various research possibilities. Inspired by doctoral students from around the world and intrigued by the growing number of immigrant students attending local schools, I designed a longitudinal project to explore the literacy trajectories of children in immigrant families. With the help of a team of graduate students, I am tracking the school experiences of eight students from immigrant families as they move through school. We interview children, parents, and teachers multiple times each year and collect student-created documents (e.g., self-portraits, depictions of native country, photographs of homes). Adam is a senior in high school and has participated in the study for 12 years.

Inspired by the work of critical ethnographers (i.e., Barton & Hamilton, 1998; Heath, 1983; Street, 1995) who documented literacy and language practices in thoughtful and respectful ways, I adopted ethnographic methods as I observed, listened, and documented children's literacy practices over time. In both longitudinal studies, children and parents were asked to describe their reading practices, their use of technology, and their satisfaction with school. Over time, children and families increasingly commented on the challenges they faced at school; identity, future plans, and peer relationships became increasingly salient.

Across my initial longitudinal study, data analysis involved grounded coding of interviews and field notes (Strauss & Corbin, 1990). Eventually, it became apparent that those coding practices were insufficient. I realized that data collected during early phases of the project gained significance when viewed in relation to data collected years later. Longitudinal patterns were obfuscated by sequential grounded coding of data from each phase of the project. Exploring longitudinal patterns required rereading stacks of data and using the search function on my word processor to locate words and ideas across the dataset.

My more recent study, which included Adam, was intentionally designed to attend to longitudinal patterns and literacy practices across time. We collected parallel data, asking participants to complete the same tasks and answer the same – or similar – interview questions each year. In some cases, modifications were made to accommodate change as the children grew older (e.g., documenting Facebook pages) and changes in technology (e.g., using cell phones rather than iPods to store music). We coded data using a combination of a priori codes – reflecting our initial research interests – and revised grounded codes over time.

While some scholars have referenced *critical incidents* from research projects, I have selected three *critical dimensions* to represent Peter's and Adam's beings/becomings. Unlike *incidents*, critical dimensions represent sets of properties and events that contribute to vectors of experience – ways of being – that inform being/becoming. These dimensions are described as critical because they mattered to participants and to me as I have written about Peter and Adam. I intentionally use the term *being/becoming* to reference the longitudinal nature of being. In short, I argue that any moment is a space of both being and becoming. Being always involves who we have been, who we are, and what we envision for the future. Likewise, trajectories of becoming selectively draw upon moments of being (Table 1.1).

Table 1.1 Critical dimensions

Peter 1996–2007	Adam 2009–2020
Elementary school	**Elementary school**
Home collection of books Brings books to school Value placed on reading by Peter's mother, grandmother, and great-grandmother Being a good reader	Images of Morocco, sunshine, and beaches Family visits to the beach Family stories related to the beach and swimming
Middle school	**Middle school**
Dangerous neighborhood and fights Doing well in school Being/Becoming a writer	Islamophobia and being Muslim Threats and danger Sharing information about Islam
High school	**High school**
Writing with friends Reading novels Going to college Being/Becoming a writer Writing poetry and being a poet	Recognizing bias, cathedrals, and mosques Attention to global humanity Environmental issues

1.2   Longitudinal Reflexivity

I maintain that longitudinal qualitative research provides a powerful space for researcher reflexivity. As Grenfell (2012) argued, research must be "iterative and cyclic, so that outcomes remain open to revision in the light of further investigations" (p. 195). Revisiting findings, reworking claims, and complicating conclusions inherently involve reflexivity. For example, I have often revisited findings presented in my early writing as I revisited students and collected additional data (Compton-Lilly, 2003, 2007, 2012, 2016a). Longitudinal research requires researchers to revisit our analyses as children's lives emerge and shift. Thus, my gaze became suspect as my claims were complicated, revealing the emergent and situated nature of knowing. I continually grappled with layers of reflexivity that require eternally tentative and emergent stances that continually trouble my research.

1.2.1   A Traditional Statement of Reflexivity

In this section, I describe a traditional and decidedly incomplete statement of my reflexivity as a researcher. I offer this account to consider what is included – and omitted – in traditional reflexivity statements. I follow this statement with a more honest and complete statement.

In most of my publications, I position myself as a White, currently middle-class, female, American scholar who grew up at the poverty line. I often highlight my teaching in a high-poverty urban community. Sometimes I write about the unique juxtaposition of growing up in a highly academic family alongside our lack of economic resources. I describe my 18 years as a classroom teacher, my interest in teacher research, and my frustration with teaching in underfunded schools in high-poverty communities. While I disclose different aspects of my experiences in different papers, these markers of my identity are typical.

1.2.2   A Reflexive Entanglement

However, there is much more that could be considered when thinking reflexively. Bourdieu maintained that researchers must acknowledge their struggle for legitimation within academic fields, the scholarly capital they accumulate, and how capital operates within academic fields (Grenfell, 2012, 2018). For example, my scholarly being/becoming was constrained by accepted methodological practices. This was the case when I conducted my dissertation as a short-term grounded theory study (Compton-Lilly, 2003). I have clear memories of repeatedly reading Strauss and Corbin's (1990) book to discern the appropriate process for conducting a grounded theory study. My focus was on doing things correctly; correctness was shattered by my longitudinal efforts and the need to adapt methodologies and analytics to accommodate longitudinal data (Compton-Lilly, 2014a, 2015).

Longitudinal trajectories do not unfold in empty spaces. Being/becoming always occurs within spaces populated by histories. Racism, colonization, inequity, and cruelty affect children's learning trajectories – including Peter's and Adam's. While the details of their experiences – an African American boy growing up in an under-resourced city in the 1990s and a Muslim youth growing up in the shadow of 9/11 – are significant, both trajectories were informed by historical moments. Likewise, my being/becoming a researcher has been subject to these same historical moments, as negotiated by my white skin. Thus, my readings of these data are inseparable from the field. The field, these data, and my positionality invite me to read in particular ways, launch particular ways of thinking, and discourage me from other directions. There are no readings of data that are not part of these data. This is what Grenfell (2018) means when he suggests that we "be" rather than "do research."

1.3 Peter's Being/Becoming Literate: Three Critical Dimensions

As I considered critical dimensions of Peter's case, I confronted hundreds of pages of transcripts, coded data, field notes, and writing samples. I recognized that no matter how I justified my selection of critical dimensions of Peter's case, a degree of preference, propensity, and partiality would lead me toward particular choices. In this chapter, I highlight three critical dimensions that have informed how I have made sense of Peter's longitudinal being/becoming (Compton-Lilly, 2014b). I focus on what resonated, intrigued, and captivated me as I wrote about Peter in elementary, middle, and high school. These dimensions are both separate and linked. They operate as examples of literacy practices at particular points in time, connected through my omniscient researcher gaze. For Peter, I focus on home literacy experiences, his temporary move to New York City, and his college plans.

1.3.1 Critical Dimension #1: Peter's Home Library

When Peter was in my first grade class, Peter and his mother described their ever-growing collection of children's books. Peter owned over a hundred books, and Ms. Horner was preparing a book order for the next day's mail. Peter regularly brought his favorite books to school, reading them aloud to younger children on the bus and sharing them with his classmates. This presence of books was intentional. Drawing on her memories of her own childhood, Ms. Horner described being "surrounded by books" and how her mother was always buying books. She described her own grandmother encouraging her to "say the ABCs to him and count to him one to twenty every single day." Literacy was deeply embedded across generations.

Peter described himself as a good reader, explaining, "[I] be reading a lot of words" and "I be using the sounds." Peter bragged about being a "great speller" who got "hundreds" on his spelling tests. In grade 5, Peter, his brother, and his friends were all reading books from the *Goosebumps* series (Stine, 1992–1997). Stine was Peter's favorite author, and he excitedly recounted the plot of the *Goosebumps* book he had just finished reading. Peter brought me the book and encouraged me to read it – inviting me into his fellowship of *Goosebumps* fans.

1.3.2   Critical Dimension #2: Moving to New York City

For a few months, while Peter was in eighth grade, his family moved to New York City. Attending school in New York was difficult. Ms. Horner noted that when Peter got to New York "unfortunately everything went just downhill." Peter explained that to attend his progressive math and science enrichment school, he had to walk through an unfamiliar neighborhood where the older boys tried to start fights. He stopped attending school, saying, "cause it was a little bit too dangerous out there for me. I got into a lot of fights down there."

As his family prepared to return to the city where I taught, Peter visited his English teacher to say goodbye. He reported, "Before I left, she said I was her best student in class. She told me I could be a writer with all the stuff I would be coming up with." During subsequent interviews, Peter consistently discussed his writing. While Peter's grades had suffered and he was warned that he might not be promoted to ninth grade, Peter committed himself to his schoolwork, passed the eighth grade English Language Arts test, and was promoted to grade 9.

1.3.3   Critical Dimension #3: College Plans

By high school, Peter described writing as a favorite activity among his friends. He mused that I might "be surprised [by] how many people [at school] you find writing stories or writing poetry." Peter compared the novel he was writing to *Scorpions* (Myers, 1988), calling it a "story of the streets, like a ghetto story." He identified *The Outsiders* (Hinton, 2003) – a book dealing with similar themes – as the best book he had ever read in school. Peter wrote poetry with his friends and his girlfriend, including a poem in which he ironically denied being a poet (Fig. 1.1).

In 11th grade, Peter shared his dream of studying journalism at Columbia. However, his being/becoming was tempered by "Bs" and "Cs" on his report card and the fact that Columbia does not have an undergraduate journalism program. In

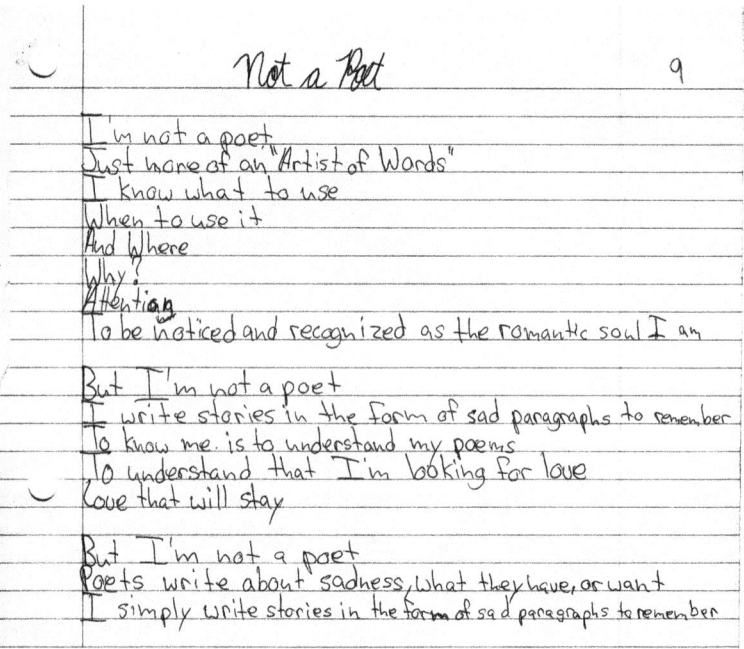

Fig. 1.1 Not a poet. (With permissions from Peter)

May of his junior year, Peter admitted that he had not taken the PSAT or the SAT.[1] He had not met with his college counselor and had no timeline for completing college applications. His high school ELA teacher was dubious, explaining, "He's one of the honors kids that's just coasting." He described Peter's writing as adequate but not "on par with what it was earlier in the year," adding, "Maybe it's just he's not trying as hard." While his teacher was confident that Peter would pass the course and the state ELA test, he was doubtful that Peter would become a writer. At age 17, Peter's goal of becoming a journalist was complicated by his teacher's lukewarm assessment, his lack of preparation for college, and his diffracted interests in various colleges. In addition to Columbia, Peter was considering Ohio State because he liked football and a private arts college in California that had sent a glossy brochure in the mail.

---

[1] The PSAT is the Preliminary Stanford Achievement Test, which is used to help students prepare for the SAT. The SAT test is a standardized test that is widely used for college admission in the United States.

1.4   Adam's Being/Becoming Literate: Three Critical Dimensions

As I considered writing about Adam, I was confronted with an even larger dataset. With Peter, I had conducted 11 interviews over 10 years; with Adam, I had conducted 35 interviews over 12 years. Thus, for Adam, there were thousands of pages of transcripts, coded data, field notes, photographs, student drawings, and writing samples. As with Peter, I selected three critical dimensions that I have written about in the past (Compton-Lilly, 2019, in review). Specifically, I draw on his descriptions of Moroccan beaches, mosques and being Muslim, and burning of mosques and cathedrals.

1.4.1   Critical Dimension #1: The Beaches of Morocco

Adam associated Morocco with sunshine and beaches. When asked to draw a self-portrait during grade 1, Adam portrayed himself in Morocco surrounded by a sunny sky filled with birds. He spoke of his grandmother, explaining, "she died and right now she is with Allah." He wrote in first-person:

> I am looking at the sckieey and I meyde a smymyas in eid and I am hipp in Eid.
> (I am looking at the sky and I made a smile in Eid and I am happy in Eid).

When asked about Morocco, Adam responded, "It's hot most of the time. And, I go to the beach and swim. I play tennis in the sand." He told us, "There's no swimming pools in Morocco. There's only the beach and it's much funner than swimming pools." He then admitted, "Well, there is swimming pools. The swimming pools in Morocco like much bigger. They're very big… almost a hundred people can fit [in the pools]." Adam fondly recalled the beach near his aunt's house that had "so much rocks that you have to climb over them" (see Fig. 1.2).

The beach and swimming were recurring motifs in Adam's family. Adam's sister recounted the story of how her mother almost drowned as a child. Adam described his uncle as the "best swimmer" who "almost made it to Olympics." Recollections of Morocco are infused with family, sunny days, and trips to the beach. The skies are blue; Adam is happy with his family, and even the swimming pools are bigger.

1.4.2   Critical Dimension #2: Mosques and Being Muslim

By middle school, Adam was becoming aware of what it meant to be Muslim and live in the United States. Adam described his preference for living in Morocco, saying, "You have like your culture, you don't have to fear like Islamophobia [and there's] not much racism." By seventh grade, issues related to immigration and hate

Fig. 1.2 Adam's grade 1 self-portrait

crimes directed at Muslims were national news. Adam witnessed the aftermath of a shooting at a gas station near his home. However, it was the proximity to the mosque and the Qur'anic school that concerned Adam: "there was like five policemen outside just our building. It was super strange but, I mean like they [the shooters] might be racist." When I posed that police might have been called because children were present, Adam was dubious, noting, "maybe, or cause like everyone's wearing hijabs."

Adam reported confronting peers at school when they used hateful language. He explained:

> Well, there isn't really hate, but people don't understand. Like I'm walking around the hall and I just hear people saying stuff like they don't even know [what it means]. Like they're just yelling like "Allahu Akbar" And I'm like, "Do you even know what that means?" [Adam's peers are] like "Oh, it's something terrorists say." I'm like, "That's definitely not what it means." Yeah, I just look at them and I'm like, "You don't even know what it means and you're just saying it... It's what we say in a prayer. It means 'God is great.' It's not something you say to spread hate or fear."

Not only did Adam challenge hateful rhetoric used at school; he also made me more aware of Muslim experiences in the United States.

1.4.3   Critical Dimension #3: Mosques and Cathedrals

On the day I visited Adam's ninth grade English Language Arts class, they were discussing the fire at Notre Dame Cathedral. Later during our interview, Adam commented, "Yeah, that was bad… *but* you know a 900-year-old mosque in China was destroyed and [it's] all rubble now." He continued, "Yeah, I just thought it was interesting how like Notre Dame is just iconic, like it burned down. When they're destroying like numerous mosques in other places. Even in Syria, there's mosques that are thousands of years old, [from] before even the Prophet, like [during] the time of Jesus. And those have been destroyed and people don't even talk about them." Across the high school interviews, Adam commented on Muslim people interned in Chinese concentration camps, Yemeni people facing starvation, and the continued American bombing of Syrian civilians. This interest in global humanity was reflected in Adam's emerging interest in studying global history in college.

By 11th grade, Adam wanted to establish a club for immigrant students, explaining that "a majority of my friends are immigrants living here." Club members would discuss "world problems during the meetings… like global issues." As Adam reported, "I'm more interested in environment because it seems like a *major problem* that we're going through right now… like the CO_2 emissions, and our water systems, we have to get those cleaned and fixed."

1.5   Reflections on Being/Becoming a Researcher

In this section, I reflect on my own being/becoming a researcher. As I consider the critical dimensions of Peter's being/becoming that I have highlighted in my writing, the significance of me being a teacher is clear. My focus was on Peter being/becoming literate and attending college. I was secretly thrilled that he wanted to become a writer, and since I had taught Peter to read, I claimed a small role in that dream. The longitudinal data set highlighted pedagogical issues: new State tests implemented as part of No Child Left Behind, my involvement with Whole Language, and my work as a Reading Recovery teacher. My writing reflected the collective ire of progressive educators distraught by increased testing, the implementation of scientifically based instruction, and the privileging of best practices and the five pillars of reading. Through my writing, I presented myself as a progressive educator with a commitment to children. Although I did not realize it, the field had directed me to attend to some things and not others, to see things in particular ways, and to think what was thinkable for a progressive educator. While this does not imply that the commitments of progressive educators are misguided, it acknowledges the field in which I operated and how I established myself as a progressive educator.

While at my school, my views and "expertise" were not always appreciated, I became recognized locally as an accomplished reading teacher and was invited by my district to coach other teachers. I began to present at national conferences, publish in teacher-oriented journals, sign book contracts, and was one of the few teacher/researchers ever to be awarded a National Academy of Education/Spencer Postdoctoral Fellowship. As Bourdieu (1993) maintained, every field brings its own set of stakes and interests in order to operate successfully, and people must play the game. However, it was after I was recruited by a Tier 1 university that I began to realize that I might be becoming a researcher/scholar; I recall the moment when a senior scholar recognized the significance of a 10-year dataset, telling me, "Almost nobody has data like that."

The data I collected with Adam in my second longitudinal study was less tightly bound with my identity as a teacher. I had benefitted from the privilege of *retiring* from public school teaching (Swartz, 1997), which allowed me whole mornings to think and write about small groups of students that I had followed across time. As Bourdieu maintained, "leisure time" to write and reflect and a "pure gaze" uninhibited by the need for ongoing decision-making and action are "luxuries unavailable to practitioners who are immersed in the flow of everyday life" (Grenfell, 2008, p. 225). I was in the early years as an assistant professor at an internationally recognized university that attracted students from around the world. My own global awareness exploded through my work with graduate students from around the globe. These graduate students inspired me to focus on my next longitudinal project on immigrant families.

Significantly, I was a tenure track professor at a top-ranked university. As I grew into that position, it become apparent that tenure involved a complicated dance – establishing a presence in the field, publishing in the right journals, adhering to established writing formats, and citing the right scholars. What I studied and how I wrote were influenced by ongoing academic conversations, the IRB process, my relationships with senior scholars, and the politics of professional organizations. I operated within an established field in which we all read and cited Heath (1983) and Street (1995). We recognized people's literacy practices, honored cultural and linguistic dimensions of literacy, and challenged the institutional mechanisms that privileged some students. Situating my work in relation to these scholars and their ideas was a good career move. Bourdieu questioned these "small circles of mutual admiration" (Wacquant, 1992, p. 57) and an accompanying lack of reflexivity (Swartz, 1997). As Swartz explained, "Reflexivity means viewing intellectual practices as being interest-oriented rather than being motivated exclusively by objective ideas or values" (Swartz, 1997, p. 279).

My researcher stance allowed me to be selectively reflexive – to decide what stories to tell and how to tell them. I decided what was and was not worthy of research. In my early work, I challenged deficit discourses related to parents in Peter's poor urban community. This focus served the interests of progressive academic researchers and reflected ongoing conversations about the prevalence of deficit discourses imposed on students and their families. I made the right argument at the right time and was rewarded. Having chosen this productive path, I moved through the tenure and promotion process. Specifically, I learned to manipulate methodology and theory to craft compelling arguments and establish myself as a scholar. Eventually, my foray into longitudinal research led to rich theoretical (Compton-Lilly, 2016b) and novel analytic spaces (Compton-Lilly 2014a, 2015).

In addition to academic spaces in which I operate, it is essential to recognize historical and societal spaces. As an American scholar, the history of race in America affects every question I ask and every classroom I enter. This entire chapter could have – and perhaps should have – been focused on my role as a White educator documenting the being/becoming of children of color. As an African American youth growing up in an under-resourced urban community, Peter attended an elementary school where most Spanish-speaking children were in "bilingual classes," leaving Peter and his African American peers in the "regular" classes, with fewer resources, a less culturally relevant curriculum, and fewer teachers who shared their cultural and linguistic background. Most of us were White teachers working in primarily African American classrooms. Our principal and several of my colleagues were literally self-described missionaries intent on saving children from their families.

Adam attended a better-resourced school in a more affluent community. He was generally the only Muslim student in his classes and recalled only one Muslim teacher across his school career. Both Adam and his mother were dedicated to helping people in schools and the community to recognize Islam as a religion grounded in love and peace; Adam routinely spoke about his faith in class and with friends. While Adam had many school friends, his primary social space was the mosque, where he learned formal Arabic, memorized sections of the Qur'an, and interacted with Muslim peers. Growing up in the post-9/11 United States, Adam sometimes witnessed and received hateful comments from peers and community members. While he treated these as opportunities to educate others, he was deeply concerned, especially for his mother who routinely wore a hijab in public.

Unlike Peter, Adam benefitted from his olive-colored skin and handsome physique. By middle school, Peter was a dark-skinned African American male who was 6-feet tall with a heavy build. While people who knew Peter recognized his gentle disposition, teachers and peers sometimes made assumptions based on his size and dark skin; other boys challenged him to fight, while teachers assumed he might cause trouble. Anti-Blackness (Dumas & ross, 2016) affected Peter's school experiences and the assumptions routinely made about him. As his teacher in a school that brought a missionary zeal to our work, I am certain that I oscillated between an emergent critical and emancipatory stance – discernable through class projects dedicated to addressing social inequities (e.g., lead paint, community violence, accessible school playground) – and the "fake love" (p. 48) described by Johnson et al. (2019), which involved fixing students, privileging White-centric curricula, and pressuring students into compliant student roles. My teaching and my research did little to enhance Peter's being/becoming. While with Adam, I was released from my obligations as a teacher, I did not use my position at the university to advocate for Adam's faith being recognized in school (i.e., he was not provided with time/space for daily prayers or accommodations during Ramadan); instead, I placed him in the formidable position of educating me, in addition to educating his teachers, peers, and community members, about his Muslim faith. Despite my increasing accomplishments as scholar, I did not:

> ... resist, agitate, and tear down the educational survival complex... [by working] in solidarity with their community to achieve incremental changes in their classrooms and schools for students in the present day, while simultaneously freedom dreaming and vigorously creating a vision for what schools will be. (Love, 2019, p. 89)

1.6   A Reflexive Coda

As I reflect on my research with Peter and Adam, I thought I was telling their longitudinal stories. Yet, I was also writing my career and claiming my place in the literacy research community. I generally ignored the orthodoxy of the field, my goals, and the limits of my experiences. Bourdieu believed that "a reflexive practice can help free the researcher from the particular economic, cultural, and social interests that distort that singular pursuit of ideal interests of scientific knowledge" (Swartz, 1997, p. 282). Too often "researchers do not know, and do not want to know, the limits of their thoughts or to acknowledge the social conditions of its construction" (Grenfell, 2011, p. 215). While it is highly questionable whether this exposé of my reflective shortcomings, written years after data were collected and hundreds of pages of manuscript have been published, alters anything, it is my hope that it serves as an unsettling example and a reminder of the limits of the researcher's gaze and our need to continuously peel back layers of analysis with an eye to the academic fields in which we operate, the social histories that define people's experiences, and the humanity of participants.

References

Barton, D., & Hamilton, M. (1998). *Local literacies: Reading and writing in one community*. Routledge.

Bourdieu, P. (1993). *Sociology in question*. Thousand Oaks.

Compton-Lilly, C. (2003). *Reading families: The literate lives of urban children*. Teachers College Press.

Compton-Lilly, C. (2007). *Re-reading families: The literate lives of urban children, four years later*. Teachers College Press.

Compton-Lilly, C. (2012). *Reading time: The literate lives of urban secondary students and their families*. Teachers College Press.

Compton-Lilly, C. (2014a). Temporal discourse analysis. In P. Albers, T. Holbrook, & A. Flint (Eds.), *New methods in literacy research*. Routledge.

Compton-Lilly, C. (2014b). The development of writing habitus: A ten-year case study of a young writer. *Written Communication, 31*, 371–403.

Compton-Lilly, C. (2015). Revisiting children and families: Temporal discourse analysis and the longitudinal construction of meaning. In J. Sefton-Green & J. Rowsell (Eds.), *Learning and literacy over time: Longitudinal perspectives*. Routledge.

Compton-Lilly, C. (2016a). *Reading students' lives: Literacy learning across time*. Routledge.

Compton-Lilly, C. (2016b). Time in education: Intertwined dimensions and theoretical possibilities. *Time and Society, 25*(3), 575–593.

Compton-Lilly, C. (2019). Being child-centered and focusing on children: A longitudinal case study. *Michigan Reading Journal, 51*(3), 50–57.

Compton-Lilly, C. (in review). *Transnationalism, global awareness and critical cosmopolitanism in the lives of immigrant youth.*

Dumas, M. J., & ross, k. m. (2016). "Be real black for me" imagining BlackCrit in education. *Urban Education, 51*(4), 415–442.

Elder, G. H. (2018). *Children of the great depression.* Routledge.

Elder, G. H., Jr. (1995). The life course paradigm: Social change and individual development. In P. E. Moen, G. H. Elder, & K. E. Lüscher (Eds.), *Examining lives in context: Perspectives on the ecology of human development* (pp. 101–139). American Psychological Association.

Grenfell, M. (2008). Postscript: Methodological principles. In M. Grenfell (Ed.), *Pierre Bourdieu: Key concepts.* Routledge.

Grenfell, M. (2011). Towards a study of language and linguistic study. In M. Grenfell (Ed.), *Bourdieu, language, and linguistics* (pp. 197–225). Continuum Press.

Grenfell, M. (2012). A future synthesis: Bourdieu, ethnography, and new literacy studies. In M. Grenfell, D. Bloome, C. Hardy, K. Pahl, J. Rowsell, & B. Street (Eds.), *Language, ethnography, and education: Bridging new literacy studies and Bourdieu* (pp. 174–196). Routledge.

Grenfell, M. (2018). Reflexivity. In M. Grenfell & K. Pahl (Eds.), *Bourdieu, language-based ethnographies and reflexivity: Putting theory into practice* (pp. 19–36). Routledge.

Heath, S. B. (1983). *Ways with words: Language, life and work in communities and classrooms.* Cambridge University Press.

Johnson, L. L., Bryan, N., & Boutte, G. (2019). Show us the love: Revolutionary teaching in (un) critical times. *The Urban Review, 51*(1), 46–64.

Love, B. L. (2019). *We want to do more than survive: Abolitionist teaching and the pursuit of educational freedom.* Beacon Press.

Parkin, D. (2016). From multilingual classification to translingual ontology: A turning point. In K. Arnaut, J. Blommeart, B. Rampton, & M. Spotti (Eds.), *Language and superdiversity* (pp. 77–88). Routledge.

Strauss, A., & Corbin, J. (1990). *The basics of qualitative research: Grounded theory procedures and techniques.* Sage.

Street, B. (1995). *Social literacies: Critical approaches to literacy in development, ethnography, and education.* Longman Publisher.

Swartz, D. (1997). *Culture and power: The sociology of Pierre Bourdieu.* Chicago University Press.

Wacquant, J. D. (1992). Toward a social praxeology: The structure and logic of Bourdieu's sociology. In P. Bourdieu & J. D. Wacquant (Eds.), *An invitation to reflexive sociology.* University of Chicago Press.

Literature References

Hinton, S. E. (2003). *The outsiders.* Puffin.

Myers, W. D. (1988). *Scorpions.* HarperCollins.

Stine, R. L. (1992–1997). *The Goosebumps series.* Scholastic Press.

Chapter 2
Can a Research Space Be a Third Space? Methodology and Hierarchies in Participatory Literacy Research

Sara Hawley and John Potter

Abstract This chapter argues that we should apply Ingold's notion of a 'dwelling perspective' to participatory research practices around literacy. We argue that a dwelling perspective allows us to cultivate research spaces as generative Third Spaces, emphasising possibilities and potentials rather than certainties and allowing the emergence of non-dominant voices in the search for solutions to some of society's most pressing problems. A dwelling perspective approach to research, which sees meanings as discovered through our embroilment in the world rather than constructed, takes us further away from the idea of researcher as disembodied intellect. We argue that, as we tune into our emotional responses to our material and natural surroundings during the research process, theory becomes lived in the immediate, emerging from our embodied experience. The chapter takes two particular instances of research space as Third Space – one involving child co-researchers and one involving a teacher-researcher, examining what it means to dwell in these lived and liminal spaces. We argue that the liminality of Third Space in research spaces can be seen to work in two ways – allowing new participants over the threshold into the hallowed, elite research space and allowing the self to be undone and redone, as the researcher and participants 'become-other' during the process.

Keywords Third Space · Participatory research · Dwelling

> *I dwell in Possibility –*
>> *A fairer House than Prose –*
>> *More numerous of Windows –*
>> *Superior – for Doors.* (Emily Dickinson, 1890)

> *Something, I felt, must be wrong somewhere, if the only way to understand our own creative involvement in the world is by taking ourselves out of it.* (Ingold, 2000, p. 173)

> *When thought's courage stems from the bidding of Being, then destiny's language thrives.* (Heidegger, 1971, p. 5)

S. Hawley (✉) · J. Potter
University College of London (UCL), Oxford, UK
e-mail: s.hawley@ucl.ac.uk

© The Author(s), under exclusive license to Springer Nature Singapore Pte Ltd. 2022
C. Lee et al. (eds.), *Unsettling Literacies*, Cultural Studies and Transdisciplinarity in Education 15, https://doi.org/10.1007/978-981-16-6944-6_2

This chapter explores the idea of 'dwelling in possibility' in times of precarity. What new openings might appear to us as we yield to our imaginations and the sensory as Dickinson suggests? An 'ontology of dwelling' is something which anthropologist, Tim Ingold, proposes (following Heidegger, 1971) as he pushes back against an enduring logocentrism in our pursuit of knowledge and the persisting characterisation of the human being as a 'disembodied intellect moving in a subjective space in which are represented the problems it seeks to solve' (Ingold, 2000, p. 186). The dwelling perspective requires us to see our understanding of the world as not so much about making views '*of* the world but of taking up a view *in* it' (Ingold, 2000, p. 43). We argue that a dwelling perspective allows us to cultivate research spaces as Third Spaces (Gutierrez, 2008), giving real voice to participants not always heard in the academy and allowing 'destiny's language' to thrive (Heidegger, 1971). Opening up the scope of theory to fresh perspectives in this way seems more important than ever in a world so fractured and fragile.

The metaphor of the 'theoretical lens' (Flewitt et al., 2015, p. 2) is often invoked to describe what researchers 'visualise and apply... to make sense of "what is going on here"'. Both authors of this chapter have used Third Space (Lefebvre, 1991; Soja, 1996; Bhabha, 1994) as a theoretical lens for unsettling our understanding of literacies. But we now wonder how research spaces themselves can be characterised as Third Spaces, as both lived and liminal, agreeing with Pahl (2014, p. 190) that 'methodologies for research are not separate from the research'. As Routledge (1996, p. 401) argues, 'to enact a third space within and between academia and activism is to attempt to live theory in the immediate'. This chapter is an account of our attempts to do so in two different settings, as a practitioner-researcher and in work with children as co-researchers. We approach this by thinking about how a focus on 'dwelling' may encourage us to cultivate research spaces as Third Spaces, paying greater attention at the same time to the way in which selfhood emerges in those liminal sites.

2.1 'Dwelling' in the Third Space

The idea of the atomised researcher in pursuit of higher truths has persisted long beyond the academic demolition of the Cartesian cut which it reflects. Somerville (2007, p. 227) notes how: 'At every stage of the research process the unacknowledged pedagogical processes for doing research – the structure of the research proposal, ethics applications and the structure of the thesis – emphasize conventions based on logics and the scientific paradigm of empiricist research.' However, as this book shows, the sands are finally shifting, and new architecture is emerging as an embodied, world-dwelling researcher comes into focus.

Ingold (2000), in his ontology of dwelling, makes several moves away from a cognitivist, rationalist account of intelligence. First, he sees learning not as 'an internalization of collective representations or...*enculturation*' but rather as 'a process of *enskilment*, in which learning is inseparable from doing and in which both are embedded in the context of a practical engagement in the world' (2000, p. 416). Second, he reverses the direction of our engagement with the world from the detached 'intelligent subject who has then to construct' it to an embodied subject who has 'then to detach himself from the current of his activity in order to reflect upon it' (2000, p. 417). But this reflection for Ingold is not intelligence but 'imagining'. We argue that a focus on reflection as imagining is, as Facer (2019, p. 10) notes, 'future-oriented' and thus open to possibility.

So what do Third Space theory and a dwelling perspective have in common, and what are the implications of thinking of ourselves as researchers both dwelling in the world and inhabiting some sort of Third Space? Charles Peirce's (1867) category of Thirdness, which several characterisations of Third Space draw on, is about the generative – what emerges and what might become. Third Space is a place of reconciliation, possibility and transformation but always, as Lefebvre (1991) noted, a 'lived space', a consequence of its origin in architecture and designs for living. It is 'a fluid site ... of permanent oscillation ... within and between enunciatory sites, physical locations, political positionings, effecting a web of interconnected conditions of possibility. Emotions, memories, life histories, bodily experiences emerge from this space and breathe life into our words' (Routledge, 1996, p. 412). Further, Ingold builds on Heidegger's discussion about how dwelling is an affective state of being at one with our surroundings. 'As soon as we have the thing before our eyes, and in our hearts an ear for the word, thinking prospers' (Heidegger, 1971, p. 5).

If Third Space involves living in different spaces at once, 'we must believe that we can inhabit these different sites, making each a space of relative comfort' (Routledge, 1996, p. 406). Becoming at ease though in these different places and positionings may involve an 'undoing' and 'redoing' of the self. Considering research space as Third Space allows us to foreground the emergence of selfhood through the research process along with the 'possibility for disrupting epistemological hierarchies' (Vasudevan, 2011, p. 1160), especially if we include participants as our co-researchers. Such disruption needs to involve far more than 'polyvocal ventriloquism' (Harrison, 1993, p. 402) as we incorporate new voices. If we can achieve this, 'dwelling' can be a useful framing of participatory work in research spaces, constituting an amalgam of insider and outsider perspectives in which researcher lifeworlds are present through 'their affectivity of being in the world' (Probyn, 1992, p. 506). This focus and framing also suggests a reworking of research spaces as Third Space, which we will now go on to address.

2.2 Research Space as Third Space

Taking a step back and thinking about the origin stories of Third Space theory leads us from linguistics and cultural studies (Bhabha, 1994) into spatial studies in urban planning (Lefebvre, 1991; Soja, 1996) and, in the latter cases, the opportunity to consider its 'polyvocal' nature, as Soja described it. Gutiérrrez (2008) recognised its potential in providing a legitimising force for social change in education. The learners with whom she was working were in transition between two spaces, home culture and a new, formal 'host nation', represented as an education system, with their own sense of themselves as learners becoming problematic, not least in terms of their identity as migrants. In what sense could they occupy a learning space in which they would not 'misrecognise' themselves as learners, learners with a deficit model imposed by the host culture? The suggested answer was a space which valued their cultural heritage and tacit understandings in their autobiographical work, not by simply admitting it into the curriculum but by generating a space in which the traditional hierarchies were flattened.

With its origins in both Bhabha and Soja, then, the Third Space of Gutiérrrez shared important characteristics relating to the need to change and adapt. It later became a useful theoretical metaphor when applied to digital media, culture and education in the context of flux and change in the texts, practices and artefacts of the twenty-first century, the 'dynamic literacies' of which they are generative (Potter & McDougall, 2017). Building on these theoretical perspectives, we further understand Third Space always to be relational and sociomaterial, a site for the emergence of practices, identities and knowledge-building, which are potentially transformative and, like all space, constantly constructed through the action that derives from human agency.

Space, like literacy, then, is always ideological, contested and contingent, and we understand that research space is no different. It is disingenuous and, as Lefebvre points out, in the interests of the dominant class, to pretend otherwise. For him:

> ...theoretical practice' produces a *mental space* which is apparently but only apparently, extra-ideological. In an inevitably circular manner, this mental space then becomes the locus of a 'theoretical practice' which is separated from social practice and which sets itself up as the axis, pivot or central reference point of Knowledge. (1991, p. 6)

The problem with such circularity is that it reinforces consensus and ends up being 'nothing more than the egocentric thinking of specialized Western individuals' (Lefebvre, 1991, p. 24). If we 'live theory in the immediate' and think of research space as liminal, we open it up to newcomers, allowing people to dwell there who do not just hail from the elites Lefebvre mentions. 'Conceptualising space as open, multiple and relational, unfinished and always becoming, is a prerequisite for... the possibility of politics' (Massey, 2005, p. 59). We argue that the liminality of Third Space in research spaces might be seen to work in two ways – allowing new participants over the threshold into the hallowed, elite research space and allowing the self to be undone and redone, as the researcher and participants 'become-other' during the process.

This chapter explores both types of liminality in participatory research practices around literacy, looking at a particular instance of each: one involving child co-researchers and one involving a teacher-researcher. The research stories which follow reflect both different accounts of research space as Third Space and different styles: the first one (John's story), which represents a synthesis of heterogeneous voices, strikes a more detached tone than the second (Sara's story), which is a more personal reflection on the hybrid positioning of being both teacher and researcher.

In a methodological Third Space, problematising and re-energising the idea of researcher reflexivity also becomes important. To be reflexive is not just to know oneself but also to get in the habit of 'unknowing – an act of **dwelling** [our emphasis] in the imaginative space between declarative acts of knowledge and not knowing; an invitation to wrest our modes of inquiry and our beings away from the clutches of finite definitions of knowledge and instead rest our endeavours in the beauty of myriad ways of knowing' (Vasudevan, 2011, p. 1157). Somerville (2007, p. 235), in her advocacy of a methodology of postmodern emergence, asks us not just to do research in a 'space of unknowing' but to 'undo the self' as part of 'the messiness, unfolding, open-ended and irrational nature of becoming-other through research engagement'. She notes that rubrics on grounded theory mention emergence repeatedly, but it is concepts, categories and theory that emerge. What happens if we start to consider the emergence of selfhood as part of the research process? For her, emergence occurs in the 'play between data, representing grounded (but unknowable) material reality and analysis as the act of meaning-making' (Somerville, 2007, p. 230). It is in this space that we develop as researchers and are ourselves changed during the research process, as we learn to occupy each other's subject positions (Spivak, 1990).

2.3 Research Spaces as Third Spaces: Working with Children as Co-researchers

From a dwelling perspective, developing as a researcher involves an 'education of attention' (Gibson, 1979; Ingold, 2000) and, as with any craft, an apprenticeship through our embroilment in the world. In such an education of attention, novices learn from more experienced practitioners how to attune their perceptual skills in the process not of constructing truths but uncovering them. This section analyses how recent experiences of fieldwork focused attention on the process of 'change', 'becoming' and 'dwelling' in a Third Space in the context of participatory research with children. It is John's story. In this space, we, the university researchers, were the more experienced practitioners alongside whom the children were uncovering truths. Yet we were also ourselves altered in the process as we learned to work alongside child co-researchers and witnessed their voices shaping the theory that emerged.

The project in question, 'Playing the Archive', was located in the space of the school playground, thereby mixing metaphor and materiality. This was a 2-year funded research project based around an archive of children's games in the UK, collected over a number of years in the second-half of the twentieth century (Opie, 1994; Opie & Opie, 1954). There were many strands to this work, some of which sought to digitise and catalogue the vast Opie collection while others sought to bring contemporary children's play into juxtaposition with the play of the past, by way of making digital artefacts and stories which unlocked them for use by present-day children and into the future.

The relevant part of the study for this chapter was ethnographic work in two London playgrounds, in which we sought to investigate the current playworlds of children, in their games, rhymes, songs, digital, media-based and imaginative play (Burn et al., 2018; Potter & Cowan, 2020). To do this, we recruited teams of children as researchers alongside us, exploring and analysing their own play lives. The idea was to bring media production to the documentary research by the children themselves, using some artefacts which were familiar to them (tablets for filming) and some which were not but which soon came to be (voice recorders). We wanted to:

> …describe and re-theorise the playground as a rich and complex meaning-makerspace, full of invention and child-led agency with both the raw material of popular culture and traditional forms of games. (Potter & Cowan, 2020, p. 249)

We were already therefore looking at this space through a lens (Flewitt et al., 2015), but, more than that, we were adopting a position with relation to our research subjects as 'co-producers' of the work in the spaces in which they were playing. In this way, *co-production* enabled the 'becoming selves' mentioned above to be placed front and centre of the research. In doing this, the intention was to resist colonising the play or attempting to confer some kind of status on the games being played and the children who were playing them. They already owned these facets of their experience; they already had status and selfhood in their playworlds, and they were already 'dwelling' there. Our 'becoming selves', as researchers, sought ways to enable the children to story their selfhood in the space, in the way that they wanted to construct it, by acknowledging and representing their tacit understandings and their cultural repertoires and flattening the hierarchies.

With this flattening of hierarchies and with the children in role as co-producers of the research, a Third Space was arguably formed out of the texts made and practices enacted. Using the available tools and resources, the children made video tours of the playground, filmed on iPads and GoPros; they made drawings and maps; they took photographs of playspaces; they made videos of their games; and they made voice recordings of interviews with one other. Of course, they were also in role as 'schoolchildren', the context was still 'institutional', and they were still representing themselves *for* someone. But given the embeddedness of the cultures of play in their lives, the latitude to represent their 'selfhoods' in the space meant they retained a degree of control over the resources of meaning-making. From our point of view, this experience and the freedom enabled by working with this form of data gathering allowed us to see things which we had not previously apprehended and which we could bring into our own representations and selfhoods as researchers. One example of this seeing of the previously unseen and swapping and overlapping of roles and 'selfhoods' occurred during an early site visit to one of the playgrounds when three pairs of children filmed tours for the researchers in an empty playspace. For one of the pairs of girls, the iPad was used to record the spaces where particular events habitually occurred, certain types of games and conversations, as well as spaces where personal histories had left traces (Marsh et al., 2019). As the researcher accompanied the children, the moments being recorded by them became difficult to film because the children wished to enact and relive one of the more intense episodes of play, the 'shark game', for which they needed hands to clamber onto benches and eyes to watch each other, which were not concerned with filmmaking, framing and staring at the iPad screen. Without asking, the iPad was handed over to the researcher like a baton in a relay race to carry on the recording and, as the episode completed, was demanded by gesture and handed back, all seamlessly, wordlessly and with no interruption to the flow of the game, nor to its being recorded. Roles and recordings were merged.

Viewing the work alongside them during the project – games and songs composed from half-quoted media resources, video games, TV shows, rhyming templates from the past and community resources in the present – we found that our young researchers had provided evidence of four interacting and intersecting domains which, arguably, we would not have seen in positivist-researcher mode, namely:

> *Lifeworlds, Folkloric imagination, play as media remix, Community and belonging…* operating in the space of the playground in different ways at different times but …frequently co-present in the production of meaning therein. They operate in a process of "lamination" in which the laminates retain "some of their original distinctiveness, although in a different configuration" in the words of Holland and Leander (2004, p. 131)… Each contributes in different proportion in different situations to the creation of meaning in the moment of play. (Potter & Cowan, 2020, p. 261)

It is true that we learned about these facets of their lives and playworlds because the children were still in some senses *being* researched. In other words, the locus of control did not wholly shift towards them; the children would not have been researching these aspects of their lived experience if we had not been there, and they did not devise the overarching parameters of the study. However, the working method of participation and self-efficacy as researcher was *designed into* the project, and the children themselves contributed substantial, mediated *co-production* of the research (Bergold & Thomas, 2012). Using material artefacts, texts and practices drawn from the children's own lives, a Third Space was created and generated findings which drew on their cultural resources and tacit understandings of play in ways which would not have emerged in the traditional hierarchies of power inherent in traditional forms of research practice. In this way, for a period of time, we were all dwelling together in the space as witnesses to aspects of play, and we also took part in the 'becoming selves' of both researcher and researched.

In the section which follows, we connect these themes to the perspective of the insider teacher-researcher in the setting, and we consider the further implications for the practitioner-researcher of these notions of 'dwelling' and 'Third Space'.

2.4   Research Spaces as Third Spaces: The Experience of Being a Teacher-Researcher

As we think of research space as Third Space, allowing children over the threshold to dwell alongside us as researchers constitutes one type of liminality. A second sort of liminality involves the melding of different subject positions as our researcher selves emerge. This section analyses the work of a teacher-researcher and the process of 'becoming-other' that took place during the long process of researching and writing a PhD part-time about digital literacy practices while working in a school. It is Sara's story. The setting for the research was in an inner London primary school where I was also teaching. Thus, liminality was key: moving between the spaces of the university and the school and oscillating between the different practices and discourses of those settings and between the empiricist paradigm of research proposal, research question and methods and the sights and sounds of the classroom. How was this research space a Third Space, and how did it allow me to 'become-other' and create possibilities for action? How did learning and transformation take place when seen from the dwelling perspective?

First of all, seeing research as taking up a view *in* the world rather than *of* it requires us to take note of what St Pierre (1997) calls 'transgressive data' – emotional data, sensual data and response data that emerge in tandem with our subjectivity, the data that escape discourse and which the traditional paradigm of qualitative methodology hasn't always made space for. For me, my sensory experience as a teacher-researcher was an important part of the liminality, with sights, sounds and touch experienced differently in the different settings I found myself in as a researcher. The quiet physical space of the library for reading, imagining and writing afforded a space for becoming a different sort of self – imbricated with the screen in a peaceful escape from the cacophony of children at work and home, the gentle touch on the keyboard, a less tiring gesture than the postures of authority necessary at school. Both the research process and the writing-up can be seen as sociomaterial. Writing is not what Goody (1977, p. 151) called a 'technology of the intellect' but rather a sociomaterial achievement of the situated researcher. As Ingold (2000, p. 403) notes, there is 'no inscription without incorporation – without … the building of habitual patterns of posture and gesture into the bodily modus operandi of the skilled practitioner.' Writing was only possible after days of immersion in the pages and screens of physical and digital texts, only possible in the early hours of the morning after some sleepless hours when reflections materialised as representation, the patterns of posture developed through watching others involved in similar practices, concentrating in their stillness for hours on end.

In the university space, it was necessary and possible to undo my teacher-self and redo a researcher-self. The process was gradual and part of a larger process of undoing, redoing and emergence. Like St Pierre (1997) who was researching a community she grew up in, I was implicated in the discourse and practices of one site (the school) but had a foot in another camp (the university) with its different discourses and practices. The importance of *the other* is well-established in sociological and sociocultural theories of identity going back to G H Mead's (1934) distinction between the *me*, others' response to us, and the *I*, our response to the *me*. Deleuze's (1993) metaphor of the fold disrupts and problematises the binary between inside and outside, self and other. St Pierre (1997, p. 178) takes up this concept of 'folded subjectivity' to describe the researcher's changing identity as boundaries blur between the researcher and researched/knower and known/self and other in a constant process of unfolding and refolding. For St Pierre (1997, p. 184):

> Traditional qualitative methodology does provide a function for the Other in the research process through activities such as peer debriefing and member checks... The purpose of both of these activities has been to lend credibility to qualitative research projects by bringing the outside – ... in the form of members and peers – into the process, but only to a limited extent.

St Pierre's concept of 'response data' broadens the field of *the other*, suggesting the role of many others in helping form our subjectivity as researcher-selves. For me, as for St Pierre, response data came not just from inside the academy – from supervisors, the PhD upgrade committee, seminar and conference audiences and the authors whose work influenced me – but also from fellow teachers at school, pupils, their parents and my family members all helping me to 'become-other'. As St Pierre (1997, p. 185) notes, 'All these others move me out of the self-evidence of my work and into its absences and give me the gift of different language and practice with which to trouble my common sense understanding of the world.' So for me, the development of my researcher-self involved the response of others to my explanations of my work, both formally in written documents and in conversation. In school, pupils, other staff and their families also responded to the different postures and gestures I adopted in small group interviews when I was being researcher rather than teacher. The blurring of boundaries between inside and outside in the research process meant not just the merging of insider and outsider perspectives but also notions of interiority and exteriority separated only by a permeable membrane, the researcher-self always absorbing both the social and material encountered outside and emerging in response to them.

Finally in the painful search for validity as a researcher, we turn to the notion of agency or 'making a difference'. Developing Arendt's idea of non-sovereign agency, Krause (2017, paras 4–5) points out that agency is always socially and materially distributed. Rather than being somehow 'contained' in individuals, it 'is constituted through social and material processes... and depends in a constitutive way on other people's uptake and the things that help shape our impact on the world.' As Denzin (2002, p. 483) notes, researchers can make a difference because 'our interpretive practices have a material effect on the world; there is a materiality to the text... We change the world by changing the way we make it visible'. Yet for teacher-researchers and indeed anyone conducting research with young people, we need to go further both in our search for validity and in making a difference. In terms of validity, practitioner-researchers are urged to demonstrate not just theoretical and interpretive validity as other researchers would but also what Pappas and Tucker-Raymond (2011, p. 7) call 'catalytic validity'. For Pappas and Tucker-Raymond

(2011, p. 7) 'a study has catalytic validity to the extent that it caused a teacher to take action... [and] transform their practice' as a result of their research. This chimes with the widespread concern among those working in the field of Childhood Studies 'to highlight the restrictions that operate on the lives of children' and their insistence that 'research must be aimed at improving the lives of children... by challenging those restrictions, rather than simply documenting their lives' (Clark et al., 2014, pp. 3–4). Teacher research of literacy involves three dimensions, as Zeichner and Noffke (2001) suggest: the *personal*, which links to questioning and improving our practice; the *professional*, which links to challenging and building on current theories and practice around literacy teaching; and the *political*, where we are asking how we can 'change and transform literacy education to challenge existing structures of power and privilege so that literacy education and the world are fairer and more just' (Pappas & Tucker Raymond, 2011, p. 266). Yet not all teachers will find the 'politics of resistance' (Giroux, 2001) straightforward in their setting. One advantage of working in the same setting as you do research is that, by virtue of that position, you may be able to achieve impact on the ground relatively quickly and easily. Of course, the teacher-researcher's agency is determined by others' response to it; they can effect change in their setting only if there is uptake of their ideas in school. I was fortunate that this was possible for me because I worked with colleagues who allowed and valued questioning and resistance.

Pascal and Bertram (2014, p. 28) talk of how their 'experience has shown that to achieve impact requires an extended commitment to the process, deep attachment within the context where change or impact is desired and a firmly-held belief in equitable, distributed, social action'. This was the case in our school – other people were willing to engage with the findings of the research. Because of their uptake, agency was distributed as a result of the research: new practices were disseminated and taken up by other staff, and new staff members were hired to carry on some of the digital practices studied and to support groups of children who might need intervention based on the outcomes of the research. Agency was also distributed materially, with investment in equipment and new software and hardware making those new digital practices possible.

2.5   Conclusion

The focus of Third Space is on becoming and emergence, and these are characteristics not just of research subjects and their assemblages but also of the researchers themselves as they develop during the research process. This is true particularly of those who are new to research, such as child co-researchers or practitioner-researchers whose identity changes as they start to dwell in new camps. If we are to 'dwell in possibility', we must acknowledge both our sensory response to the material and the uptake to us of others as we 'redo' ourselves as researchers. The process of 'becoming-other' in research involves an undoing or 'deidentification of the self' (Spivak,

1989, p. 130), which goes beyond accounts of researcher reflexivity demanded in the qualitative tradition to incorporate the possibility of making a difference.

Hannah Arendt, working with Heidegger in the phenomenologist tradition which Ingold draws upon, has, as Debarbieux (2017) notes, a three-part spatial ontology which focuses on the material, the social and the political conditions for human action. First, there exists the **Earth** as the material framing for the human condition. Second is the **world** which is the way the world appears to us as humans. 'If nature and the earth generally constitute the condition of human life, then the world and the things of the world constitute the condition under which this specifically human life can be at home on earth' (Arendt, 1958, p. 134). This second spatial concept is about how we dwell on Earth, in relation to the things as they appear to us. The third spatial frame she adduces is a praxeological space, the 'space of appearance' where we can make a difference. Such a space is both fragile and contingent, unlike 'the spaces which are the work of our hands... wherever people gather together, it is potentially there, but only potentially, not necessarily and not forever' (1958, p. 199). The fact of being together is not enough: words and deeds are necessary for political action. This space of appearance has a lot in common with Third Space, a space where action is possible. In both of the research spaces we have identified as Third Space, agency was possible but was determined by the way in which others took up the findings, the potential for agency in both spaces framed by the social and material conditions.

2.6 Reflective Coda

Participatory research, which listens to the 'richness of the meanwhile' (Facer, 2019) so that competing narratives and voices are heard, may be a particularly fruitful Third Space, but any research space has characteristics of Thirdness if the researcher takes up the invitation to 'unknow' (Vasudevan, 2011) in order to know more fully. We argue that a 'dwelling perspective' allows us to 'unknow' and 're-know' more effectively as we take up views not *of* the world but *in* it. For Ingold (2000, p. 387), there is no difference between acquiring a practical skill and one which involves language and communication. 'There is no "reading" of words or deeds that is not part of the novice's own practical orientation to his or her environment.' By 'dwelling' as researchers, we can 'live theory in the immediate' (Routledge, 1996) and enact spaces where academia and activism are brought into conversation.

Acknowledging ideas of Thirdness moves us away from a linear approach to research and to seeing the world as the 'mess' that it is (Law, 2004) with all its 'folds, wrinkles, back alleys and whirlpools' (Davies, 2015, p. 35). It also allows us to shine the lens on social justice as hitherto marginalised voices get the microphone or megaphone. In this way, literacy research can be seen as an activist project, where the voices of those involved in struggles help shape the critical literature and theory that conceptualises those struggles. Taking into account these perspectives is only a first step though. Understanding how the agency of participatory researchers is distributed both socially and materially is crucial to thinking about how we might dwell in the possibility of a more optimistic and just future.

References

Arendt, H. (1958). *The human condition*. University of Chicago Press.
Bergold, J., & Thomas, S. (2012). Participatory research methods: A methodological approach in motion. *Historical Social Research/Historische Sozialforschung, 37*(142), 191–222.
Bhabha, H. (1994). *The location of culture*. Routledge.
Burn, A., Potter, J., Marsh, J., Hudson-Smith, A., Woolley, H., Bishop, J., Hay, D., Cowan, K., Signorelli, V., Brickhill, A., Bannister, C., & Somerset-Ward, A. (2018). *Playing the archive*. [EPSRC funded project]. Retrieved October 22, 2020, from playingthearchive.net
Clark, A., Flewitt, R., Hammersley, M., & Robb, M. (Eds.). (2014). *Understanding research with children and young people*. Sage.
Davies, E. (2015). Meanings and mess in collaborative participatory research. *Literacy, 49*(1).
Debarbieux, B. (2017). Hannah Arendt's spatial thinking: An introduction. *Territory, Politics, Governance, 5*(4), 351–367. https://doi.org/10.1080/21622671.2016.1234407
Deleuze, G. (1993). *The fold: Leibniz and the baroque* (T. Conley, Trans.). University of Minnesota Press.
Denzin, N. K. (2002). Confronting ethnography's crisis of representation. *Journal of Contemporary Ethnography, 31*(4), 482–490.
Facer, K. (2019). Storytelling in troubled times: What is the role for educators in the deep crises of the 21st century. *Literacy, 53*(1).
Flewitt, R., Pahl, K., & Smith, A. (2015). Methodology matters. *Literacy, 49*(1).
Gibson, J. (1979). *The ecological approach to visual perception*. Houghton Mifflin.
Giroux, H. (2001). *Theory and resistance in education: Towards a pedagogy for the opposition*. Bergin & Garvey.
Goody, J. (1977). *The domestication of the savage mind*. Cambridge University Press.
Gutiérrez, K. (2008). Developing a sociocritical literacy in the Third Space. *Reading Research Quarterly, 43*(2), 148–164.
Harrison, F. (1993). Writing against the grain: Cultural politics of difference in the work of Alice Walker. *Critique of Anthropology, 13*, 401–427. https://doi.org/10.1177/0308275X9301300407
Heidegger, M. (1971). *Poetry, language, thought* (A. Hofstadter, Trans.). Harper and Row.
Holland, D., & Leander, K. (2004). Ethnographic studies of positioning and subjectivity: An introduction. *Ethos, 32*(2), 127–139.
Ingold, T. (2000). *The perception of the environment: Essays on livelihood, dwelling and skill*. Routledge.
Krause, S. (2017). *Agency*. Online chapter. https://www.politicalconcepts.org/agency-sharon-krause/. Accessed 27 Sept 2020.
Law, J. (2004). *After method: Mess in social science research*. Routledge.
Lefebvre, H. (1991). *The production of space* (English translation). Basil Blackwell.
Marsh, J., Bishop, J., Burn, A., & Potter, J. (2019). *Meshwork, playlines and palimpsests: A tracing of play over time*. Paper presented at UK Literacy Association (UKLA) 55th International Conference, July, 2019, Sheffield Hallam University.
Massey, D. (2005). *For space*. Sage.
Mead, G. (1934). *Mind, self and society from the standpoint of a social behaviorist*. University of Chicago Press.
Opie, I. (1994). *The people in the playground*. Oxford University Press.
Opie, I., & Opie, P. (1954). *The lore and language of schoolchildren*. Oxford University Press.

Pahl, K. (2014). *Materializing literacies in communities*. Bloomsbury.

Pappas, C., & Tucker-Raymond, E. (2011). *Becoming a teacher researcher in literacy teaching and learning*. Routledge.

Pascal, C., & Bertram, T. (2014). Transformative dialogues. The impact of participatory research on practice. In A. Clark, R. Flewitt, M. Hammersley, & M. Robb (Eds.), *Understanding research with children and young people*. Sage.

Peirce, C. S. (1867). On a new list of categories. *Proceedings of the American Academy of Arts and Sciences, 7*(1868), 287–298.

Potter, J., & Cowan, K. (2020). Playground as meaning-making space: Multimodal making and re-making of meaning in the (virtual) playground. *Global Studies of Childhood, 10*(3), 248–263.

Potter, J., & McDougall, J. (2017). *Digital media, culture and education: Theorising Third Space literacies*. Palgrave Macmillan.

Probyn, E. (1992). Technologizing the self: A future anterior for cultural studies. In L. Grossberg, C. Nelson, & P. A. Treichler (Eds.), *Cultural studies* (pp. 501–511). Routledge.

Routledge, P. (1996). The Third Space as critical engagement. *Antipode, 28*, 399–419.

Soja, E. (1996). *Thirdspace: Journeys to Los Angeles and other real-and-imagined places*. Basil Blackwell.

Somerville, M. (2007). Postmodern emergence. *International Journal of Qualitative Studies in Education, 20*(2), 225–243. https://doi.org/10.1080/09518390601159750

Spivak, G. (1989). *In a word*. Interview with Ellen Rooney. *Differences, 1*, 124–156.

Spivak, G. (1990). *The post-colonial critic*. Routledge.

St Pierre, E. (1997). Methodology in the fold and the irruption of transgressive data. *International Journal of Qualitative Studies in Education, 10*(2), 175–189.

Vasudevan, L. (2011). An invitation to unknowing. *Teachers College Record, 113*(6), 1154–1174.

Zeichner, K. M., & Noffke, S. (2001). Practitioner research. In V. Richardson (Ed.), *Handbook of research on teaching* (4th ed.). American Educational Research Association.

Chapter 3
Sharing the Screen: Reconfiguring Participatory Methodologies for Digitally Mediated Literacy Research

Bethany Monea

Abstract This chapter examines what happens when participatory methodologies for literacy research are enacted through screens and across physical distance. It is based on data from a year-long participatory video project in which nine Latinx youth and I co-created a film series exploring their transitions to college during a global pandemic. The COVID-19 pandemic also reconfigured the sociomaterial conditions of our participatory research processes, including the platforms we used, the roles and rituals we adopted, and the ways in which we articulated our goals and contributions across screens. In this chapter, I use the guiding concept of "sharing the screen" to illustrate how these sociomaterial arrangements shaped the way that participation, power, and perspectives were distributed across and through our collaborative inquiry. I suggest that conducting participatory research that is attuned to equity in virtual environments necessitates critical attention to the sociomaterial arrangements of screen sharing and the interplay of distributing access, control, and stories across digital contexts.

Keywords Participatory research · Literacy studies · Sociomaterialism · Youth media · COVID-19 · Digital research methods

A lot of people don't know what it's like to be Latina …right now, we're women of color – like all of us – we're first-gen, going to college, in the middle of a pandemic. I want people to see what that's like. – Clementine

We are all Latinas and we are all women, but for me, when people think about a group or identity, they think about it as a universal thing - that all women or Hispanics have the same experience. For me it's important to kind of break away from that and understand that not every single person's the same, and that even though we have similarities, there's different aspects, different facets of our life that have to be accounted for. – Dani

B. Monea (✉)
University of Pennsylvania, Philadelphia, PA, USA
e-mail: bmonea@upenn.edu

© The Author(s), under exclusive license to Springer Nature Singapore Pte Ltd. 2022
C. Lee et al. (eds.), *Unsettling Literacies*, Cultural Studies and Transdisciplinarity in Education 15, https://doi.org/10.1007/978-981-16-6944-6_3

3.1 Introduction

The quotes above were spoken aloud by Clementine and Dani[1] in a Zoom room populated by six female Latinx[2] high school students and me, a non-Latinx adult researcher, in April 2020. We were discussing their goals for a participatory visual research project in which we were all engaged: the creation of a film series documenting students' transition from high school to college in the middle of the COVID-19 pandemic, which the students decided to share on a YouTube channel they named "Latinx Stories." In their responses, Clementine's and Dani's use of the phrases "we are all" and "all of us" indicate they were articulating ownership of goals they claimed for themselves and the other Latinx youth participants in the group; in this moment, my goals for the project as a non-Latinx, white researcher were peripheral to the conversation. Significantly, the students' articulation of control over the project's purpose in this moment aligned with a moment where Dani also had control over the "screen sharing" function of Zoom and her screen was being shared with the group: a moment that represents how power was distributed by the converging social and material configurations of our work together and a starting point for thinking about how the sharing of screens is entangled with the ethical implications of digitally mediated participatory research.

3.1.1 Background of the Latinx Stories Project

I met the nine youth participants involved in the creation of Latinx Stories in the summer of 2019, when I was volunteering with an extracurricular College Bridge Program in a metropolitan area of the United States. This program supported students who would be the first in their family to attend college throughout the process of preparing for, applying to, and transitioning into college, and I was serving as a writing coach and a video project facilitator. During students' last year of high school, I asked for volunteers to participate in a filmmaking project and research study about their literacy practices as they transitioned from high school to college, and nine students and I began working together to create the Latinx Stories YouTube channel. In February of 2020, I convened our first (and only) 4-hour, in-person Saturday workshop, which consisted of community-building activities, planning, and goal-setting for the series. Although transportation was arranged for all participants, only three were able to attend this in-person event because of school, family, extracurricular, and work commitments. At the end of the workshop, I asked the

---

[1] Participant names and the name of the series are pseudonyms. Participants were given the option to choose their own pseudonyms.

[2] Some participants used the terms Latino, Latina, or Latinx to describe their ethnicity, some used the term Hispanic, and some used multiple terms. In this chapter, I use the term "Latinx," in congruence with the name they chose for their film series.

students to choose a platform for group communication, and they set up a group chat within the social media application Snapchat.

Less than a month later, the COVID-19 pandemic closed schools and put a halt to our plans for further in-person research, and I notified participants that we would shift our project to a virtual format. As a group, we remained in communication asynchronously via the Snapchat group, and we began to meet weekly via Zoom to discuss our lives, research, and the filmmaking project. I sent filmmaking kits to each participant that enhanced the capacities of their phones with a microphone and tripod, and we began using a collaborative video-editing platform, WeVideo. In total, we produced 12 videos for the Latinx Stories YouTube channel.

3.1.2 Shifting Toward Sharing the Screen

The onset of the COVID-19 pandemic shifted the priorities, logistics, and sociomaterial conditions for the project in multiple ways. This chapter will explore these entangled shiftings, in order to elucidate the ways in which temporal and physical arrangements are intertwined with the arrangement of goals, literacies, and selves in the context of participatory research. Over the course of the year-long project, the youth participants and I only shared a physical collaboration space one time – during our single in-person workshop. However, our computer and phone screens were filled with each other's faces, voices, writing, and avatars as we connected through Zoom, Snapchat, Google Docs, WeVideo, and other platforms. Although we stopped sharing physical space in March, we shifted toward a "shared screen" in many different ways: we contributed to the screens of shared platforms (synchronously and asynchronously), we shared our screens with each other on Zoom, and youth participants shared themselves and their stories via the screens through which viewers watched the Latinx Stories YouTube channel. This chapter explores how such shiftings across different permutations of "sharing screens" distributed opportunities for participation across our digitally mediated collaboration and how these opportunities were connected to the distribution of power within the project and students' distribution of perspectives on being Latinx, first-gen students in 2020. In what follows, I explore how shifting sociomaterial configurations – from goal-setting to Zoom settings – reshaped three vectors of distribution (participation, power, and perspectives) and suggest their entanglements with "sharing the screen."

3.2 Theoretical Frameworks

The design of the Latinx Stories project is inspired by participatory educational research paradigms (e.g., Barley & Russell, 2019; Caraballo et al., 2017) that are "deeply rooted in the struggle for social justice and educational equity" (Irizarry, 2009, p. 194). Following Burnett et al.'s (2019) exploration of digital tools in a participatory theater project, I adopt a sociomaterialist orientation to this work through which I see "technologies as participants, foregrounding what they do when they come *into relation* with other participants" (p. 683, emphasis in original). I detail these theoretical underpinnings to my study design and analysis below.

3.2.1 Participatory Approaches to Literacy Research with Marginalized Youth

I invited students to participate in the knowledge construction process using participatory filmmaking, drawing on traditions of visual and participatory research methodologies that have been widely used across sociological, anthropological, educational, and community development research and that rely on including participants in co-constructing and interpreting visual data about their own experiences (e.g., Gubrium & Harper, 2013; Mannay, 2016; Mitchell et al., 2017; Pauwels, 2015; Pink, 2021; Wang & Burris, 1997). When used with populations whose contributions to academic research are often overlooked, sidelined, or repressed, such methods offer a way of centering the epistemic privilege (Campano et al., 2016; Moya, 2002) that participants from marginalized communities can contribute to examinations of social inequities, as well as foregrounding participants' "right to research" their own experiences (Appadurai, 2006, p. 167). Educational researchers have used participatory visual methods, such as student-produced photography, map-making, and scrapbooking, to center youths' perspectives in the knowledge construction process and incorporate students' visual meaning-making processes into inquiries about their literacy and learning practices (e.g. Call-Cummings et al., 2019; Lutrell, 2010; Orellana, 1999; Pahl & Allan, 2011; Templeton, 2018; Tuck & Habtom, 2019). In this study, I specifically drew upon the methodological traditions of participatory video, collaborative filmmaking, and community video, methods employed by participatory researchers to invite participants into the processes of shooting and editing films that capture their perspectives and sharing these films with each other, their peers, researchers, and other stakeholders (e.g., Elder, 1994; Chalfen & Rich, 2004; Mitchell et al., 2016; Muir & Mason, 2012; Cardinal, 2019). In the Latinx Stories project, we adapted participatory video methods by creating a series of short episodes documenting the participants' college transition journeys and changes over time. We hosted this episodic web series on a YouTube channel collaboratively created by the participants.

Participatory visual methods can de-center and augment researchers' perspectives by including participants in shaping the project and data, and Barley and Russell (2019) argue that they can reduce power differentials between participants and researchers. However, it is important to remember that participant-constructed visual data is always partial, mediated, and open to mis- and over-interpretation (Shankur, 2016). When employing participatory visual methodologies, reflexive acknowledgment of these realities, attention to the limits of what can and should be represented, and critical interrogation into how power is distributed among participants, the researcher, and the research apparatus are integral to an equity-oriented research design (Burkholder et al., 2015, Whiting et al., 2018). Considering the sociomaterial configuration of the research design is one element of this process.

3.2.2 Sociomaterial Dimensions of Literacy Research

I approached my analysis of this project with an orientation toward the sociomaterial, through which I understand the literacies that participants leveraged in making Latinx Stories as multiple, materially mediated, and mobile (Burnett et al., 2014; Stornaiuolo et al., 2017). Education researchers adopting a sociomaterialist orientation have drawn on actor-network theory (Latour, 2005) to foreground the ontological inseparability of social and material factors in literacy activity and research and to trace the complex web of relationships between people, things, places, and practices (Burnett & Merchant, 2020; Fenwick et al., 2011). An example of turning a sociomaterialist lens toward the research process itself is offered by de Roock (2020) in his tracing of researcher-participant-tool-platform interactions across data generated by video cameras, screen recording software, and participant observation. By unpacking the ways in which a group of students interacted with him and the physical and digital apparatus of his research, de Roock (2020) underscores the materiality of these platforms and their co-construction of the research process. This type of critical sociomaterial analysis of how bodies, devices, platforms, and social structures are arranged in relationship to each other in the process of conducting research has ethical implications for designing projects with "methodological dignity" (Garcia, 2020) that are attuned to respectful representation and accountable to participants and their goals.

3.2.2.1 A Sociomaterial Approach to a Shifting Inquiry

The COVID-19 pandemic unsettled our lives, literacies, and research as we collaborated on Latinx Stories. However, with a sociomaterial perspective that emphasizes how the "ongoing, shifting relationships" between people and material artifacts contribute to the construction of meaning-making practices (Burnett et al., 2019, p. 697), these unsettlings also offered opportunities to critically reflect on how the (re)arrangements of our collaboration affected the (re)distribution of power, participation, and perspectives within it. Just as material objects and arrangements regularize activity and patterns, they are also open to rearrangement that can unsettle the status quo (Schatzki, ctd. in Burnett, 2016, p. 571). In the Latinx Stories project, the unexpected shift to an entirely screen-mediated collaboration opened opportunities for new insights and imaginings into how virtual collaborations can forward ethical commitments to access and equity.

3.3   Participants, Identities, and Roles in the Latinx Stories Project

All nine of the student participants involved in the Latinx Stories project were the first in their family to attend college in the United States. Their families have immigrated from El Salvador, Bolivia, Peru, and the Dominican Republic, and they live in homes where Spanish and English are spoken. They were all selected in middle school for enrollment in the extracurricular College Bridge Program where I met them during their senior year. When we began the project, they attended nine different public high schools and participated in a range of activities, such as cosmetology, soccer, and dance; they cared for siblings, volunteered in their communities, and worked a variety of jobs. They went on to attend four different universities and a local community college, and one participant delayed college enrollment.

My own lived experiences differ significantly from those of my youth collaborators. I am a white, non-Latinx, monolingual English-speaking adult; I was not the first in my family to go to college, and neither I nor my parents are immigrants. In these and other ways, I am an outsider to many of the experiences and identifications my youth collaborators shared. Additionally, my status as a researcher, the convener of the project, and their former tutor often positioned me as an authority figure within our group. As a white, non-Latinx researcher working in collaboration with racialized Latinx students who are often denied power within the same systems that have bestowed it on me, I have tried to remain "cognizant of how any [research] apparatus creates a reality and requires me to be aware of how my whiteness is part of that construction" (Cardinal, 2019, p. 43). I frequently interrogated how aspects of my identity and role inflected the project's trajectory through weekly reflective memos and discussions about these inflections with my youth collaborators. In recognition of myself and my tools as "co-participants in the research process" (de Roock, 2020, p. 200), I included artifacts, notes, recordings, and reflections on my own participation and goals throughout data collection and analysis.

3.4   Data Collection and Analysis

In total, I made 52 audiovisual recordings of our collaborative work together in group video calls and 62 recordings of individual, unstructured video calls with participants. I also conducted, recorded, and transcribed four rounds of individual, hour-long semistructured interviews with each participant (in Feb. 2020, Jul. 2020, Oct. 2020, and Jan. 2021). I wrote 320 pages of field notes about our interactions across Snapchat, Zoom, text messaging, and other platforms and 40 weekly reflective memos about my affective experiences and role within the project. I collected 121 artifacts of participants' literacy practices, such as artwork and essays, in addition to 12 episodes of the Latinx Stories series they created for the YouTube channel. Episodes of the Latinx Stories project were created both collaboratively and individually; for example, an episode about the COVID-19 pandemic's disruption to students' high school experiences was co-created by all nine participants, while other episodes were created by a single participant or smaller groups. After transcribing interview data and creating content logs for video recordings of our Zoom meetings, I began analysis for this chapter by coding sections of interview transcripts in which I asked participants about the advantages and disadvantages of shifting our collaboration online. I also coded my weekly reflective memos to trace how my own evolving goals and perspectives impacted the project. These codes coalesced around a common theme of "distribution," realized across three dimensions: participation, power, and perspectives. After creating this three-pronged analytic heuristic, I referenced field notes and content logs to identify focal scenarios within artifacts and recordings to which I could apply it (Table 3.1). I then

Table 3.1 Codes generated from interviews and memos, correlated to themes and focal scenarios

Themes	Example codes	Examples of coded data	Focal scenarios
Distributed participation	• Time • Access • Busy lives • Tools • Logistics	"a pro about having it online was definitely like it's accessible to everyone." (Interview, Oct. 17, 2020) "it's really good the way we've worked it, because like we're not all like huddled on one little, small screen. Also like, sharing our screen is just way more effective. It's also easier for me because we're all [spread out]…I can't drive." (Interview, Oct. 16, 2020)	Making participation visible in Snapchat
Distributed power	• Goals • Roles • Positions • Relationships	"So just being able to like establish what we want to make and that it doesn't have to be right away." (Interview, Oct. 12, 2020) "This is making me realize that holding space for students to talk to each other may be another way of checking my privilege and power and sidelining my perspective as a white researcher working with Latinx youth." (Reflective Memo, Mar. 29, 2020)	Changing the screen-sharing settings in Zoom
Distributed perspectives	• Expression • Representation • Audience • Collaboration	"We all have different perspectives. We all have our own opinions, but that's what makes us a really good team." (Interview, Oct. 13, 2020) "I feel like when you're watching those videos, you kind of also gained a sense of how they view everything else, like how they viewed the world." (Interview, Oct. 17, 2020) "I like when someone else can show me exactly on their computer what they're doing – and we're literally making videos. So just being able to watch them and be like, hey guys, I'm sharing my personal thing." (Interview, Oct. 21, 2020)	Collaborating via screen share in Zoom Sharing stories on the YouTube channel

conducted multimodal analysis (Jewitt, 2009) of these recordings and artifacts, tracing the sociomaterial conditions across which these dimensions were distributed, which revealed how they were related to the sharing of screens throughout the project. After completing this analysis, I shared my findings with my participants to elicit and incorporate their feedback.

3.5 Sharing the Screen and Distributions of Participation, Power, and Perspective

When analyzing these distributions of participation, power, and perspective in the context of the focal scenarios across which they were enacted, the ways in which we shared and were shared through screens became a unifying concept for understanding the social and technological apparatus of our collaborative inquiry. Below, I explore how different permutations of the concept of screen sharing (both synchronous and asynchronous) illuminate these distributions and their entanglements.

3.5.1 Distributing Participation Across Shared Screens

When I asked participants about "pros and cons" of enacting our project virtually during semistructured interviews, they collectively named more pros than cons. These "pros" usually centered around the possibility for increased participation that the virtual nature of the project afforded. In contrast to the limited number of participants who were able to attend our one in-person workshop (three), over the course of the virtual phase of the project, all nine participants were active in the Snapchat group and attended group Zoom calls. Students who had busy work schedules or family responsibilities during our meetings were able to contribute asynchronously via the Snapchat group, in Google Docs, or by making videos for the YouTube channel. Participants were able to join the Zoom calls without worrying about transportation, and some even joined while running errands. It was not only the virtual format of our weekly Zoom meetings that made them more accessible but also their duration and frequency; if someone could not make it to a meeting one week, they could watch the recording, catch up in the Snapchat group, and join the next week. In this way, participants had multiple ways to control how, when, and to what degree they participated in the project. In other words, rather than making contributions to the group around a shared table at the same time, we contributed to the project across shared platforms at different times, with our names, ideas, voices, avatars, and faces sharing a screen instead of a room.

However, when participation is distributed across time and space, it can also be hidden; participants may not be able to see and build upon each other's contributions as easily when they are enacted asynchronously and across different platforms. Creating opportunities for each other's participation to be seen on screen is therefore a necessary component of building a sense of community across asynchronous collaboration – of making it known that the group chat or Google Doc to which we contribute at different times is in fact a "shared" space. Snapchat is useful in this regard because it makes multiple types of participation visible by showing who has sent or is typing a message, who has seen a message, and which participants have the app open at the same time. For example, one participant in the Latinx Stories project did not regularly attend our weekly Zoom calls but often participated in our ongoing conversation via Snapchat. In an interview, we discussed how her activities in Snapchat made her participation visible within the group. She told me "I'm like, 'I'm here!'" as I responded: "Yes! I see you popping in and out [of the Snapchat conversation]" (Interview, 13 Oct. 2020). In making multiple forms of interaction visible, Snapchat created opportunities for us to see and be seen by each other, whether or not we shared the screen in real time (Fig. 3.1).

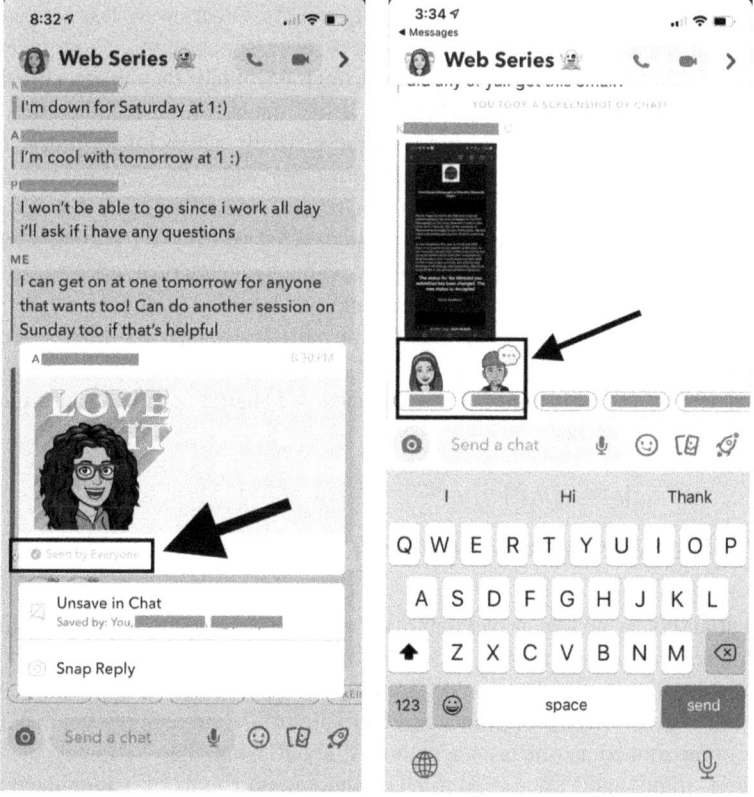

Fig. 3.1 Two screenshots from our group chat in Snapchat. The screenshot on the left demonstrates how the application shows who has seen each message. The screenshot on the right demonstrates how the application shows who is viewing or typing into the chat

However, when participation is distributed across time and platforms, it can be hard to create a sense of collaboration and community. Distributing participation across digital contexts can also mean distributing it more thinly across time, changing the timescale and pacing of collaborative work. In interviews, some participants mentioned that we might be "getting more stuff done" if we were working together for extended periods in the same room (i.e., Saturday workshops) instead of working across shorter, more frequent, and virtual intervals. Others felt that the potential for relational depth was limited by the project's virtual format: "for me personally, like I need to meet people in order for me to get closer to them. Texting and you know, doing all these things. That's ... for me, still very superficial" (Interview, 17 Oct. 2020). Although this participant acknowledged that some people could form deep and intimate relationships without meeting in person, she indicated that – for her – sustained, embodied interaction is necessary for building relational depth.

These differences in how participants felt and developed relational depth have implications for how and when participants made themselves and their ideas visible, as well as which screens they felt comfortable sharing with me and with one other. For example, some participants used the Snapchat group to share personal anecdotes about their daily lives, emotions, and questions. Others were less active in the Snapchat group and were more active in the weekly, synchronous Zoom meetings. Still others contributed their perspectives through the videos they made, edited, and shared on the YouTube channel. While the virtual nature of our collaboration fragmented it in ways that may have stretched it more thinly across longer timescales or kept certain relationships from deepening, in other ways, this fragmentation also allowed us to exercise control over the form, timing, and visibility of that participation. The ability to control when and through what screens we participated also opened opportunities for participants to stay up late working on a video together, or for us to also share our homes, our pets, and our families with each other on the screen. In sum, distributing opportunities for participation across time, space, and platform may have extended timescales and limited relational depth, but it also distributed access, visibility, and control over how we shared our ideas, our time, and our lives with each other.

3.5.2   Distributing Power Through Screen Sharing

A potential (but by no means inevitable) corollary to the distribution of participation within a collaborative project is the distribution of power. Platforms and rituals of participation distribute control in different ways that are often hierarchically structured. For example, as the convener and facilitator of the project, my youth collaborators often looked to me as an authority about what they "should" or "were supposed" to do, and I often tried to reconfigure these rituals by asking them about their own goals for participating in the project. For example, I was determined that I would not be the person to name the YouTube channel, although I often brought up the need to do so and encouraged participants to come to a consensus. While they did eventually create and agree on the name "Latinx Stories," this decision was the result of a months-long process as participants brainstormed and negotiated ideas asynchronously and across platforms. This distribution of control (my pushing for a decision and them choosing a name) represents an ongoing negotiation of power that spanned the project and platforms as I acknowledged that my role came with a responsibility for leading the group toward shared goals while also trying to ensure that goals and decisions were shared by all participants.

Sharing goals and decision-making within a virtual collaboration are also entangled with the platforms and screens through which they are mediated. A material instantiation of the distribution of power within our project was the convening of our weekly Zoom meetings. As the project coordinator, I hosted the weekly Zoom meetings from my own account, and I often outlined goals for the call and decided when they should end. However, in the Zoom call recounted at the beginning of this chapter, which occurred a little over a month after our shift to virtual collaboration, power was redistributed in a new way when screens were shared differently from usual, as recounted in the following field note excerpt:

> Today was one of the best video calls we've had. We spent the first half hour or so looking at our [vlogging] kits and talking about how to use them [...] Then we started talking about the episode – I asked someone to open WeVideo and share their screen, and [Dani] volunteered. She then kind of took the lead on asking some pointed questions about how we should focus the series and the episodes. She asked everyone to go around and talk about the purpose of the series (and I said that it could have changed from what we originally thought because our group has changed [...]) and each person gave a really beautiful and poignant talk about what the series meant to them and why they got involved. (Field Note, 25 Apr. 2020)

During the meeting described above, Dani's sharing of the screen opened up a conversation in which each youth participant present articulated her personal goals for the series. When this meeting began, the default settings of Zoom were configured to give me control of the screen and what we shared there, mirroring the "default settings" of many adult-youth collaborations. However, when Dani volunteered to share her screen and I adjusted the default setting on Zoom so that she could do so, her screen assumed prominence, overlaid across all of our screens. As our conversation progressed with Dani's screen taking center stage, Dani also assumed control over the direction of the conversation, suggesting that we "go around and each state our goals for the series" (Content Log, 25 Apr. 2020). During Dani's and Clementine's turns, they shared the goals quoted at the beginning of this chapter, goals framed as specifically relevant to the Latinx youth participants in the group. In this meeting, adjusting the settings on my device changed how screens were configured across all of our devices, exemplifying how these devices, the software installed on them, and the screens they shared co-constructed the interactions they mediated, both socially and materially. While it is possible that Dani would have assumed the same role and participants would have stated the same goals even without her screen being shared (in fact, later in the meeting she said she forgot it was being broadcast), the convergence of these social and material reconfigurations of control in that moment represent the entanglement of platforms, roles, and ritual in redistributing power across virtual spaces of collaboration.

As Garcia (2020) explains, the platforms through which we conduct our research "are shaped by the contexts, values, and interests of their participants. Resistance to and endorsement of rituals, cultural tropes, and collective values can be held by the communities on particular platforms or engrained within the functionality of these platforms" (p. 404). Reconfiguring the sociomaterial arrangements of the platform during that call correlated with a redistribution of power within the group, and the conversation initiated by Dani that day resonated throughout our work together for the duration of the project. This demonstrates how arranging the tools, spaces, and structures of collaborative inquiry in particular ways can make or constrain space for power to be shared and accessed by multiple participants within a project. The distribution of power within a project also shapes how the power of that project is shared among wider networks and digital publics.

3.5.3   Sharing on Screens and Distributing Perspectives

Dani's and Clementine's goals quoted at the opening of this chapter echo those shared aloud by other participants as they took turns articulating them in that Zoom call (i.e., "to understand what other people are going through at this time because we're all taking this hit [the pandemic] at a different angle," and "I want our stories to be heard" [Content Log, 25 Apr. 2020]). These goals were rearticulated and remained central to our participatory filmmaking work throughout the year, as participants strove to broaden the landscape of available "going-to-college" narratives on YouTube by telling their stories as first-gen, Latinx students and to distribute a range of perspectives on what it meant to hold those identities in the United States in 2020. Participants created episodes for the YouTube channel that represented multiple aspects of themselves and their college-going journeys, opening multiple windows into their lives across the screens through which the public watched their videos. In their episodes, they shared reflections on their families, their heritages, their passions, and their insecurities. They screened videos about successes and struggles as they dealt with cancelled high school graduations, disrupted college plans, and attending college online, and they often included messages of hope and encouragement to themselves and their viewers. In creating videos together and alone, they wove a rich tapestry of experiences across the shared screen of the Latinx Stories YouTube channel, and viewers responded by leaving comments on their videos, such as "I loved this episode; it is great to have a window into others' experiences during these unusual times. Keep up the good work!" (YouTube Comment, Aug. 2020).

Not all participants chose to share their stories and perspectives on such a public screen. However, even those who chose not to share their faces or voices on the public-facing channel contributed ideas, music, and feedback across our platforms of collaborations that were picked up and woven into the tapestry of Latinx Stories.

Thus, the ways in which multiple perspectives are distributed through participatory digital projects are dependent upon the control that participants exert over which perspectives they share, with whom, and on what screens.

In other words, distributing perspectives in participatory research projects does not only mean distributing a range of points of view through research outputs – the videos, publications, photographs, and reports that emerge from such collaborations. Considering the distribution of perspectives also entails considering how participants' stories, opinions, and perceptions are shared within the collaboration process itself. Consider the following paragraph from the same field note excerpted above:

> [Clementine] had some really great questions prepared, one of which was about assigning roles for each episode, which we ended up doing. [...] They all agreed that they wanted some sort of structure or outline that would help them to focus – so [Dani] made a Google Doc template of roles and we went through each role and said what that person would be responsible for. [...] We ended up talking for over two hours, even though I tried to wrap it up a couple of times. (Field Note, 25 Apr. 2020)

Not only did students share their goals for distributing perspectives in this meeting; they also determined how roles might be configured that would help them realize these goals through film production (i.e., "director," "editor, "videographer"). These roles were solidified and made visible as Dani shared her screen and typed their descriptions into a Google Doc as we discussed them together. Alex was also taking notes during this meeting but on a separate screen because she had joined the Zoom call from her phone while typing on a laptop. Therefore, our screens were oriented to center Dani's note-taking, while Alex's were rendered invisible to us in that moment through the configuration of her devices, and, consequently, our conversation often oriented around the notes that Dani was typing during this meeting. While Alex's verbal contributions were represented in Dani's notes, the invisibility of her own written interpretation of the conversation serves as a reminder of how the sociomaterial configurations of collaboration can also constrain the distribution and visibility of perspectives. In other words, the way perspectives were shared in our project was not only externalized through the sharing of Latinx Stories on YouTube; it was also entangled with the sharing of screens within the project, the visibility of participation, and whether participants were able (or willing) to share their perspectives on screen (Fig. 3.2).

In sum, the distribution of perspectives within and through screens is tied to who is invited to participate, along with when, where, and by what means. As one participant explained in an interview, "I think in terms of accessibility the technology really helps in that [...] you're able to talk to people from all different places. And that can be very great because you get a broader perspective" (Interview, 17 Oct. 2020). Through the stories they shared across Snapchat, Zoom, and YouTube screens, participants invited each other and, in some cases, the broader public into their lives, maintaining control over who had access to which perspectives by making informed decisions about what platforms on which they were distributed. Considering how screens are shared (and what is shared across them) can not only serve as a guiding principle for thinking about how power and participation can be

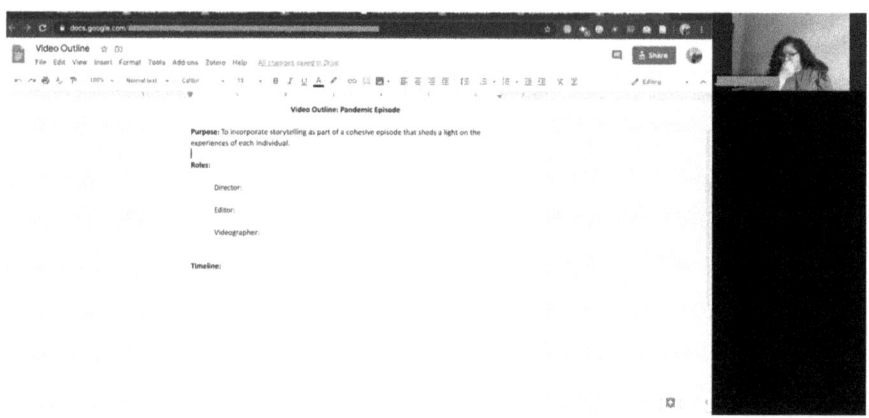

Fig. 3.2 Screenshot from a recording of our Zoom call. Dani's screen (with the Google Doc she created) is being shared, and Alex's face is visible as she verbally shares her ideas with the group

distributed within screen-mediated participatory projects but also help researchers configure the sociomaterial arrangements of these projects to distribute a range of perspectives within and through them.

3.6 Discussion: Entangled and Uneven Distributions

In conducting virtual participatory projects, researchers can make reflexive decisions about how screens are shared by considering the ways in which these arrangements facilitate or constrain the distribution of participation, power, and perspectives. In the Latinx Stories project, participants' abilities to participate in the project on their own terms and across multiple screens, to exert control over the screen and the goals of the project, and to distribute multiple perspectives on being a Latinx student across different platforms were entangled with each other and the sociomaterial arrangements of our work together – arrangements for which I was often responsible as the convener of the project. In other words, the distribution of participation, power, and perspectives was recursive and contingent upon each other. Considering their entanglements, along with the relationships, platforms, and rituals that configure them, is an important part of making decisions about screen sharing that forward the ethical commitments of a digitally mediated participatory project.

It is also important to consider the balance of these distributions. In the Latinx Stories project, for example, participation was not distributed evenly among participants, and we talked openly and often about how we each had different capacities and goals for participating in the project. This contributed to an often unbalanced distribution of responsibilities and ideas as some participants chose to participate with less frequency or in less visible ways than others. Power was also unequally distributed: my position as the researcher and my responsibilities as the convener of the project meant that I often exerted more control over the logistical arrangements and parameters of the project than other participants. Inevitably, the way that participation and power were unequally shared within the project ultimately affected how perspectives were shared through Latinx Stories, and some participants' perspectives have more screen time than others. While it is important to be attentive to these imbalanced distributions and strive to correct them when necessary, my point is not to suggest that screens should be shared equally among all participants at all times or that participation, power, and perspectives should always be evenly distributed. Rather, I suggest critical attention to the sociomaterial conditions that shape and reshape these three vectors of distribution, a willingness to unsettle and shift relational and technological arrangements when necessary, and continued striving toward "methodological dignity" (Garcia, 2020) when (re)configuring the sharing of screens.

3.7   Coda

Throughout this chapter, I have used the concept of "sharing the screen" to explore how my and my participants' choices about the social and material arrangements of our collaboration facilitated or constrained our goals for the Latinx Stories project. I have done so by considering how three dimensions of distribution within the project (participation, power, and perspective) were intertwined with these choices, with each other, and with the ethical implications of the project. I have emphasized that sharing a screen does not automatically produce horizontality, community, or transparency in a participatory research project. Rather, how screens are set up to be shared, who controls what is shared on them, and which screens are shared with which audiences can all contribute to or detract from these common goals of participatory visual research, particularly when it is enacted virtually.

Neither the youth co-creators of "Latinx Stories" nor I know when, or if, we will be able to share stories, laughter, and maybe some pizza together in person as we originally imagined we would. We *do* know that our screen-based interactions have expanded our own and others' perspectives and that "Latinx Stories" are being shared across the screens of our peer, community, and academic networks. Our work together toward these goals has demonstrated how considering the sociomaterial configurations of screen sharing – across multiple vectors of distribution – is a critical component of designing participatory research in digital contexts.

References

Appadurai, A. (2006). The right to research. *Globalisation, Societies and Education, 4*(2), 167–177.
Barley, R., & Russell, L. (2019). Participatory visual methods: Exploring young people's identities, hopes and feelings. *Ethnography and Education, 14*(2), 223–241.

Burkholder, C., Makramalla, M., Abdou, E., Khoja, N., & Khan, F. (2015). Why study power in digital spaces anyway? Considering power and participatory visual methods. *Perspectives in Education, 33*(4), 6–22.

Burnett, C. (2016). Being together in classrooms at the interface of the physical and virtual: Implications for collaboration in on/off-screen sites. *Learning, Media and Technology, 41*(4), 566–589.

Burnett, C., & Merchant, G. (2020). *Undoing the digital: Sociomaterialism and literacy education.* Routledge.

Burnett, C., Merchant, G., Pahl, K., & Rowsell, J. (2014). The (im)materiality of literacy: The significance of subjectivity to new literacies research. *Discourse: Studies in the Cultural Politics of Education, 35*(1), 90–103.

Burnett, C., Merchant, G., Parry, B., & Storey, V. (2019). Conceptualising digital technology integration in participatory theatre from a sociomaterialist perspective: ways forward for research. *Research Papers in Education, 34*(6), 680–700.

Call-Cummings, M., Hauber-Özer, M., Byers, C., & Mancuso, G. P. (2019). The power of/in photovoice. *International Journal of Research & Method in Education, 42*(4), 399–413.

Campano, Ghiso, & Welch. (2016). *Partnering with immigrant communities.* Teachers College Press.

Caraballo, L., Lozenski, B. D., Lyiscott, J. J., & Morrell, E. (2017). YPAR and critical epistemologies: Rethinking education research. *Review of Research in Education, 41*(1), 311–336.

Cardinal, A. (2019). Participatory video: An apparatus for ethically researching literacy, power and embodiment. *Computers and Composition, 53*, 34–46.

Chalfen, R., & Rich, M. (2004). Applying visual research patients teaching physicians through visual illness narratives. *Visual Anthropology Review, 20*(1), 17–30.

de Roock, R. S. (2020). Digital selves, material bodies, and participant research tools: Towards material semiotic video ethnography. *International Journal of Social Research Methodology, 23*(2), 199–213.

Elder, S. (1994). Collaborative filmmaking: An open space for making meaning, a moral ground for ethnographic film. *Visual Anthropology Review, 11*(2), 94–101.

Fenwick, T., Edwards, R., & Sawchuk, P. (2011). *Emerging approaches to educational research: Tracing the sociomaterial.* Routledge.

Garcia, A. (2020). "Electric word life": Methodological dignity in equity-driven research. *Equity & Excellence in Education, 53*(3), 399–411.

Gubrium, A., & Harper, K. (2013). *Participatory visual and digital methods.* Taylor & Francis.

Irizarry, J. G. (2009). Reinvigorating multicultural education through Youth Participatory Action Research. *Multicultural Perspectives, 11*(4), 194–199.

Jewitt, C. (Ed.). (2009). *The Routledge handbook of multimodal analysis.* Routledge.

Latour, B. (2005). *Reassembling the social: An introduction to actor-network theory.* Oxford University Press.

Luttrell, W. (2010). "A camera is a big responsibility": A lens for analysing children's visual voices. *Visual Studies, 25*(3), 224–237.

Mannay, D. (2016). *Visual, narrative, and creative research methods: Application, reflection, and ethics.* Routledge.

Mitchell, C., De Lange, N., & Moletsane, R. (2016). Me and my cellphone: Constructing change from the inside through cellphilms and participatory video in a rural community: Me and my cellphone. *Area, 48*(4), 435–441.

Mitchell, C., de Lange, N., & Moletsane, R. (2017). *Participatory visual methodologies: Social change, community and policy.* Sage.

Moya, P. M. L. (2002). *Learning from experience: Minority identities, multicultural struggles.* University of California Press.

Muir, S., & Mason, J. (2012). Capturing Christmas: The sensory potential of data from participant produced video. *Sociological Research Online, 17*(1), 1–19.

Orellana, M. F. (1999). Space and place in an Urban Landscape: Learning from children's views of their social worlds. *Visual Sociology, 14*(1), 73–89.

Pahl, K., & Allan, C. (2011). *'I don't know what literacy is'*: Uncovering hidden literacies in a community library using ecological and participatory research methodologies with children. *Journal of Early Childhood Literacy, 11*(2), 190–123.

Pauwels, L. (2015). 'Participatory' visual research revisited: A critical-constructive assessment of epistemological, methodological and social activist tenets. *Ethnography, 16*(1), 95–117.

Pink, S. (2021). *Doing visual ethnography* (4th ed.). Sage.

Shankur, A. (2016). Auteurship and image-making: A (gentle) critique of the photovoice method. *Visual Anthropology Review, 32*(2), 157–166.

Stornaiuolo, A., Smith, A., & Phillips, N. C. (2017). Developing a transliteracies framework for a connected world. *Journal of Literacy Research, 49*(1), 68–91.

Templeton, T. N. (2018). *'That street is taking us to home'*: Young children's photographs of public spaces. *Children's Geographies, 18*(1), 1–15.

Tuck, E., & Habtom, S. (2019). Unforgetting place in urban education through creative participatory visual methods. *Educational Theory, 69*(2), 241–256.

Wang, C. C., & Burris, M. (1997). Photovoice: Concept, methodology, and use for participatory needs assessment. *Health Education and Behavior, 24*, 369–387.

Whiting, R., Symon, G., Roby, H., & Chamakiotis, P. (2018). Who's behind the lens? A reflexive analysis of roles in participatory video research. *Organizational Research Methods, 21*(2), 316–340.

Chapter 4
A Felt Presence: Affect, Emotion, and Memory as Literacy Researchers

Bronwyn T. Williams

Abstract The disruptions of the pandemic highlighted the role of the presence of the researcher and participants in our conceptions of literacy research and allowed us for a moment to reflect on the implications of our embodied presences as researchers. In this chapter, I draw from theories of affect, emotion, and memory to explore how we have constructed and understood the physical presence of the researcher in literacy research and how the challenges of research during the pandemic, as well as other social and political disruptions, challenge us to rethink the purpose and significance of that presence. In particular, I explore how embodied, affective experiences and physical locations not only shape our interactions with participants but also construct our identities as researchers and writers. The experiences we have doing research, and how we process those experiences as emotion and memory, create our individual stances and meanings of research and would benefit from reflection as individuals and as a field.

Keywords Affect · Emotion · Memory · Researcher position · Research ethics

In winter 2020, I was planning a research project involving in-person interviews with university students in the United States about cultural attitudes toward writing and their effects on student perceptions of agency. With a divisive presidential election on the horizon, I wanted to understand how cultural perceptions of education and writing were influencing perceptions of individual literacy practices. On a Thursday in early March, I received my ethics approval for the project. By the next week, the onrush of the COVID-19 pandemic had closed the physical university and moved our work – and lives – online. I realized, once I had a moment to breathe after the initial shock of the lockdown and the work of moving my teaching and administrative work online, that the significant cultural event of our time was happening, quietly, all around me. As I amended the ethics documents, the changes

B. T. Williams (✉)
University of Louisville, Louisville, USA
e-mail: bronwyn.williams@louisville.edu

© The Author(s), under exclusive license to Springer Nature Singapore Pte Ltd. 2022
C. Lee et al. (eds.), *Unsettling Literacies*, Cultural Studies and Transdisciplinarity in Education 15, https://doi.org/10.1007/978-981-16-6944-6_4

seemed deceptively straightforward. I would now conduct interviews online to focus on how literacy practices – and the emotions and perceptions surrounding them – were shifting with the pandemic. Even so, I could sense, if not yet articulate, that the changes in the research, and in my experience and stance as a researcher, would feel more significant.

In literacy studies research, the image of the literacy researcher in the field has often meant a person visiting a home, working in a community center, observing a classroom. As the field has focused on literacy as a social practice, the importance of being present in the social worlds of writers has been more than simply a methodological approach. The idea of the researcher in the home or workplace or community or school has been a symbolic foundation on which conceptions of literacy research are often constructed. When I think about literacy research, I think of Susan Jones (2018) spending hours in a public library or Marcelle Haddix (2012) in a summer writing institute for Black adolescent males or Dan Keller (2013) watching youth play video games in their living rooms or Lalitha Vasudevan (2014) working with adolescents in an alternative to detention program or Brice Nordquist (2017) talking to research participants as he rode with them on city buses. There were many reasons I was drawn to teach and research writing, but the vision of research I saw in the scholarship, sitting with people in coffee shops or classrooms, listening to their stories, observing their activities, and the relationships of those around me are not just activities that I have learned how to do, but are things I love to do.

The presence of the literacy researcher is more than a methodological conception in our field, however. Indeed, describing the presence of the researcher, and the relationships with participants that presence affords, has become an expected genre convention in research writing. Literacy studies scholarship commonly includes descriptions of research sites and participants, but also reflections by the researcher about the effects of their presence on the participants. The researcher in the field has become part of a constituting narrative of literacy research.

In the spring of 2020, as the pandemic halted research in the field indefinitely, the idea of the researcher's presence changed dramatically. For many, projects were suspended, hovering out of reach as everyone waited for a change in conditions that no one could predict. For others, interviews and focus groups relocated to online formats and screen-sized interactions. I had projects in both situations – community collaborations that stopped as schools and libraries closed their doors, and my interviews about culture and agency that moved online.

The disruptions of the pandemic highlighted the role of the presence of the researcher and participants in our conceptions of literacy research and allowed us for a moment to reflect on the implications of our embodied presences as researchers. In this chapter, I draw from theories of affect, emotion, and memory to explore how we have constructed and understood the physical presence of the researcher in literacy research and how the challenges of research during the pandemic, as well as other social and political disruptions, challenge us to rethink the purpose and significance of that presence. In particular, I explore how embodied, affective experiences and physical locations not only shape our interactions with participants but also construct our identities as researchers and writers. The experiences we have doing research, and how we process those experiences as emotion and memory, create our individual stances and meanings of research and would benefit from reflection as individuals and as a field.

4.1 The Position of the Researcher

In literacy studies, the question of the "position of the researcher" has received consistent attention for a number of years. Scholarship has considered how the position of the researcher affects the willingness of people to participate in research or cautions about coercing participation (Mortensen & Kirsch, 1996; Ryen, 2011). Others discussed how to work respectfully and reciprocally with participants (Powell & Takayoshi, 2003), while others pointed out inevitable power relationships and issues of identity at work between researchers and participants, and studied their effects on data gathering and representing participants in research writing (Anderson, 1998; Brydon-Miller, 2004; Newkirk, 1996; Sullivan 1996). And still other writers examined questions of researcher positions in online settings (Kelley, 2016; McKee & Porter, 2009). All this work, with its emphasis on understanding that, as researchers, we were developing relationships with other people, not just gathering data from objective participants, has been important in the ethical planning and conducting of research and in teaching research methods. Considering the "position of the researcher" has become so central to our understanding of research that for it not to be addressed in scholarship is notable. Such discussions are not just part of our approach to epistemology but have become familiar genre conventions in scholarship and are often included as explicit sections in articles, books, and research proposals.

Like most in our field, I value the importance of considering the position of the researcher in terms of issues of ethics, representation, identity, and power to try to mitigate any harm or problems we might cause people who are generous enough to help us in research. Quite reasonably, the emphasis of much of the discussion of the position of the researcher has focused on how it affects the participants of a study, not the researcher. Even when scholars write about the personal effects of research experiences on their position as a researcher, the discussion then tends to turn to how such effects might have shaped the data gathering and analysis in ways that might affect the participants. To discuss the "position of the researcher" implies a certain level of detachment, of stepping outside ourselves to consider, analytically, the effects of our decisions and actions. It can almost feel that we are talking about someone distinct from ourselves. Not only does such detachment reflect the normalized conventions of analysis in academic research, but it avoids the language of emotion and affect and uses of narrative that academics often regard as messy, unreliable, and even uncomfortable.

Less prominent in scholarship, however, have been discussions of the affective experience of research on the researcher. We all have thought at times about how the experiences of research have had an impact on us, both in the embodied moment and later as we process emotions and memories. Often we keep such thoughts to ourselves. When we do talk about these experiences professionally, it is mostly in moments of conversations in our offices or over drinks at conferences. Writers who do write more directly about the affective experiences of research (Brydon-Miller, 2004; Newkirk, 2017; Behar, 1996) have come in for criticism for work that is deemed "too personal" or "too emotional." It is still easy to find substantial resistance from scholars in the field who regard addressing issues of personal experience or affect and emotion in research as the antithesis of the rational, objective creation of knowledge.

4.2   Affect Theory

The recent turn, in literacy studies, to more engagement with affect and emotion offers us the moment to rethink and reengage with the idea of how the experiences of research shape the individual who is doing the research (Anwaruddin, 2016; Burnett & Merchant, 2016; Leander & Ehret, 2019). In particular, affect theory has been used as a lens through which to consider our immediate and ongoing embodied experiences. Affect theory reminds us that there are intensities to our ongoing experiences that are beyond our abilities to represent them in language (Massumi, 2015). We all understand the concept that we feel the moments of our lives in ways that we cannot represent semiotically. Yet conventional approaches to research and how it creates knowledge in our culture are grounded in ideas of detachment and representation. It is by standing back, apprehending, and analyzing that we interpret social phenomena for each other. Most scholarship tries vigorously to elide, or even erase, the intensities of our bodies and experiences in the midst of research. Affect theory reminds us, however, that as much as we try to stand back from and represent people and events, "our experiences aren't objects. They're us, they're what we're made of. We are our situations, we are moving through them. We are our participation – not some abstract entity that is somehow outside looking in at it all" (Massumi, 2015, p. 14). We can no more escape affect during our research, or any moment of our lives, than we can escape the weather.

In our field, exploring the contours of affect theory often focuses on the context of what we see – and feel – in research in the field. In particular, researchers are questioning how the desire and necessity to represent research in traditionally positivist and rationalist ways flattens and distorts the experiences and affective moments and how we might explore new ways of communicating our ideas and research (Burnett & Merchant, 2016, 2020; Gourlay, 2019; Pandian, 2019; Sheridan et al., 2020). What I think – and what I feel – is that it is important to extend these conversations to our experience as researchers. How does the affective moment, the feeling of research, not only shape what we are seeing and writing but also change us as people – people who also happen to be doing research?

Affect and embodiment are always shaping us as researchers. However, the disruptions of the pandemic, as well as the concurrent social upheavals in the United States, created fissures in daily experiences and customs that made the intensities of affect more tangible and explicit. Just as weather grasps our attention, and concern, when storms descend and make explicit our embodied concerns of shelter and safety, the conditions of daily life during the pandemic were altered in disorienting, and even traumatic, ways that made explicit affective intensities, both for the people I interviewed and for myself.

4.3 Interviews and Intensities

In spring 2020, I interviewed 41 university students, from first-year undergraduates to doctoral students. Six months later, as cases of the virus rose and winter approached, I did follow-up interviews, with a third set of interviews to follow in November, 2021. My initial interest was to understand what was happening in their writing and reading practices, both for school and for themselves, as the university moved all instruction online and as the city was under a stay-at-home order. Given the unprecedented circumstances, for all of us, while I had a range of questions about what they had been doing, I had not identified a focused "research question" I was pursuing. What I did feel was an impetus to talk to people to find out what was happening, both to document and to enable people to tell their stories to someone. An email announcement seeking participants resulted in the 41 students who responded, and who represented a broad range of identifications of race, gender, nationality, age, social class, and more. Though I had questions prepared, and while we did talk about writing, the conversations often escaped the boundaries of those questions and evolved into combinations of narrating, testifying, documenting, and simply sharing of their experiences. I was grateful for their time and their trust, as I always feel when I do research.

Yet there was more happening in the embodied, affective experiences of those conversations than simply gathering information about literacy practices and expressing gratitude for their participation. The affective intensities could be, well, intense. Among some of the people I talked with, there was a palpable need to be heard – and to have someone to talk to – and to talk through the mixture of emotions and metaphors marking this unsettling moment. There was sometimes joy in having someone to tell their story to, or appreciation for reassurances that they were not alone in struggling to complete online work, or desperation to talk to someone about the struggle, not just of work, but of daily life.

When I interviewed Phillip in early May, 2020, he was clearly struggling with effects of the stay-at-home order. He talked of the stress of living at home again, in close proximity to a large family, all of whom were trying to work or attend school online, with little respite from each other. More than that, he talked about his anxieties during the pandemic. He was worried about whether he would be able to attend graduate school in the fall as he had planned and what he would do for income over the summer and about his now long-distance relationship with his girlfriend, as well as worried about the virus itself. The previous sentence does not adequately reflect, however, the intensity of the conversation. Phillip's anxieties, his struggles, his affect came flooding through the screen onto my lap, raw and unavoidable. I found myself listening to what he was saying about his experiences with reading and writing, sure, but also listening and responding to the anxieties he was expressing. As an empathetic person, I felt a responsibility to respond to the affect Phillip was displaying, and I was feeling in that moment. When the call was over, and I logged off the computer, I felt exhausted, both emotionally and physically. My affective experience of the interview was intense and inescapable. Over the next week, that experience returned to me as I continued to think, and worry, about Phillip (and follow up with him to see how he was doing).

Although there have been other times, as a researcher, when the affective intensities of a moment registered so directly, there is no doubt that the disruptions of the pandemic made Phillip's experience rawer, more intense for him, and more willing to say it to me. What's more, the precarity that people I interviewed were feeling was not just from the medical facts of the virus. My university, like many around the world, found that the campus shutdowns and move to online instruction revealed and exacerbated systemic problems created by years of budget cuts and neoliberal ideological approaches to institutional structures and planning. The economic imperatives of the university, long driven by reduced government support and neoliberal ideologies, meant that during the pandemic, staff were kept at risk to keep enrollments up and avoid furloughs and job losses. Phillip, and others, were anxious but also angry and frustrated at the tradeoffs of economic and physical safety they felt they were being asked to make. As part of that system, I shared that anger and frustration.

The affective, embodied response of the people I talked with varied, of course. Some talked of feeling the guilty pleasures of introverts being able to stay home; others expressed anger around the social justice protests that took to the streets over the summer. For many of them, however, the pandemic seemed to open fissures in conventional research interactions to emphasize more unusual and disruptive moments of affect that were more on the surface of our conversations.

In my previous experiences of research, which took place in more typical settings of classrooms or writing centers or public spaces such as coffee shops, the conversations and the affect were mediated by the setting and the social roles that setting implied. In a classroom, for example, whatever else happened, there would always be the inescapable cultural conventions of the school and the student-teacher relationship in the background. The conversations, in general, stayed relatively close to the issues of reading and writing we were discussing, even if those might also involve talking about frustrating or painful classroom memories. If a student was upset in the classroom or discussed a troubling experience in an interview, I always tried to be sympathetic as well as interested. Still, even those moments in which the affect seemed noteworthy, the experience for both of us was mediated, and made less disruptive, by the social conventions structured by the settings. Yet, again, the anxieties and personal and social disruptions of the pandemic emphasized different elements of my experience and response in these moments.

4.4   Screens and Locations

One central disruption created by the pandemic that had a substantial impact on affect was the shift to home as the sole location for work, school, and daily life and the simultaneous move to online platforms for most interactions with anyone outside. Recent new materialist critiques have argued that the locations and objects that we act with and through are inextricable from our actions and our experiences (Gourlay, 2019; Lemieux & Rowsell, 2020; Sheridan, et al. 2020). For years, as we have become familiar with what have become foundational and conventional approaches to literacy research, we have been both able to attend to the importance of location and objects in literacy practices (Barton & Hamilton, 1998; Brandt, 2001; Heath, 1983) while at the same time taking for granted the culturally conventional ordinariness of the homes, schools, neighborhoods, and workplaces where we did our research. We had a conventional sense of what a classroom or library or home was conceived to be, and what people expected in being there, and we carried out our research looking for ways in which literacy practices supported or pushed against those conventional understandings. And we understood that our place, as researchers, was in the sites where reading and writing was taking place.

Initially, I thought the biggest change in interviewing people online would be in what I could see. The small screen makes it harder to see details of body language, and a person in front of a webcam moves less. Also, details glimpsed in the background can be distracting or unclear and more difficult to interpret. There is also a different concern about intruding when looking through a video screen and knowing that the person on the other end may not have a choice about where they are having the conversation. These were typical "position of the researcher" kinds of concerns.

Soon, however, I recognized unexpected affective components to online interviews. It mattered not only that the person I was talking to was in a kitchen or bedroom, but also that I was sitting at *our* dining room table. We not only had limited views of each other; we were also not sharing our material experiences. When I interviewed Nora, a single mother, I could hear her child off screen, and see Nora's distracted glances, but had no clear understanding of what was taking place or what the effect might be on Nora. And when I talked to Marina, and she spoke of feeling trapped in her small apartment, it was impossible for me to know what that setting was like and connect her description with what I might see. Conversely, the person I was interviewing wouldn't know that my glance to the side during the interview was prompted by a squirrel running along the tree branch in my neighbor's garden. Our affective experiences were altered by the disconnect between the embodied setting in which I was sitting and the person on whom I was focused on the screen.

At the same time, there were ways in which our mutual focus on the digital screen intensified affect. Peering at a small image of a person, listening carefully to sometimes distorted audio and trying not to be distracted, and having so much of their performance of emotion play out in front of you in close-ups of faces meant that the diffusion of affect that might happen in an in-person encounter, in a larger space with perhaps other people around, did not always take place. While the screen might limit engagement in some ways, it focused the intensity in others and acted as an extension of our embodiment, a membrane that affect pushed through. In addition, for me the distraction of an image of myself in the corner of the screen made me aware of my presence in very different ways in on-screen encounters from in-person ones. In past projects, if I was interviewing someone in a classroom or my campus office, I had a clearer sense of how that might be read (or thought I did) and how I would respond in the interview setting to try to put people more at ease or to understand what traditional connotations the space would have. But, in the online conversations, my home had also become a research image.

The affective intensities of these interviews were also changing my position – or my person – as a researcher in ways that I could feel, if not always name. Was I researcher as empathizer? Researcher as lifeline? Researcher as window to another world? Researcher as therapist? At such moments, we may find ourselves in roles we did not choose or feel ready for or comfortable with.

Though scholars have discussed questions about the position of the researcher as activist (Brydon-Miller, 2004), the idea of researcher as a lifeline or therapist, I know, raises even more concerns. I'm not a therapist, and don't pretend to be one when talking to people in distress. If I'm concerned, I often recommend they talk to a professional, and I provide resources if they want them. At the same time, I am human, and, as such, I am compelled to respond humanely when encountering someone in distress. The issue at hand is not simply a matter of whether my position as a researcher might affect the data or how I represent it. In that moment, my response could not be limited to just asking a follow-up question about writing processes or only recommending professional support. I have to respond to the needs of the person in front of me. When talking with Phillip, we were two people living through a genuine and pervasive crisis, which made affective and embodied experiences more explicit for both of us. Even if other researchers would choose not to respond as I did, and would see their role as detached researcher unchanged in that moment, the affective experience would still have an impact and still leave an imprint on them as researchers. If such moments made a researcher uncomfortable, for example, that person might try to avoid them in the future and set up a research site or interview questions differently the next time.

The affective experiences didn't end with the close of each interview. After an hour or more of listening to descriptions of the pains and pleasures of working from home, I would log off, to turn to my own home. Like many people, I try to leave the experiences of work in the office or at the research setting and look forward to a different affect when I go home. Like many people during the pandemic, those settings and experiences overlapped in sometimes wearying, but sometimes gratifying ways. The energy of positive conversations was with me at home, but I also could not distance myself from the impact and concerns of talking to those who were struggling. My own anxieties about the pandemic, about friends and politics and inequality, blended with those I was hearing online.

4.5 Emotion, Memory, and Processing Affect

Some of the recent research on literacy practices and affect has emphasized the importance of focusing on affect, which is embodied, immediate, and resistant to representation, rather than emotion, which they argue has garnered more attention because of how it is categorized and represented in language. In terms of understanding how the intensity of experience shapes us as researchers, however, I find it important to engage with both the embodied moment of affect as well as the socially constructed processes of emotion and autobiographical memory. The ways we process experiences in terms of both our earlier experiences and the social roles and customs in which we live has a crucial effect on how those sedimented experiences shape who we understand ourselves to be as researchers.

If affect is an embodied reality in the moment, emotion is how we process and pattern affect to form dispositions or personas. Our construction of emotion begins almost instantaneously; as soon as our senses and body feel, our brain begins to construct meaning from those sensations (Barrett, 2006). Should the loud sound in the street be understood as fear or joy? Is the person I am talking to amused or anxious? Our senses and brain work in rapid, reciprocal waves to pattern what is taking place in terms of our previous experiences and respond to the stimulus as a recognizable emotion. If we come across a long line at a shop, our possible frustration, while feeling immediate and internal, is learned through previous experiences and social conventions. If we are interacting with another person, our recognition and performance of emotion is often part of what Wetherell (2012) calls a "normative back and forth…The affective pattern is in fact *distributed* across the relational field and each partner's part becomes meaningful in relation to the whole affective dance" (p. 87). When I talk with someone like Phillip, whether I feel sympathy, concern, guilt, or some other emotion develops through how I understand, name, and pattern emotion through the interanimating effects of sensation and sociality. When I think about the interview just after it ends, or the following day before I do the next interview, I continue to process and pattern the emotions in response to a combination of cultural cues and previous experiences, including our roles as researchers.

The dispositions we develop as we process affect create the emotional landscapes we inhabit as we move forward with research. My response to the next angry, troubled, or joyful person I encounter is determined by how I have constructed and internalized previous emotions. I might feel anxious, or eager, before I'm fully aware of what experiences and conventions have created the framework for these emotions. My emotions shape who I feel I am as a researcher, what I will plan, and how I will pattern the next affective moment, even if it is not as distinctive or vivid as during a pandemic.

If emotional processing is social, but immediate, the person of the researcher is also constructed by the ways autobiographical memories are formed and narrated. As Fernyhough (2012) points out, memories are not retrieved intact from metaphorical shelves in our brains but reconstructed and narrated every time we construct a memory. What's more, a memory is shaped by the context in which it is constructed. The memories we have of the research we have engaged in are not pristine when we tell them to ourselves. Like the stories of our research that we tell at a conference, or to students we are mentoring, the memories are reconstructed in the moment as narratives and shaped by current contexts of emotion, motivation, culture, and relationships. Yet, such autobiographical memories are integral to how we understand ourselves and portray ourselves to others. The autobiographical memories that we tell ourselves and others about our work, and our embodied responses to doing research, are what we use to give context and meaning to our lives. So, for example, my interview with Phillip, as a memory that I access and narrate to myself, and now to you, may mean different things to me as I remember it and may have different emphases as contexts change. At one point, just after the interview, the memory may be one of confusion and exhaustion. Now, months later, and after I have talked about it and also had a follow-up interview with Phillip, my memory of the original interview may contain those initial elements but also now seems to be about finding purpose in work during a time when the world was spiraling.

Memory, however, is not only about the past. Fernyhough (2012) points out that memory plays a crucial role in how we imagine and plan for the future. What we create in the way of autobiographical memory, and the identity it constructs, will also shape the person of the researcher. Part of what I was unprepared for in the pandemic was understanding how, for many, the crisis was not directly about the virus but, instead, about isolation, about the toll of unending, unfocused anxiety and how all of that affect would be focused into our online interactions. What I need to imagine now is not just the effects of the pandemic but how we all respond to precarious times and events in our lives and in writing. Just as important, I need to work to understand more fully the self I am building as a researcher through my emotional dispositions and my autobiographical memories. It will not be the same after this.

4.6 Conclusion: Unsettling Literacies and Stances of Researchers

Gail Boldt (2019), therapist and teacher, notes both teaching or working with a client "means attending to the flow of affect and energy as well as being alive to rhythms of the work and the improvisational possibilities of the moment" (p. 39). Approaching her work in this way, she says, offers the possibility of a new experience of the self. In the same way, research offers us new experiences of the self. If we attend not just to data collection or conventional conceptions of researcher positions but also to the affective intensities that are simultaneously individual and shared, we enable a richer understanding not just of others, but of ourselves. Such understanding isn't limited to dramatic moments where we might feel we are acting as a lifeline or empathetic set of ears. Every engagement we have with another person, and the subsequent processing of our actions as researchers, changes who we are. The disruptions and intensities of the pandemic created opportunities to apprehend these intensities more clearly, more vividly, but should also be a reminder that they are always happening as we research and live. Other scholars have urged us to consider the multiple nature of our narratives and understandings of what we observe and the complexities of the relations we have with the participants in our research (Burnett & Merchant, 2016; Rowsell, 2020; Sheridan et al. 2020). To these considerations, I believe we need to add an ongoing recognition of, and reflection on, how affect, emotions, and autobiographical memory shape us as researchers and the research and writing in which we engage.

I find resonances here with Rowsell's (2020) articulation of "stance." Rowsell argues that stances are distinct from positions in that they are *made*, not just taken, and combine both intellectual and rhetorical perspectives with embodied and sentient practices (p. 627-8). Stances reflect imagination and desires for agency. If many previous articulations of the "position of the researcher" are not adequate to address the affective experiences of research, we can instead consider how affect, emotion, and memory create the stances we inhabit as researchers. Like all conceptions of self, even as our sedimented experiences accumulate, such stances are multiple, and we perform them in different ways depending on the context. Still, there is a role for considering how we might work to understand how we continually construct our stances as researchers from affect, emotion, and memory and then narrate them to ourselves and others.

What I tell myself about my research, and how I do everything from forming initial questions to completing the final edits on a book, is bound up and formed by these experiences. Recognizing and reflecting on how I am constructing such stances will help me understand more about the motivations, and hesitations, that define my work and my life as a researcher. My decisions as a researcher are not simply a set of ethical and intellectual calculations (though it is worth remembering that rationality and detachment are emotional states as much as they are intellectual positions) but are built from embodied and affective experiences as well. We all have a tendency to rationalize memories and emotions in ways that construct us as generally well-intentioned and ethical leading characters in the narratives of autobiographical memories. Reflecting on researcher stances in ways that recognize the complexity of the emotions, and the instability of the memories, may help us understand more fully why we act and think as we have.

Such reflection is a disposition toward asking questions as much as it is a set of concrete steps. In the future, as I plan research, I wonder how I will carry forward my experiences from those that marked the pandemic. How will I remember and feel about what happened – the good, the bad, the precarious? Although the pandemic and the protests of the past year may have made questions of bodies and presence particularly pressing, the issues and experiences of precarity will continue to be intense, for those we research and for us as well. The affective intensities of research, whether because of a pandemic or because of other effects of precarity, such as budget cuts, privatization, climate change, systemic inequalities, political polarization, and other traumas, will continue to shape our future. In ongoing precarious times, as a researcher and a person, I must ask myself what my obligations are to the people with whom I am talking, not just in regard to data gathering and representation but in our mutual affective encounters. Who am I to them and them to me? How and when should I account for affect, emotion, and memory when I describe research projects to possible participants and check in on those same issues as the research moves forward? And how do I handle the emotional labor of conducting research in this way?

There is also the question of how we talk about our experiences to others. Certainly the project of this book, as well as other recent research that connects to affect, is offering opportunities for more discussions of the implications of affect in our work. I would argue that we need to engage more with questions of affect and memory and stance in these conversations. In talking to my students about "my experience" as a researcher, I can remember to do more than performing it as instruction – or even wisdom – and instead be more attentive and honest about the emotions and memories that linger, both good and bad. There is also a place in writing about research for addressing more than just our position as a researcher, but more of our affective and embodied stances and how those shaped our work throughout a project. Although we need to be careful not to wander down self-interrogating but directionless rabbit holes of memories and emotions, I think there are times when more conversations about understanding what we are learning, and becoming, as researchers will be valuable and relevant. For myself, I know that I am not going to run from affect and emotion – or from the moments where I might need to be a lifeline and an empathizer. Yet, even when that is not asked of me, I will be more attentive to the affect and improvisational possibilities of the moment and to how I process them afterward. The intensity of this year has been like opening windows on a stormy day, but the question is how we will understand the effect of the weather on us when the storms have passed.

References

Anderson, P. V. (1998). Simple gifts: Ethical issues in the conduct of person-based composition research. *College Composition and Communication, 49*(1), 63–89.

Anwaruddin, S. M. (2016). Why critical literacy should turn to 'the affective turn': Making a case for critical affective literacy. *Discourse: Studies in the Cultural Politics of Education, 37*(3), 381–396.

Barrett, L. F. (2006). Solving the emotion paradox: Categorization and the experience of emotion. *Personality and social psychology review, 10*(1), 20–46.

Barton, D., & Hamilton, M. (1998). *Local literacies: Reading and writing in one community.* Routledge.

Behar, R. (1996). *The vulnerable observer: Anthropology that breaks your heart.* Beacon Press.

Boldt, G. (2019). Affective flows in the clinic and the classroom. In K. Leander & C. Ehret (Eds.), *Affect in literacy learning and teaching: Pedagogies, politics and coming to know* (pp. 25–42). Routledge.

Brandt, D. (2001). *Literacy in American lives.* Cambridge University Press.

Brydon-Miller, M. (2004). The terrifying truth: Interrogating systems of power and privilege and choosing to act. In M. Brydon-Miller, P. Maguire, & A. McIntyre (Eds.), *Traveling companions: Feminism, teaching, and action research* (pp. 3–19). New York University Press.

Burnett, C., & Merchant, G. (2020). Literacy-as-event: Accounting for relationality in literacy research. *Discourse: Studies in the cultural politics of education, 41*(1), 45–56.

Burnett, C., & Merchant, G. (2016). Boxes of poison: Baroque technique as antidote to simple views of literacy. *Journal of Literacy Research, 48*(3), 258–279.

Fernyhough, C. (2012). *Pieces of light: The new science of memory*. Harper Collins.

Gourlay, L. (2019). Textual practices as already-posthuman: Re-imagining text, authorship and meaning-making in higher education. In C. Kuby, K. Spector, & J. Thiel (Eds.), *Posthumanism and higher education* (pp. 237–254). Palgrave Macmillan.

Haddix, M. (2012). Reclaiming and rebuilding the writer identities of black adolescent males. In D. Alvermann & K. Hinchman (Eds.), *Reconceptualizing the literacies in adolescents' lives: Bridging the everyday/academic divide* (pp. 112–131). Routledge.

Heath, S. B. (1983). *Ways with words: Language, life and work in communities and classrooms*. Cambridge University Press.

Jones, S. (2018). *Portraits of everyday literacy for social justice: Reframing the debate for families and communities*. Springer.

Keller, D. (2013). *Chasing literacy: Reading and writing in an age of acceleration*. Utah State University Press.

Kelley, B. (2016). Toward a goodwill ethics of online research methods. *Transformative Works and Cultures, 22*.

Leander, K. M., & Ehret, C. (2019). *Affect in literacy learning and teaching: Pedagogies, politics and coming to know*. Routledge.

Lemieux, A., & Rowsell, J. (2020). On the relational autonomy of materials: Entanglements in maker literacies research. *Literacy, 54*(3), 144–152.

Massumi, B. (2015). *Politics of affect*. Wiley.

McKee, H. A., & Porter, J. E. (2009). *The ethics of internet research: A rhetorical, case-based process* (Vol. 59). Peter Lang.

Mortensen, P., & Kirsch, G. E. (1996). *Ethics and representation in qualitative studies of literacy*. NCTE.

Newkirk, T. (1996). Seduction and betrayal in qualitative research. In P. Mortensen & G. Kirsch (Eds.), *Ethics and representation in qualitative studies of literacy* (pp. 3–16). NCTE.

Newkirk, T. (2017). *Embarrassment: And the emotional underlife of learning*. Heinemann.

Nordquist, B. (2017). *Literacy and mobility: Complexity, uncertainty, and agency at the nexus of high school and college*. Routledge.

Pandian, A. (2019). *A possible anthropology: Methods for uneasy times*. Duke University Press.

Powell, K. M., & Takayoshi, P. (2003). Accepting roles created for us: The ethics of reciprocity. *College Composition and Communication, 54*(3), 394–422.

Rowsell, J. (2020). "How emotional do I make it?": Making a stance in multimodal compositions. *Journal of Adolescent & Adult Literacy, 63*(6), 627–637.

Ryen, A. (2011). Ethics and qualitative research. *Qualitative research, 3*, 416–538.

Sheridan, M. P., Lemieux, A., De Nascimento, A., & Arnseth, H. C. (2020). Intra-active entanglements: What posthuman and new materialist frameworks can offer the learning sciences. *British Journal of Educational Technology*.

Sullivan, P. A. (1996). Ethnography and the problem of the 'other'. In P. Mortensen & G. Kirsch (Eds.), *Ethics and representation in qualitative studies of literacy* (pp. 97–114). NCTE.

Vasudevan, L. M. (2014). Multimodal cosmopolitanism: Cultivating belonging in everyday moments with youth. *Curriculum Inquiry, 44*(1), 45–67.

Wetherell, M. (2012). *Affect and emotion: A new social science understanding*. Sage.

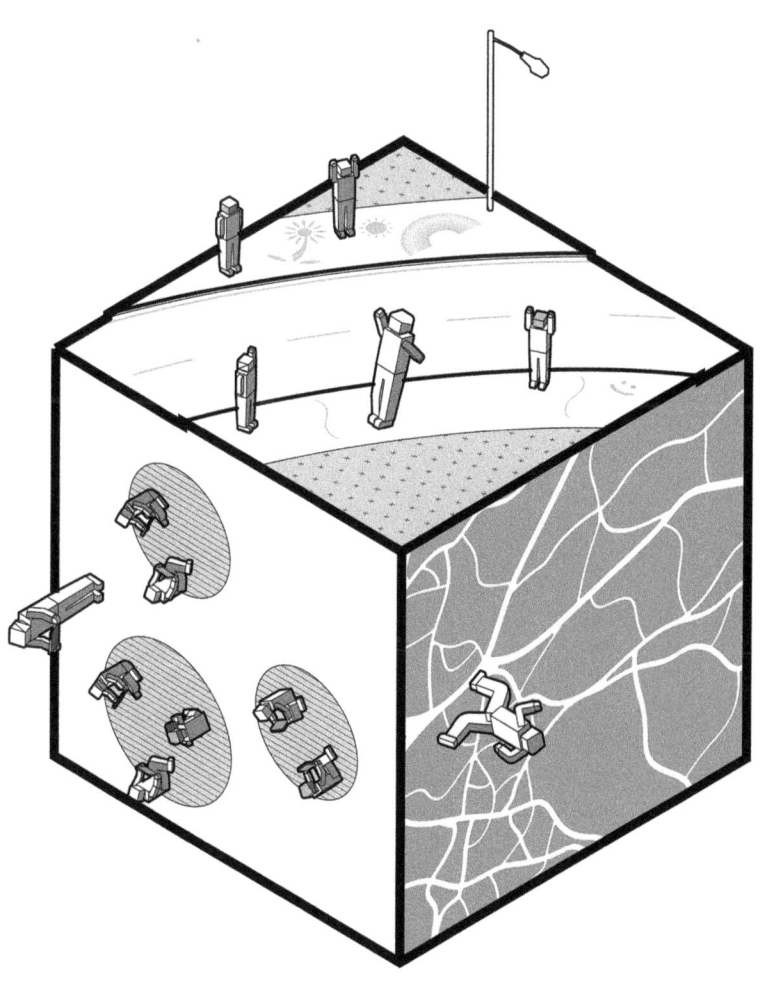

Chapter 5
Attending to Our Response-abilities: Diff/Reading Data Through Pedagogies of the Other-wise

Amélie Lemieux, Kelly C. Johnston, and Fiona Scott

Abstract In times of global emergencies and shifting social priorities worldwide, literacy researchers must recognize how ethnographic methods—foregrounded by New Literacy Studies researchers—may be rendered temporarily and persistently inaccessible. These conditions force us to work other-wise, employing new materialism to contemplate methodologies of the other-wise by channelling our response-abilities (Barad, 2007). Our theorizing extends emerging literature of the other-wise (Kuby and Gutshall Rucker, 2020; Wohlwend, 2019) to make the matter of literacy research come through the dynamics of working remotely, across different time zones and political climates. Across the United States, England, and Canada, our inquiry asks: How do diffractive methodologies help literacy researchers attune to the other-wise? How do these methodologies help us reimagine literacies in ways that support equitable and fully lived futures? We examine these questions by diffractively reading our data and each other's over time—rethinking our methodologies in previous research sites, the literacies that mattered in them, and the literacies that matter now. Datasets come from studies of (a) middle school youths' literacies in an English Language Arts classroom, (b) preschool children's digital literacies at home, and (c) a high school youths' stop-motion environmental literacy project. These diffractive readings extend NLS methodological principles through attention to how sociomaterial assemblages (Burnett and Merchant, 2020) and affective dimensions of literacies (Rowsell, 2020) come to matter differently in the midst of unprecedented global unrest. Attuning to the shift from NLS in its text-mode oriented combinations towards an ontology of postqualitative literacies, our chapter elucidates diffractive readings to attend to time, situatedness, and political tensions.

A. Lemieux (✉)
Faculty of Education, University of Montreal, Montreal, QC, Canada
e-mail: amelie.lemieux.1@umontreal.ca

K. C. Johnston
School of Education, Baylor University, Waco, TX, USA

F. Scott
School of Education, University of Sheffield, Sheffield, UK

© The Author(s), under exclusive license to Springer Nature Singapore Pte Ltd. 2022

C. Lee et al. (eds.), *Unsettling Literacies*, Cultural Studies and Transdisciplinarity in Education 15, https://doi.org/10.1007/978-981-16-6944-6_5

Keywords New materialism · Diffraction · New Literacy Studies · Sociomateriality · Literacy

5.1 Coming Together as *Other-wises* in a Global Pandemic

This chapter emerges from early conversations about collaborative research into the methodologies that mattered before the COVID-19 pandemic and those methodologies which came to matter in the midst of a worldwide pandemic. The three of us knew each other from different outlets, mostly through conferences and shared affinities, despite living and working in different geographical contexts and institutions. In May 2020, in an effort to reach out to each other when human contact was cut from us, we met through Skype and asked ourselves, and one another, questions about how we were doing and the state of our respective research projects. We shared our initial frustrations that data collection was on hold and our feelings that work felt secondary, as hospitalizations and deaths were peaking. Human contact with colleagues came with a newly defined sense of utopian dis/comfort, careful hope, and rationalized understanding of our own and each other's conditions, which entangled a range of responsibilities—some similar and some different. Because the three of us worked across time zones, political decisions affected the public health and sociomaterial conditions that dictated our daily activities, from new conditions at work with emergency remote teaching to being and becoming a parent in a pandemic. Negotiating these newly minted, always changing identities, we acknowledged how our ethico-onto-epistemologies brought about questions of positionalities as well as response-abilities (Dernikos et al., 2020; Zapata et al., 2018).

We found ourselves collectively constructing and re/negotiating *what* was valuable in data (and the notion of *value* thereof) and trusting one another's expertise as opposed to (simply) ourselves as experts of our research. When research expertise is confined to one individual, who might be too immersed in the process, we argue that the potential for emergent meanings to take shape is significantly reduced. Our meetings, beyond the materialities and flattenings of the screen, quickly reminded us of the joys of now defunct face-to-face research project planning. Our encounters reminded us of a friendly academic book club, where we found ourselves scribbling and documenting ideas for collaboration, and theories that 'stuck' with us throughout the pandemic. Our conversations centred agential realism (Barad, 2007) and suggested using diffraction to read (through) one another's data, as a framework that would help us attend to each other's projects with a renewed sense of altruism we felt was much needed in such isolating times. This process involved developing a methodology (or anti-methodology in the traditional, qualitative sense) of the *other-wise*, which required trusting one another as well-intentioned, critical readers of each other's work.

This work involved allowing each other to make data their own, responding to excerpts, listening to project stories, and looking at what might emerge. For this purpose, we define the *other-wise* as people entities, other than us as primary researchers of our studies, that are wise and that come from different epistemologies, sociopolitical situations, institutions, and disciplines. We hyphenate otherwise to emphasise the other's wise(ness), looking at how their reading diffracts original data. Our research question became: How do diffractive methodologies help literacy researchers attune to the other-wise? We acknowledge how the notion of the other-wise has been explored recently in varying contexts from classroom-based studies to ways of conferencing and to early childhood play (see Dernikos, 2020; Kuby & Gutshall Rucker, 2020; Osgood et al., 2020; Wohlwend, 2019). For example, *feeling otherwise* invites humans to experience and sense more-than-human worlds that exist outside the classroom (Dernikos, 2020). On their end, Kuby and Gutshall Rucker (2020) frame humans' complex subjectivities as a dimension of the other-wise, whereby literacies decentre meaning-making and fixed representations, to consider, instead or in addition, literacy *desirings.* The latter are defined as fluid and dynamic understandings of literacy events, uncovering needed dimensions of the 'not-yet-known' (p. 30). Osgood et al. (2020) provide another important, posthuman contribution to the other-wise by exploring experimental ways of redefining the academic conference and what this might produce. Elsewhere, Wohlwend (2019) theorizes play as a literacy for imagining other-wise. Play, here, is a literacy that writes with bodies rather than print to produce action texts. Built on constant negotiations amongst its players, social play then allows for shifting compositions, allowing an alternative, critical approach to literacies in early childhood. This body of research on the other-wise demonstrates pivotal avenues to advance, and perhaps unsettle, literacy research.

5.2   Diff/Reading Data Through the *Other-wise*

Our process was iterative, building on ideas forged through Skype meetings, individual readings, and exchanges through shared Google Documents, between May and December 2020. This process involved, in June 2020, submitting an AERA symposium on postqualitative research (St. Pierre, 2016) with invited scholars, namely, Sarah Truman, Susan Nordstrom, Jessica Cira Rubin, and Jennifer Rowsell, who contributed in dynamizing these exchanges. We came from an understanding that diffractive reading (Barad, 2007) would be central to our inquiry (Cira Rubin, 2020; Mazzei, 2014), though our contribution addressed what and how data came to matter in pandemic times—where usually trusted systems, in our respective research worlds, became quickly unreliable, disrupted, or simply gone. We selected datasets that glowed (MacLure, 2013) and engaged in diffractive reading—the latter meant clarifying what data produced for each of us and how we would (re)present these diffractions. Because this section of the volume engages with new possibilities for inquiry, it seems critical to report on this (anti)method, and we realise that readers might adapt this freely (St. Pierre, 2016). We call this trusting process of reading one another's data 'diff/reading'.

Diff/reading involved, first and foremost, naming sometimes reluctantly what we were doing, taking risks, and extending qualitative research. We acknowledged how we would get used to simultaneously being uncomfortable with, and trusting of, such an exercise. In our meetings, we asked ourselves: What data do I select; what if it does not align? What do my colleagues think about my data, and how do we negotiate these choices with one another? In a shared document, we inserted our data and set a date by which we would each have individual responses written, focusing on what the data *produced* for each of us. We met via Zoom and read one another's responses at the same time, simultaneously taking notes of each other's reactions—bodily and other-wise. We debriefed, shared responses and provided more contextual information, and reflected on what the diff/readings produced— these inform the coda at the end of this chapter. Below are contextualizations of each research site, followed by data diff/readings.

5.3   Diff/Reading Amélie's Data

Reading on screen, opening new browser tabs, picking up the iPhone, closing said tabs, going back to writing-reading-writing-not/reading-daydreaming—what was the term again? What page? This short, yet repetitively familiar cycle of situated engagement across platforms has hit us all since the beginning of the COVID-19 pandemic in March 2020. Lockdowns affected each of us, with our respective universities turning to emergency remote teaching in mid-March 2020. As an assistant professor of literacies, I quickly became the token digital literacy expert, from being interviewed by the media about ideal screen time for children to offering faculty advice on best practices for online learning. The readings I did necessarily permeated how my human-centred perceptions were entangled with statistics that surfaced and that echoed my daily engagements with scholarly productivity. While Jennifer Rowsell and I had co-conducted research on online learning in Canadian secondary schools (Lemieux & Rowsell, 2019) prior to this request for shared expertise, these public events crystallized through needs emergency, i.e. perceived best practices for online pedagogies. These new surges of information duties short-circuited my daily doings and propelled me into a public-oriented role as I became-with the emergency. Online conferencing and data sharing became accessible, with less time, travel, and money involved.

I shared with Kelly and Fiona that before the lockdown, I had completed data collection for a literacies project with tenth-grade adolescents (14–15-year-olds) who were critically studying climate change using maker and multimodal platforms (Stop Motion, 3D printing, film-making). Spanning over 8 weeks in fall 2019, this project followed previous research done collaboratively (e.g., Lemieux & Rowsell, 2020; Rowsell et al., 2018). It took place in a lower-income high school. I facilitated workshops (Lemieux, 2020; Lemieux et al., 2020), and the research involved several professionals (Rowsell, 2016), including a program developer, a school board consultant, the teacher, and myself as researcher. GoPro video footage, audio interviews, maps, and field notes were collected. Volunteer students were given a GoPro headset to record, from a personal angle, their making; the interviews served as an unstructured opportunity to speak to unforeseen literacy events that happened in the makerspace; maps were designed to give students a chance to express their processes through drawing; and the research field notes helped me remember what took place and the vicarious moments that emerged at that time.

Entangled Intensities 1
October 10 2019

Today, I went in at 10:10 am. I wore leggings, a white pullover, and my grey wool shoes—attire that is not intimidating for students. As an outsider to the school and temporary member of that classroom culture, Stacy asked me what I wanted them to call me, and I answered my first name as it was more approachable. I wanted to come in as an equal, not as an expert, as a vulnerable human. Another way I did this in this first class was to ask the class: 'Where are my gamers in this class?' Eight boys raised their hands, and we chatted for 30 seconds about the games we played. I was struck that no girl raised their hand, corroborating how technofeminist research has shown how girls are less prone than boys to engage in STEM-related activities including gaming. Scanning the room with my seemingly innocent question had a result that was twofold: having boys engage in a conversation with a woman who knows about technology, and two, have girls engage and reflect on what it means to have someone they might look up to, who is approachable and who plays 'boys' video games. I made a radical decision as I was planning for this project to deconstruct my go-to methodologies, and this new sense involved playing with a GoPro and adjusting as I went ahead with this project (Fig. 5.1).

Kelly's Diff/Reading of Amélie's Data
My approach to a diffractive analysis through a methodology of the other-wise is to immerse myself in the assemblaging entanglement of bodies in the data. For me, that means imagining myself there in the midst of the data and naming the material-discursive productions (Barad, 2007; Bozalek & Zembylas, 2017). Amélie's

GOPR0085

Fig. 5.1 Messy entanglements between GoPro-hands-camera-researcher

entrance into this new makerspace (and her desire for decentring the adult-student hierarchies through name and attire) with students-teacher-materials-high school-gaming produced a new assemblage, a coming-together of human and nonhumans, bringing about particular realities and social engagement. Even more so, Amélie's intentional talk, to position herself as an inviter to girls who may feel marginalized in a gaming space, as well as a co-technologist with boys who may not be accustomed to seeing a woman leading in the makerspace, also changes the assemblage. And yet, these materialities and talk produce assemblages that will function in particular ways, hindering some possibilities while opening up others (Johnston, 2019), many of which we cannot predict or control. Thus, as a researcher I must ask: How might assemblages function to open up spaces for not-yet-experienced literacies, particularly in schooled spaces? The other-wise speaks to our expectancies as educators and researchers; that is, how we expect and invite engagement opens up possibilities.

Amélie's research choice to bring in the GoPro produces a force that again morphs the assemblage into new possibilities for production. The GoPro shifts the assemblage to value the mundane, reminding us that literacies of the other-wise include literacies of the everyday from the ordinary to the overlooked (Pahl & Rowsell, 2020). Though the other-wise might not yet be experienced, or even thought, it is the opening that positions potentials for the other-wise. In our current times of global unrest and uncertainty, in which we may need to remain open to new possibilities of schooling across space and time, perhaps now is a much-needed time to open up thought to such literacies of the other-wise.

Fiona's Diff/Reading of Amélie's Data

Reading Amélie's 'intensity', I am initially struck that I would never have had the confidence to ask the question 'where are my gamers' in her position. 'Gamer' is not an identity I feel confident to assume, despite having spent huge chunks of time in earlier life playing *The Sims* (an activity that is frequently dismissed as 'feminine' and 'not real gaming' in online gaming discussions). My thoughts move towards my past work on the MakEY project and the notion of maker literacies (Marsh et al., 2017, 2018). In particular, Amélie's 'intensity' makes me think in terms of how maker literacies are or are not constructed as important or valuable, the perceived value of maker activities as aligned with STEM (Marsh et al., 2018), and the extent to which gender plays a role. Very broadly, the present pandemic has drawn into sharp focus the reality that the world cannot function without purportedly 'low-skilled' (e.g., sanitation workers) and female-dominated (e.g., early years, nursing) professions, and yet it feels unlikely that this experience will change the perceived status of, or approach to rewarding, these skill sets. I am reminded of my past maker research and the utopian vision of makerspaces as contexts in which making might flow freely across activities and former gender boundaries, as initial ideas are translated across media and materials, from sewing to coding to electronics (Scott, 2019). The tiny window into Amélie's project awakens in me a desire to know more about how the research unfolded from here: what discussions did researchers, educators, and students engage in in relation to gender and how did these discourses intra-act with maker practices and literacies in the classroom.

5.4   Diff/Reading Kelly's Data

My research focus in these early years as a scholar has been on examining expansive forms of children's and youths' engagement with literacies. This entails attuning to time, place, and space and how people shape and are shaped by contexts through their engagement with literacies. Thus, like many working in education-based settings across the globe, as COVID-19 shook social and institutional foundations throughout the world, my perspective on my educational commitments, including research, was pushed to take on new lines of thought.

For instance, in my work with REACH (Reflective Educational Approach to Character and Health), an after-school programme that supports youth in accessing safe physical activity spaces as well as student-centred literacy-based experiences, methods continue to evolve pre- and post-COVID. The aims of REACH are to (a) engage students in literacy practices through reflective and embodied activities, (b) teach students fitness and nutrition concepts to foster a healthy lifestyle, and (c) promote positive youth development. Our team has partnered with underserved communities in New York City and Los Angeles and most recently through a partnership with the US Peace Corps, Paraguay (cf. Marttinen et al., 2020).

Since 2019, the research project in Paraguay had begun and was in process up until the COVID-19 lockdown. I was a co-researcher, along with Marko, co-creator of REACH and a university professor of health and physical education, and Marisol, a Peace Corps volunteer and recent graduate from Marko's university programme. Marisol, who had been living in the rural Paraguayan village to support health and education initiatives through the Paraguay-Peace Corps partnership, implemented REACH on the ground with approximately 30 12–14-year-olds, while Marko and I mentored and engaged in the research process from the States.

Our research examined how youth engaged in the REACH program through physical and literacy activities and, on a larger level, how their experiences reflected the health and education goals set forth between the community and the US Peace Corps. Our theoretical framework included sociocultural critical perspectives (Kalman & Street, 2013; Lewis et al., 2020) and positive youth development through sport (Holt et al., 2020). We were also interested in our methodological approach, with Marisol implementing the programme and the three of us engaging in a participatory action research methodology to inform implementation and responsive leadership. Data production included weekly field notes, weekly research team notes and reflections, and artefact analysis. The three of us checked in weekly via email or phone. Marisol would send her fieldnotes and reflective notes. Marko and I would review separately and provide responding notes via email or phone call. After these written or verbal meetings, we would decide on implementation changes. Marko and I provided the content and research expertise by offering specific action points for Marisol to try; we also provided relevant literature and resources when these applied.

Entangled Intensities 2

In response to previous weeks of email exchanges regarding how Marisol might support youth in making connections between their everyday literacy practices and their participation in REACH, Marisol wrote: '[Today], we got into a discussion as a class with one question: "Why is it important to be healthy?"' It is one of the central discussion questions provided by the REACH programme. As a class, we discussed activities/hobbies/sports our healthy bodies allow us to do and, depending on our health, how we can lose these things we like to do. During the discussion, there was an impromptu side conversation that took us down a great road! A student sang a lyric from a popular polka song (Paraguayan traditional music), and the entire class laughed and laughed because it has an inappropriate lyric in the mix. One student commented that it's not right to just drink with our friends [as suggested in the song] if we want to be healthy. I asked them that if what the song is saying is parallel to what we had discussed earlier about health as a group, and they said 'No.' So I proposed to them a creative homework assignment to rewrite the part of the song—with something that relates to health, let it be mental health, physical health, or emotional health. The class went crazy for the idea—I asked them to write it in Guaraní and Spanish. Thanks to the article [Kelly sent in previous weeks], *Preserving Indigenous Languages*, it was in my mind to have them do Guaraní assignments (Fig. 5.2).

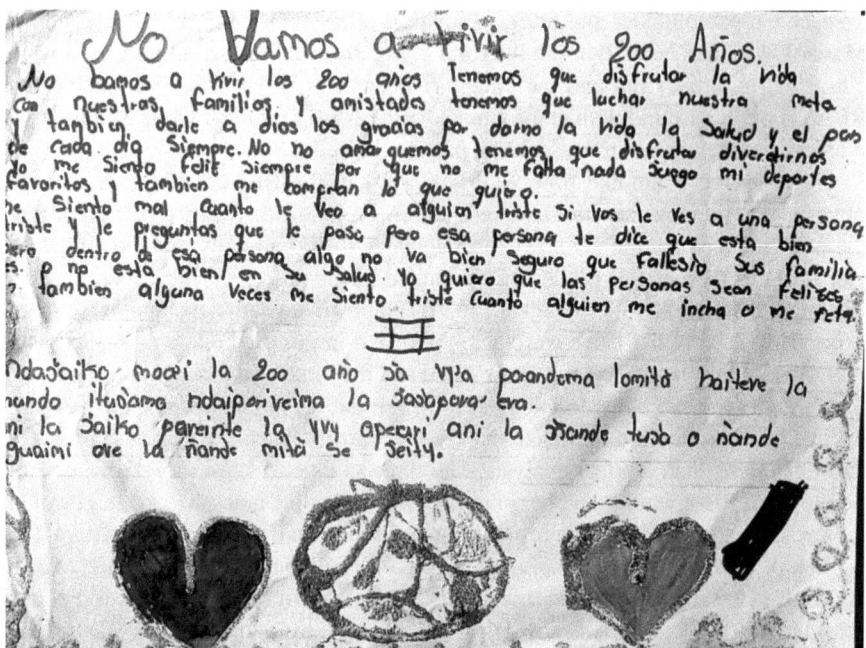

Fig. 5.2 Messy entanglements between teacher-Guarini-Spanish-English-song- laughter-researcher

Amélie's Diff/Reading of Kelly's Data

These are the cuts that trigger. As one of the 'other-wise(s)', I come to this diff/reading in a nonlinear way, as a nonlinear body with rhizomatic thoughts. I feel grateful that, as a relational ontoethical practice, Kelly shares these excerpts with us in writing in addition to the many meetings we have had where we all took turns in explaining the research projects and the sites of tensions they produced. These entangled intensities bring, at the forefront, affective reminders of situations that too often researchers face in literacy studies, that of making agential cuts (Barad, 2007) to dynamically be part of entanglements that generate lively literacy or bewildering moments (Snaza, 2019), such as introducing academic literature to participants. This agential cut (that of bringing in new texts) might, in turn, provoke or trigger unanticipated literacy events, such as literature integration, question prompting, and embodied song performances. The cut Kelly made reminded me of similar cuts co-made in a research project on maker literacies (Lemieux & Rowsell, 2020), where the teacher and I discussed posthuman inquiry as an opening for making, which in turn generated larger considerations for nonhuman materials and how they were used, often extractively, in student projects. What Kelly proposes is important in situating cuts that trigger, through texts we introduce, texts that cut, and texts that trigger. These connections point to the entangled contributions of the other-wise, whereby the experiences of diff/reading might help others in seeing the agential cuts that become to matter, that is, how introducing texts that matter for the researcher necessarily routes research moments other-wise, rhizomatically and unexpectedly.

Fiona's Diff/Reading of Kelly's Data

Kelly's 'intensity' disorients and excites me. It is unlike any research I have undertaken. Given my interest in the embodied aspects of very young children's literacies and my impression that they are somewhat ignored in formal education settings, I am surprised, impressed, and interested to learn of a project in a formal educational space, which so explicitly draws together thinking about the physicality of bodies and literacy. It strikes me that new literacy scholars have long called for formal learning to draw on established literacy practices in local contexts. Thinking about bodies as the basis of literacy curricula, then, feels like a step beyond. When a student introduces the Paraguayan polka song, I am reminded of Papen and Tusting's (2019) notion of 'authentic materials' as the basis of English literacy teaching. The song draws together the themes of health and physicality with local literacies, perhaps uncovering a deeper cultural attitude to health. My interest centres on what strikes me as the subversion of the song as a response to the given task. When the educator, Marisol, suggests that the students rewrite the lyrics to reflect something that relates to health, I am struck that the song, as it stands, already reflects (for me) something very specific relating to health. With Thiel's (2015) assertion that small, in-the-moment pedagogical decisions that adults make in their interactions with children might create boundaries around the creative potential of a child and a set of materials in mind, I am interested in the extent to which her question may have indicated to the students that the song was not the 'right' answer and needed to be rewritten to pertain to health. And in the rewritten songs!

5.5   Diff/Reading Fiona's Data

My work focuses on the literacy practices of young children in their engagements with digital texts and devices. Two events in 2020 changed my relationship with academic work (and everything). For two months post-lockdown, I worked in an iteration of the pandemic-era neoliberal university, adjusting my teaching practices while feeling a sense that working with colleagues in Canada, Australia, or the United States was perhaps (suddenly) no different from working with my colleagues down the road in the United Kingdom. My first, hopeful thought was that the new, pandemic-induced necessity of digital devices for young children's education and general well-being might perhaps be the final nail in the coffin for the media and public obsession with 'screen time'. Less hopefully, I observed the emerging discourses of the 'left-behind' child in a COVID world: with some early suggestions that inequalities for young children in the United Kingdom were widening in relation to the pandemic (Oxford University, 2020) and, later, the tale of a 16-year-old in Southern India taking his own life after accidentally breaking the smartphone he and his siblings relied on for their remote education (Singh, 2020). I felt some apprehension about focusing the debate too strongly on access to devices and connections, to the detriment of considering the complexity of human intra-actions with the digital and the minute, momentary actions that constitute practices over time, in particular in relation to family involvement in children's digital practices. I questioned how emerging discourses about the pandemic's 'left-behind' children were valuing difference in family literacy practices (the other-wise), or simply measuring them against schooled literacies. In June, my own child arrived and irreversibly changed everything for the second time in the space of a few months.

The two events were experienced so simultaneously that they will, perhaps, remain permanently entangled in my mind. As emergency funding calls for vital COVID-era literacies research came flooding in, I (partially) checked out of the emerging academic response and watched my own child begin to coo, gurgle, and babble. As formal childcare disappeared, I watched my colleagues' professional and familial lives becoming more messily intertwined. I joined the ranks of early childhood researchers (Bazalgette, 2019; Nelson, 1989), mentally *datafying* the unfolding literacy and digital literacy practices before me: the micro-intra-actions my child began to engage in in relation to her human and nonhuman surroundings and those I self-consciously noted myself producing or participating in.

My doctoral project examined precisely these micro intra-actions ethnographically: between young children and their families and things in the home, including digital and non-digital objects and texts. The project brief, which I came to as a preformed entity, suggested that the research should focus on families 'from economically and socially disadvantaged communities'. The abridged excerpt between Olivia (O; 3 years, 9 months), Teresa (T), and *CBeebies Playtime* app (CP) originated in such a community—one of top 10% most deprived[1] areas in the United Kingdom.

---

[1] Though not unproblematic, given the explicit focus on economically and socially disadvantaged communities, UK Indices of Multiple Deprivation (Ministry of Housing, Communities and Local Government, 2015) and a modified Hope-Goldthorpe (Seyd, 2002) scale were employed as proxy measures for broadly understanding relative socioeconomic status.

Entangled Intensity 3: Olivia Makes a Photo Sticker on the Tablet with Mum (Abridged)

Intra-action	Discourse in place
Olivia smiling; Teresa picks up tablet, holding in front of Olivia	(CP) Camera! Take a photo of something, and let's use it to make a picture
Olivia reaches right finger towards the tablet, presses 'x' in top right corner, closing the camera window (laughs)	(T) Go on, take a picture, go on, take a picture
Teresa taps camera icon	(CP) Camera! Take a photo of something, and let's use it to make a picture
Screen displays mirror image of Olivia. Teresa gestures to correct on-screen icon to take picture	(T) Go on, take a picture here
Olivia taps correct icon	
Screen freezes briefly, six 'stickers' appear, with Olivia's selfie photo inside. Olivia laughs	(T) Uh-ohh!
	(CP) Stickers! Choose a sticker to add to your picture
Both laughing, looking at screen	
Teresa looks at Olivia	(T) You have a sticker. Look!
Olivia reaches hand out, Teresa taps her gently on the arm, Olivia taps on sticker, tablet makes a beeping noise, and a sticker is placed on Olivia's drawing	(T) Go on, tap it
	(T) Uhh!
Olivia continues to tap, placing multiple photo stickers on drawing, tablet making corresponding beeping sound. Both laugh	
[…]	
The screen displays the six stickers	
Olivia playing with her hair, points at diamond sticker with selfie, circling it with finger	(O) What's that shape?
Teresa looks at screen. Olivia is covering eyes, tired and giggling	(T) What's that shape?
Teresa gestures towards diamond, Olivia points	(T) What's that shape? I don't know what's that shape…
	(T) … diamond?
Olivia nods head up and down, emphatically, smiling	
	(T) Diamond shape
Teresa looks momentarily at Fiona and at diamond. Points to star sticker	(T) And what's that shape?
Olivia looks at star sticker, still smiling, nodding dying away	
Teresa looks briefly at Olivia and back to screen	(O) Star
Teresa points to square sticker	(T) And this one?
	(O) Triangle
	(T) No, it's skw… (O) Square (T) Square

Fig. 5.3 Entanglements with Olivia

Kelly's Diff/Reading of Fiona's Data

As I read Fiona's data, I continue to think with assemblages in mind, which moves me to consider the material-discursive as an entanglement that produces particular realities, experiences, and relationalities (Burnett & Merchant, 2020). I imagine this network of people and things forming over this brief segment of time: CBeebies app-Olivia/daughter- Teresa/mother-tablet-beeping-digital   stickers-and-and-and (Deleuze & Guattari, 1988), and I think especially about imagining literacies of the other-wise through digital play. As I read this constellation of moments, what many would look at as ordinary and perhaps even literacy-less, I am reminded of how assemblages produce felt sensations that stick with us long after temporary assemblaging productions have passed (Fig. 5.3).

Particularly, in the present moment of rethinking schooling and learning outside of traditional bounds, often at home with parents or caretakers, I am thinking about how this assemblage produces felt sensations through digital play and offers thought on literacies of the other-wise. In this case, it is not just access to a digital device and app but considering how the assemblage and felt sensations—laughter, touch, experience—open up possibilities for meaning-making through exploration of and engagement with ideas. I am moved to consider the mundane and how what could be seen as the mundane may be felt as much more by a child whose digital play becomes agentic through what an assemblage makes possible. This experience of enacted agency (Barad, 2007) invites learners, like this child, to become-other-wise through digital play.

Amélie's Diff/Reading of Fiona's Data

Becoming a lava lamp. I craft this response of the other-wise as one that is generated from hope (Pahl & Rowsell, 2020) that children like Olivia bring about to research projects. I see parts of myself in Fiona as she is entangled in these moments between the child, the iPad, the app, the diamond, and the not-yet or the materialization in the making. I am reminded that research contexts produce different affects depending on where these affects come from and where they go. Focusing on moments where the relational becomes with and through this diff/reading, I cannot help but think about where Olivia is now, whether she is still using the app, and how this moment perhaps sparked a defining moment in her development and play with apps. From the nonhuman software micromovements to the human nods, the entangled intensities with app play generate thoughts about generating togetherness—moments where intra-actions, discourses, people, and materials operate like the traversing and bubbling waxes of a lava lamp. The unpredictability of fluid mechanics and slowly merging movements within a lava lamp, much like in the research assemblage, generate yin- and yang-like *va-et-vient* between different, non-static parts. By embracing these flowing shifts, we notice how much time it takes for the lamp (an analogy for the research assemblage) to warm up the wax so that the fluids emulsify. Diff/reading with Fiona's excerpt and attending to the movements it produces allows us to develop literacies of the capacious, breaking the normative of interpretation, attuning to a coming togetherness, playing with the other-wise, and moving from private to public.

5.6   Reflective Coda

This chapter on data diff/readings through the other-wise has generated trajectories for postqualitative inquiry in literacies research. By reading one another's data, we have theorized the other-wise—a plural, rhizomatic entity that produces alternative perspectives to that of the researcher who needs to engage with her own data in pandemic times where collaborations are halted. Attending to the diff/readings, we noted how our bodily responses to the other-wise were, sporadically and simultaneously, immediate, messy, engaged, paused, uncomfortable, risk-laden, surprising, careful, and generous. To diff/read data through the other-wise is to accept these conditions as they come and to take risks and be uncomfortable. Diff/readings provoke relational generosity, for others and the self, in seeing new directions in research. Similarly to a trust fall team-building exercise, diff/reading data through the other-wise provokes opportunities to offer care, faith, and hope, almost blindly. The other-wise, as an entangled entity, reciprocates with time and generosity, two qualities that spark much-needed togetherness in the midst of a global pandemic. Diff/reading data inspires the contemplation of dismantling the structural constraints of produced research. In so doing, it puts faith into recentering what can be seen as data mattering in neoliberal universities and how the other-wise shapes the concepts that produce data. We realize how diff/reading data is both a grounding and a transcorporeal experience, whereby time, place, and situationalities overlap each other, producing data through the other-wise.

Ethics Statement All studies have received ethics clearance.

References

Barad, K. (2007). *Meeting the universe halfway: Quantum physics and the entanglement of matter and meaning*. Duke University Press.
Bazalgette, C. (2019). *Some secret language: How toddlers learn to understand movies*. Doctoral dissertation, University College London. Retrieved from https://discovery.ucl.ac.uk/id/eprint/10041767/1/THESIS%20FINAL%20PDF.pdf
Bozalek, V., & Zembylas, M. (2017). Diffraction or reflection? Sketching the contours of two methodologies in educational research. *International Journal of Qualitative Studies in Education, 30*(2), 111–127.
Burnett, C., & Merchant, G. (2020). Literacy-as-event: Accounting for relationality in literacy research. *Discourse: Studies in the Cultural Politics of Education, 41*(1), 45–56.
Cira Rubin, J. (2020). Third spaces and tensions: Teacher experiences in an international professional development program. *Teaching and Teacher Education, 95*, 103141.
Deleuze, G., & Guattari, F. (1988). *A thousand plateaus: Capitalism and schizophrenia*. Bloomsbury Publishing.
Dernikos, B. P. (2020). Tuning into 'fleshy' frequencies: A posthuman mapping of affect, sound and de/colonized literacies with/in a primary classroom. *Journal of Early Childhood Literacy, 20*(1), 134–157.
Dernikos, B.P., Ferguson, D., & Siegel, M. (2020). The possibilities of 'humanizing' posthumanist inquiries: An intra-active conversation. *Cultural Studies, Critical Methodologies, 20*(5), 434–447.
Holt, N. L., Deal, C. J., & Pankow, K. (2020). Positive youth development through sport. In G. Tenenbaum & R. C. Eklund (Eds.), *Handbook of Sport Psychology* (4th ed.). Wiley.
Johnston, K. C. (2019). Assemblaging communities: Looking at how communities work for enacting critical literacies pedagogy in the classroom. *English Teaching: Practice & Critique, 19*(1), 121–135.
Kalman, J., & Street, B. V. (Eds.). (2013). *Literacy in Latin America*. Routledge.
Kuby, C. R., & Rucker, T. G. (2020). (Re) Thinking children as fully (in)human and literacies as otherwise through (re)etymologizing intervene and inequality. *Journal of Early Childhood Literacy, 20*(1), 13–43.
Lemieux, A. (2020). *De/constructing literacies: Considerations for engagement*. Peter Lang.
Lemieux, A., & Rowsell, J. (2019). Digital technologies and online learning in secondary education (Canada). *Bloomsbury Education and Childhood Studies*. https://doi.org/10.5040/9781474209441.0038
Lemieux, A., & Rowsell, J. (2020). On the relational autonomy of materials: Entanglements in maker literacies research. *Literacy, 54*(3), 144–152.
Lemieux, A., Smith, A., McLean, C., & Rowsell, J. (2020). Visualizing mapping as pedagogy for literacy futures. *Journal of Curriculum Theorizing, 35*(2), 36–58.
Lewis, C., Enciso, P. E., & Moje, E. B. (2020). *Reframing sociocultural research on literacy: Identity, agency, and power*. Routledge.
MacLure, M. (2013). Researching without representation? Language and materiality in postqualitative methodology. *International Journal of Qualitative Studies in Education, 26*(6), 658–667.

Marsh, J., Kumpulainen, K., Nisha, B., Velicu, A., Blum-Ross, A., Hyatt, D., Jónsdóttir, S. R., Levy, R., Little, S., Marusteru, G., Ólafsdóttir, M. E., Sandvik, K., Scott, F., Thestrup, K., Arnseth, H. C., Dýrfjörð, K., Jornet, A., Kjartansdóttir, S. H., Pahl, K., Pétursdóttir, S., & Thorsteinsson, G. (2017). *Makerspaces in the early years: A literature review. University of Sheffield: MakEY Project.* Retrieved from http://makeyproject.eu/wp-content/uploads/2017/02/ Makey_Literature_Review.pdf

Marsh, J., Arnseth, H. C., & Kumpulainen, K. (2018). Maker literacies and maker citizenship in the MakEY (Makerspaces in the Early Years) project. *Multimodal Technologies and Interaction, 2*(3), 50.

Marttinen, R., Fredrick, R. N., III, Johnston, K., Phillips, S., & Patterson, D. (2020). Implementing the REACH after-school programme for youth in urban communities: Challenges and lessons learned. *European Physical Education Review, 26*(2), 410–428.

Mazzei, L. (2014). Beyond an easy sense: A diffractive analysis. *Qualitative Inquiry, 20*(6), 742–746.

Ministry of Housing, Communities & Local Government. (2015). *English indices of deprivation 2015.* Retrieved from https://www.gov.uk/government/statistics/ english-indices-of-deprivation-2015

Nelson, K. E. (1989). *Narratives from the crib.* Harvard University Press.

Osgood, J., Taylor, C. A., Andersen, C. E., Benozzo, A., Carey, N., Elmenhorst, C., Fairchild, N., Koro-Ljungberg, M., Otterstad, M., & Rantala, T. (2020). Conferencing otherwise: A feminist new materialist writing experiment. *Cultural Studies ↔ Critical Methodologies, 20*(6), 596–609.

Oxford University (2020). UK lockdown linked to widening disadvantage gap for babies and toddlers. Retrieved from https://www.ox.ac.uk/news/2020-10-27-uk-lockdown-linked-widening-disadvantage-gap-babies-and-toddlers

Pahl, K., & Rowsell, J. (2020). *Living literacies: Literacy for social change.* MIT Press.

Papen, U., & Tusting, K. (2019). Using ethnography and 'real literacies' to develop a curriculum for English literacy teaching for young deaf adults in India. *Compare: A Journal of Comparative and International Education, 50*(8), 1140–1158.

Rowsell, J. (2016). What professionals can teach us about education: A call for change. *Cambridge Journal of Education, 46*, 81–96.

Rowsell, J. (2020). "How emotional do I make it?": Making a stance in multimodal compositions. *Journal of Adolescent & Adult Literacy, 63*(6), 627–637.

Rowsell, J., Lemieux, A., Swartz, L., Burkitt, J., & Turcotte, M. (2018). The stuff that heroes are made of: Elastic, sticky, messy literacies in children's transmedial cultures. *Language Arts, 96*(1), 7–20.

Scott, F. (2019). 'Knock, knock, it's Freddy!': Harnessing young children's digital and media skills and interests to foster creativity and digital literacy in makerspaces. *Media Education Research Journal, 8*(2), 95–104.

Seyd, S. G. (2002). *A citizen audit for Britain: Full research report.* Retrieved from http:// www.researchcatalogue.esrc.ac.uk/grants/L215252025/outputs/read/f14368a1-2896-4e4e-8c0c-ab8ddbdf8dab

Singh, N. (2020). Teenager in India kills himself after shattered mobile phone screen means he can't attend online classes. *The Independent.* Retrieved from https://www.independent.co.uk/ news/world/asia/india-teenager-suicide-mobile-phone-screen-online-classes-b1371700.html

Snaza, N. (2019). *Animate literacies: Literature, affect, and the politics of humanism.* Duke University Press.

St. Pierre, E. A. (2016). The empirical and the new empiricisms. Cultural Studies ↔ Critical Methodologies, *16*(2), 111–124.

Wohlwend, K. E. (2019). Play as the literacy of children: Imagining otherwise in contemporary early childhood education. In D. E. Alvermann, N. J. Unrau, & M. Sailors (Eds.), *Theoretical models and processes of literacy* (7th ed.). Routledge.

Zapata, A., Kuby, C. R., & Thiel, J. J. (2018). Encounters with writing: Becoming-with posthumanist ethics. *Journal of Literacy Research, 50*(4), 478–501.

Chapter 6
'Connected to the Soul': Autoethnography, Neurodiversity and Literacies in Times of Ongoing Change

Chris Bailey

Abstract The COVID-19 pandemic has seen ongoing and disruptive change on a global scale. As well as being experienced collectively, this period of uncertainty has been felt intensely and personally by individuals across the world. In this chapter, I use an autoethnographic approach to provide a personal, reflective take on recent events. Here, I emphasise how individual lives are *always* subject to and unsettled by change and disruption, both *regardless of* and *inclusive of* global contexts, in order to make a case for an approach to literacy research that takes direct account of the personal.

During the first period of 'lockdown' in the UK, I was diagnosed as autistic. Here, I reflect on this experience in the context of wider disruption, using a literacy lens to examine the texts I encountered, and created, during this period. Considering these texts—including formal diagnostic papers, a comic, mapping and song—using autoethnography, I reflect on the process and experience of being diagnosed autistic during a time of global change. I explore the multiple meanings made around these texts and the value they brought to my own 'precarious' experience of the world.

This chapter both exemplifies and argues for the use of autoethnography, and other storying methods, as valid and necessary aspects of literacy research. I also suggest that there are benefits to encouraging stories that engage with meaning-making through the use of multiple modes. Finally, I show how literacy research could be enriched by drawing on ideas from the neurodiversity (Singer, 1999) paradigm, which deal with interrelated issues of power, value and the resistance of deficit or normative models of understanding difference.

Keywords Neurodiversity · Literacies · Affect · Autism · Autoethnography

C. Bailey (✉)
Sheffield Hallam University, Sheffiled, UK
e-mail: C.Bailey@shu.ac.uk

© The Author(s), under exclusive license to Springer Nature Singapore Pte Ltd. 2022
C. Lee et al. (eds.), *Unsettling Literacies*, Cultural Studies and Transdisciplinarity in Education 15, https://doi.org/10.1007/978-981-16-6944-6_6

6.1 Introduction

This chapter offers a personal take on this book's concerns around precarity, providing an 'opening' that encourages the expansion of literacy studies through methodology and topic. Drawing on my own experiences, I exemplify and argue for the use of creative personal storying approaches as necessary methods in literacy research. At the outset of the COVID-19 pandemic, during the first period of lockdown in the UK, I was diagnosed autistic by the local authority's Adult Autism and Neurodevelopmental Service. Here, I recount this experience, exploring how I made sense of this emerging identity in relation to the texts I encountered, and created, during a time of personal and global precarity. I discuss these texts and reflect on their impact using three autoethnographic episodes. I combine perspectives from New Literacy Studies (NLS) (Street, 2012) and the neurodiversity (Singer, 1999) paradigm to demonstrate how both share concerns around power, value and the resistance of deficit or normative models of understanding difference. In spite of these synergies, there has been little connection made between these areas. I argue for the necessity of further work that unites these perspectives, particularly at a time in history where, politically and culturally, there is growing need to push back against popularist discourses around identity and normatively framed conceptions of value.

6.2 Neurodiversity

In recent years, the neurodiversity movement (Kapp, 2020) has advocated for the rights, respect and inclusion of those diverging from a socially constructed 'neurotypical' (NT) human default. The term 'neurodiversity' was first introduced by Singer (1999) to describe the naturally occurring variation between human minds, particularly in relation to autism. As a 'key force in promoting social change for autistic people' (Kapp, 2020, p. 3), those aligned with the neurodiversity paradigm argue for a view of autism and other types of neurodivergence, in 'social terms of human rights' rather than 'as a medical collection of deficits and symptoms to cure' (Kapp, 2020, p. 18). The term 'neurodivergent' (ND) is also used in relation to terms such as dyslexia, ADHD, Tourette syndrome, learning disability, etc., as a means to include anyone who does not adhere to the neurotypical default. As such, neurodivergent individuals are positioned as experiencing ways of thinking, feeling, doing and being that, in contrast with deficit, medically mediated models of understanding human worth, add value to society in ways that move beyond neurotypical conceptions of the world. Nevertheless, neurodivergent people are still subject to social power inequalities (Tisoncik, 2020), what Deleuze and Guattari (1987) might call 'minoritarian' oppression in a homogenous 'majoritarian' system.

6.3   Autism

Several characteristics are shared by autistic people. Williams (2020) suggests that being autistic involves a 'sense of being "other"' (p. 39). This feeling often results from social misalignments that arise due to communication differences between ND and NT individuals. Challenge around verbal and/or nonverbal communication is a feature of autism diagnosis (American Psychiatric Association, 2013, p. 50). Differences in sensory processing are key aspects of autism (Belek, 2019, p. 30). Sinclair (2013) writes that 'autism is a way of being. It is pervasive; it colours every experience, every sensation, perception, thought, emotion, and encounter' (n.p.). Autistic individuals experience varying degrees of hyper- or hyposensitivity to different sensory stimuli. Autistic people also generally rely strongly on routine and face challenge in managing uncertainty (American Psychiatric Association, 2013, p. 50). I understand autism as an 'assemblage' (Deleuze & Guattari, 1987, p. 4) consisting inevitably of the more pathologised medical definitions but also being constructed from more generous sociocultural accounts of autistic experience. Referring to autism as an 'assemblage' helps to resituate the language around autism in a space beyond the medical model, expanding our understanding of autism as 'both a construct and objective part of the world' (Chapman, 2020, p. 42) whilst also acknowledging the complexity of autism as an identity rather than a deficit or a disorder (Fletcher-Watson & Happe, 2019). This is not to deny the challenges faced by autistic people but to shift understanding of those challenges as stemming from societal barriers rather than internal failure. Autism is a 'heterogeneous' experience (Fletcher-Watson & Happe, 2019, p. 159), just as being NT is a heterogeneous experience. Nevertheless, it tends to be more medically mediated conceptions of autism, and other neurodivergent ways of being, that permeate the popular consciousness, often via simplified portrayals in popular culture. Whilst autism is said to be a 'spectrum' with a wide range of variation (American Psychiatric Association, 2013), this is widely misinterpreted as a linear diagnosis that somehow reflects the 'functioning level' of the autistic individual rather than the idea of a 'constellation' (Fletcher-Watson & Happe, 2019, p. 40) of different profiles which represent this diversity more accurately.

6.4   Autoethnography as 'Autistext'

Autoethnography has been described as an emancipatory method that resists objectification (Richards, 2008), providing a 'socially-just and socially-conscious' (Ellis et al., 2011, p. 273) means of exploring issues around disability and difference. As an approach to research that allows for individual voices to be heard, it involves description and analysis of personal experience to gain understanding of cultural experience. Whilst autoethnography has been critiqued for being both biased and self-absorbed (Ellis et al., 2011), these arguments tend to come via misunderstandings of the purpose of qualitative research. As such, Ellis et al. (2011) suggest that autoethnography 'attempts to disrupt the binary of science and art' (p. 283). In writing this chapter, I have considered 'relational ethics' (Turner, 2013) by obscuring the details relating to others who may appear in my writing. I am writing about my experiences because I have found comfort in the autoethnographic and narrative work of other neurodivergent writers, such as Yergeau (2018) and Ratcliffe (2020). Yergeau (2018) suggests that autistic stories, or 'autistexts', exist to 'resist the cultural inscriptions that autism as a diagnosis suggests' (p. 24), helping to complicate understandings of neurodivergence. Methodological approaches that involve self-narrative, such as autoethnography, can help to bring the lived experience of neurodivergent individuals to the fore, giving an author valuable control over their own narratives in the face of societal misrepresentation.

Neurodivergent lived experience is still misunderstood and misrepresented, in significant part due to the dominance of research located within scientific paradigms. In the work of Baron-Cohen (2010)—awarded a knighthood in 2021 for 'services to people with autism'—autistic people across the gender spectrum have been depicted as having an 'extreme male brain' (p. 167) and a lack of empathy or theory of mind (Baron-Cohen, 2000). Elsewhere, a recent study sought to understand levels of social distress in autistic children by *causing* social distress in autistic toddlers and charting their 'distress intensity' (Macari et al., 2020). To counter the damage done by what Yergeau (2009) refers to as 'the typical autism essay', research that gives voice to neurodivergent people provides a counter-narrative. My experience of neurodivergence is a lived experience of being autistic, and therefore, this chapter largely focuses on this aspect. Although my diagnosis is only recent, I have lived experience of being undiagnosed autistic for more than 40 years. Whilst my own 'autistext' does not claim to directly represent anyone other than myself in terms of how being neurodivergent influences my life, I hope there is enough commonality to make it at least indicative of one dimension of neurodivergence.

6.5   NLS and Texts

An NLS approach allows for the mobilisation of broad understandings of literacy and text. Whilst traditional, 'autonomous' conceptualisations of literacy position it as a fixed set of skills, the 'ideological' perspective frames literacies as an evolving set of social practices, culturally located in particular contexts, manifesting in the relationships between people (Street, 2012). Literacies are not neutral but are subject to power relations, with some literacies being more 'visual and influential' (Barton et al., 2000, p. 12) than others. Literacies are also connected closely with the forming of identity (Wohlwend, 2009) with the concept of 'identity text' (p. 57) helping to demonstrate how identities are shaped by the consumption and production of texts. An expansive conceptualisation of text helps us to understand texts as written (e.g., letters, books, academic writing) but also as 'multimodal artefacts' (Pahl, 2007, p. 87) that encompass other modalities (e.g., songs, images, film).

What follows are three short autoethnographic reflections, coupling descriptive reflection with theoretical analysis. Each centres on a text or series of identity texts (Wohlwend, 2009) that helped me to shape and make sense of my own identity in light of an autism diagnosis received during a period of global disruption.

6.5.1 A Letter: Language, Identity and Power

I receive a letter from the Adult Autism and Neurodevelopmental Service. It states: 'To Whom it may concern. Christopher attended this service for assessment... The assessment concluded that they do a [sic] have an Autism Spectrum Condition'. This is a relief. The long diagnostic process was not so much a means to find out but to validate what I already knew. I had been working on the assumption that I was autistic for some time, so an alternative conclusion would have potentially led to feelings of uncertainty, self-doubt and shame even. The letter continues '[...] it is important to note that Autism Spectrum Disorder is a recognised disability under the Equity Act 2010 and as such "reasonable adjustments" should be made in any relevant setting'. I had received this diagnosis verbally a few days before, via video call with the psychologist. Nevertheless, there's something reassuring about these words appearing on paper.

This letter is not written *to* me but *for* me, to use when I require accommodations at work. Unfortunately, any accommodations I negotiated prior to formal diagnosis had been overtaken by the disruption of lockdown. Regardless, there's much contained in these short sentences, and this letter marks the end of a process of diagnosis that began with a doctor's referral 14 months prior. Although the typing error (the extra 'a') is a little jarring—arguably the most important sentence in this letter doesn't *quite* make sense—other aspects are more significant. This text has meaning for me in terms of my identity: how I see and understand myself. The letter refers to my diagnosis in multiple ways: as autism spectrum *disorder* (ASD) and autism spectrum *condition* (ASC). ASD is the terminology of choice in medical literature. The DSM-5 and the ICD-10, on which diagnosis is based in the UK, both frame autism as a 'disorder'—a word which evokes deficit, a brokenness. Deficit models prevail in all aspects of life. Since its inception, New Literacy Studies (NLS) has sought to challenge the 'deficit' model that stems from 'autonomous' conceptions of literacy (Street, 2012), where one dominant set of literacy practices are positioned as valuable, whilst the sociocultural, contextual and profoundly *meaningful* literacies of everyday life are sidelined. The 'ideological' (Street, 2012) model of literacy has sought to complicate binary notions of 'literate/illiterate' by questioning dominant discourses around literacy. Similarly, the neurodiversity movement has sought to challenge dominant understandings that position autism (and other minority neurotypes) as lacking against a default understanding of what it means to be human. The reframing seen in this letter, replacing 'disorder' with 'condition', is presumably an attempt to acknowledge the potential stigmatising effect of using particular language. However, whilst 'condition' is often used synonymously with 'state of being', there is also still something pathologised about the term. My response to this is more physical than it is intellectual—there is something slightly incongruous about a feeling of relief being associated with the confirmation of a 'disorder'. However, being 'disordered' is something I'm increasingly happy to reclaim as a positive description.

There is a strong argument for using the term 'identification' rather than 'assessment' or 'diagnosis'. Self-identification is considered valid by many in the neurodivergent community, due to the barriers to diagnosis faced by many. A referral for assessment in the UK requires agreement by a general practitioner (GP). As many in the medical profession still rely on outdated perceptions of autism, a referral will be rebuffed in many cases. Denial of access to assessment leads, in particular, to underrepresentation of diagnosis for anyone who does not present as male (Lockwood Estrin et al., 2020) or is part of a racial minority (Travers & Krezmien, 2018; Zuckerman et al., 2014; Ribeiro et al. (2017), and thus the system perpetuates itself and its 'grave inequalities' (Onaiwu, 2020).

My privilege as a white academic, with access, via my workplace, to a well-informed counsellor who could advocate for me, worked in my favour. These factors likely legitimised my request for diagnosis. Those who gain a GP referral face a lengthy wait, as UK diagnostic services are largely underfunded. In many countries, diagnosis is financially prohibitive. The process requires a significant amount of emotional labour, complicated by 'bureaucratic literacies' (Jones, 2014)—a flow of correspondence that requires reading and writing of letters and diagnostic forms. There is also the resulting stigma when diagnosis is achieved, and, in spite of autism being 'a recognised disability under the Equity Act 2010', for many, 'reasonable adjustments' will remain ungranted. I am conscious of the irony here of being a white man writing about underrepresentation. However, my motivation for sharing my experience is to use my position to highlight inequalities in the system and to strengthen cross-disciplinary ties with neurodiversity to ensure that diverse perspectives *are* increasingly represented in the future.

Back to my letter, another innocuous-looking turn of phrase also positions autism in a pathologising way. I am told that I 'have' ASC/ASD. This possessive phrasing uses 'person-first language', otherwise known as 'nondisabling language', which places 'emphasis on the person first rather than the disability' (Jensen et al., 2013, p. 46). This constructs me as a 'person *with* autism' rather than, as would be the case in identity-first phrasing, 'an autistic person'. Autistic people, such as Sinclair (2013), disrupt pathological assertions about autism by suggesting that being autistic is not something that can be separated from the self—it is something that you *are*. The person-first language used in my diagnosis letter is now widely critiqued within the neurodiversity and wider disability study communities who suggest that person-first language has the potential to embed deficit understandings of disability. As Gernsbacher (2017) suggests, 'desirable attributes are normally expressed through pronouns preceding nouns' (Vivanti, 2020, p. 691), and therefore, PFL implicitly positions disability as undesirable. For these reasons, Botha et al. (2020) argue that the framing of autism through language 'has material consequences for the autistic community, especially those who are minimally verbal'. Bottema-Beutel et al. (2020) suggest that such framings have the effect of reinforcing ableist ideologies. The neurodiversity perspective, however, 'sees autism as an expression of cultural diversity, rather than pathology' (Vivanti, 2020, p. 691) and, therefore, the use of identity-first language asserts autism as an identity without presuming that this de-personifies the individual.

This letter, then, is an identity text invested with the weight of official discourse. This formal text has power to reinforce problematic medicalised conceptions of neurodiversity, reflecting the 'problem with power dynamics' in autism discussion (Yergeau, 2009). In recent years, however, the autistic community has itself sought to reframe discussions about neurodiversity using digital texts via blogs and social media. So when I read this letter, I do this having also explored autism more widely. On social media, the *#ActuallyAutistic* hashtag helps amplify autistic voices, adding detail and nuance that complicate the narrative around autism. Thus, this 'formal' diagnostic text does not exist in isolation, and the extended network of texts produced by autistic individuals has the power to recontextualise and shift discourses and personal understandings.

6.5.2   'The Schiphol Test': Affect, Assemblage and Movement

'Push push push push... moving on...'

These words repeat in my head as I run. These are the words of a song, *Schiphol Test* by Underworld, playing through noise-cancelling earphones pushed deep into my auditory canals. Many autistic people process sound in ways that differ from the neurotypical population (Davies, 2019). For me, this results in a hypersensitivity to multiple environmental sounds which compete for attention and can lead to overwhelm. Headphones help me escape from complex soundscapes into a space where sounds weave in less challenging ways. Here, electronic beats and a repeating bass pattern accompany a familiar voice, all of which merge with the motion of my body through space as my trainers make their own rhythm on the asphalt. My hands, fingers splayed wide, make repetitive, jagged patterns in the air ahead of me in time with the beat. Driving synth base, repetition, movement, *flow...*

'Got to get away...'

I rediscovered running in my mid-20s. I was put off most kinds of physical exercise as a child due to the shame involved in *always* coming last, compounded by the PE teacher who was overheard mocking my unusual running form. Running as an adult is a different experience. Since the onset of the pandemic, I have been running, compulsively, every day, because I need to. Amid reconfigured working and living patterns necessitated by new directives to prevent the spread of the virus, I have found multiple readjustments challenging. Like many autistic people, I find change difficult and rely on routine and certainty to keep myself calm. For most people, change and uncertainty has characterised lockdown. Disruption of routine. Distractions. All of these lead to overwhelm, which is characteristic of the autistic experience of the world, particularly when the world feels as unstable as it does at this point.

'Connected to the soul...'

But running whilst listening to music helps me to find release. The song's words become *my* words as movement helps me inhabit the space made by the song. The song is a text but one that is embodied and that I can move inside. As Frith (1996) suggests, music helps to define 'a space without boundaries' (p. 125). Running—movement—does not generally achieve this on its own: I need the music too. Not just this song, but this is one that has caught my attention during this time and one that I'm compelled to have on repeat. There is certainty in repetition. This does not feel like escapism—it feels like connection, as if the song is speaking *to* and *through* me. In particular, there's something about the word 'soul' that chimes with my thinking round my identity and the fact that somehow my very essence has been disrupted and, concurrently, settled by my diagnosis.

Particularly at times of disruption or precarity, music has a powerful way of resonating. A connection is formed between the world, the song, and my body. I often rely on this process to help me escape a full meltdown. There's a route I've discovered recently where, after a short section of residential roadway, a right turn takes me to the top of a hill. Reading the horizon, on a clear day, I make out the silhouettes of two coal-fired power stations 40 miles away. Soon after this expansive view, I'm led by the curve of the road, down a tree-lined hill into green fields inhabited by wildlife. I'm carried by this descent and the music and my surroundings, experiencing something close to joy, the opposite of the 'emotion dysregulation' (Swain et al., 2015) I was undergoing just minutes before. Running feels like creation, as if the energies flowing out of my body must be leaving some kind of trace. In fact, a digital record is being generated, by the GPS tracking on my watch. A map is produced, a line drawn that allows me to revisit my routes on my phone. As well as the individual map, it generates a 'heat map' of territory covered over a period of time. One such map (Fig. 6.1) shows my territory covered during 2020. Roads and paths most frequently charted are coloured 'hot'—red and thick—whilst less common routes are marked 'colder' blue. The hill descent is the thickest red line on the map.

This map recalls a process developed by Deligny (2015) to map the movement (or 'wander lines' (p. 44)) of autistic children, charting a 'mode of being' (Deligny, 2015, p. 33) in the form of a network ('the Arachnean' [p. 33]). Deligny's maps endeavoured to 'shape a gaze in order to change habits' (Ogilvie, in Deligny, 2015, p. 13), not to impose change on the observed individuals but to shift the gaze of the observer. The maps encourage the observer to identify value in places (or 'modes'), where it may otherwise not have been evident. My own lines of drift are driven by affective experience—a map of territory covered in the pursuit of positive affective experience.

The recent turn towards 'affect' in New Literacy Studies (Leander & Ehret, 2019) understands text in relation to a body situated within 'assemblages' (Deleuze & Guattari, 1987) of material, immaterial, spatial, semiotic and environmental aspects. 'Affect' names the 'prepersonal intensity' (Shouse, 2005) that arises through the

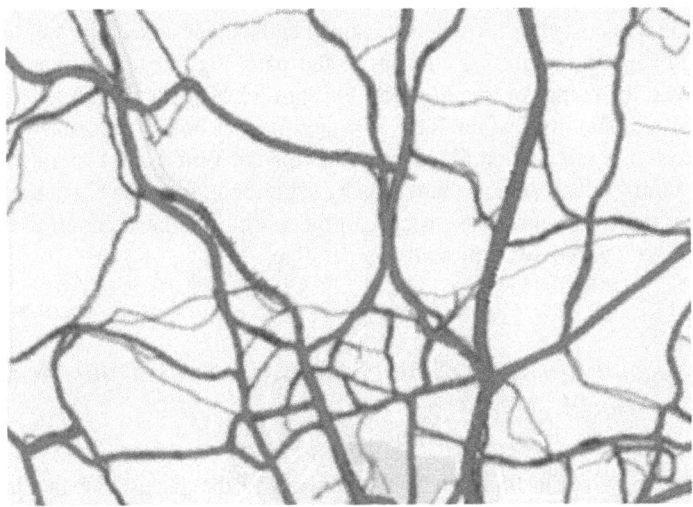

Fig. 6.1 Heat map

shifting from one bodily state to another—experiences that defy labels like 'feeling' and 'emotion' but take a powerful hold of our bodies and minds. This assemblage, involving running and song, features an affective 'intensity' (Deleuze & Guattari, 1987). In autism, the sensory self-regulation achieved through sensory means is often known as 'stimming' (Yergeau, 2018, p. 98). These self-regulatory autistic behaviours are, to advocates of behaviourist interventions such as Applied Behavioural Analysis (ABA), undesirable behaviours which should be suppressed. There is an abundance of studies looking at tracking and eliminating 'stereotopic behaviour' (e.g. Amiri et al., 2017; Tse et al., 2018; Zhou et al., 2020). Such studies deny individual agency over the body, seeking to deny the autistic need for sensory stimulation. This is the kind of perspective that would get me into trouble at school, regularly reprimanded for my facial tics that were interpreted as 'pulling faces'. Recently viewing home videos from my childhood—visual texts that help me review and re-evaluate my own history in light of my recent diagnosis—it is clear that these behaviours were neither conscious nor confrontational. The DSM-5 Criteria (APA, 2013) allows that 'many adults with autism spectrum disorder… learn to suppress repetitive behaviour in public' (p. 54), and these movements are often masked due to the kind of social/cultural engineering that comes from wanting to appear 'normal'.

The neurodiversity perspective reframes these movements as positive, empowering acts. Bakan (2014) explores the intersection between music and stimming, reframing self-stimulatory behaviour as 'productive, communicative, pleasurable and even socially valuable' (Bakan, 2014, p. 133), noting a 'fluid progression between different modes of productive engagement.' This productive engagement with multimodal texts, via music, has much in common with affective perspectives on literacies. Furthermore, just as the 'ideological' notion of literacy seeks to challenge the 'autonomous' idea of literacy as a pre-established set of skills—forcing the individual to comply with state sanctioned and narrow conceptions of literacy—the neurodiversity perspective challenges the pathologised notion that there is a standard way of being, of *moving*, that the individual must adhere to. There is a concept of 'autistic joy', which has yet to permeate academic accounts of autistic experience but is often exemplified on social media. Whilst my experience of this active 'reading' of the song is about sensory regulation, it is also about the 'autistic joy' that comes from sensory experience of the world, and the assemblage of sound, movement and space feels profoundly generative.

6.5.3   Special Interests: Photography, Aphantasia and 'Seeing' the World

Another letter arrives in June. This is a summary of the discussions that led to my diagnosis, ordered under headings 'Development and Social History', 'Social Communication and Interaction' and 'Sensory Experiences'. Comments here largely recount the challenging aspects of being autistic. The final section—'Restrictive Repetitive Patterns of Behaviour Interest or Activities'—details what are often called 'special interests' (Jordan & Caldwell-Harris, 2012) that result in hyper-focus on particular topics. The form reports that I have 'a tendency to spend long hours taking, developing, looking at and reading about photographs'. I love photography, and, particularly during lockdown, I have found comfort in 35 mm photography. Even this, however, is framed as a negative, 'restrictive' interest. As well as being a source of pleasure, absorbing interests also provide a way of making sense of the world.

I have been thinking, for instance, about the concept of 'masking' or 'camouflaging' (Livingstone et al., 2020) autistic traits in order to present as neurotypical. This thinking has involved using photography to explore my physical 'stimming' behaviours. This visual text (Fig. 6.2) is one attempt to examine my own 'autistic' movement. I shot and developed a sequence of stills capturing the motion of my own hands on black-and-white 35 mm film. The process of creating this text, as well as the text itself, assisted me in achieving some abstract distance from myself, creating a sense of space from the subject of my thinking, offering a means of thinking about the sensory self-regulation that I achieve through repetitive motion.

The fact that this text is visual, rather than written, is significant. Autistic people report differences in how they visually process and engage with the world. Grandin (2006), for example, reports a vivid experience of 'thinking in pictures'. Others, like me, are at a different point in the visualisation spectrum, with a complete inability to think using internally generated pictures. Aphantasia (Zeman et al., 2016) is an inability to visualise using the 'mind's eye', resulting in an inability to 'see' in visual imagery. I do not have the ability to visualise or remember objects, people or places by forming a mental picture of them. It is not possible to be formally diagnosed with aphantasia, but there are tools online to aid self-identification. There is

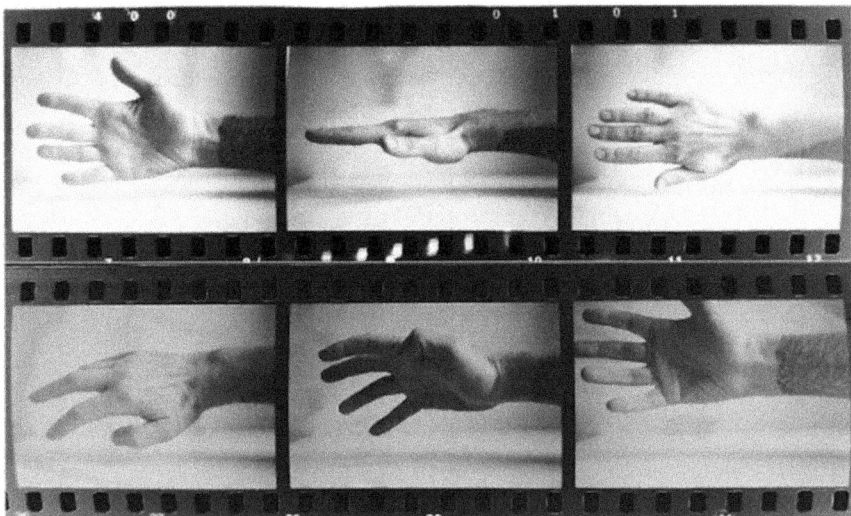

Fig. 6.2 Moving hands

little known about its implications but also less stigma involved than with other neurodivergent 'conditions'. Until very recently, I assumed that 'visualising' was just a metaphor for *conceptualising*, rather than an actual act that people could perform. Working through this idea, I created a comic to share on social media in an attempt to describe and communicate what aphantasia means for me (Fig. 6.3).

My use of photography and drawing could be explained as a method of *externalising* the process of visualisation, as a kind of extended cognition (Clark & Chalmers, 1998), helping to develop my understanding of my neurodivergent identity in a way that does not assume the primacy of language. Although I do not think *in* pictures, I find it useful to think *with* pictures. We still know little about how neurodivergent ways of being impact on thinking and learning. What is clear is that pedagogical approaches that make assumptions about how people think, learn and process information that assume a neurotypical default are not sufficient for everyone.

6.6   Future Directions

Above I have taken a personal approach to illustrate how personal storytelling can illuminate lived experience. I suggest that similar methods could be utilised in two ways: as tools to enable literacy researchers to look inwards to their own experiences and outwards in relation to others. For Smith (2016), storytelling offers a valuable counter to 'dominant disembodied research paradigms' (p. 183). With this in mind, I encourage literacy researchers to consider whether they could use autoethnography to exemplify their perspectives on the world, in relation to text and

Fig. 6.3 Aphantasia comic

textual assemblages—especially those whose perspectives are currently underrepresented. Where self-storying does not feel appropriate, I encourage engagement with other storying approaches that seek to understand people's lived experiences, particularly in relation to text, and how these intersect with neurodivergent identities.

I have also advocated for greater recognition of the diversity around individuals' meaning-making practices, here in relation to multiple modes. When engaging with stories and texts in the ways suggested above, I ask researchers to continue to pursue the more 'generous' definitions of text afforded by NLS. I also suggest that researchers consider the roles that these engagements play in their own meaning-making, as well as those of participants. By forefronting sidelined ways of engaging with the world, literacy research has the potential to embolden its status as a force for shifting dominant, normative perceptions of worth.

In conjunction with these methodological moves, I also encourage literacy researchers to engage directly with work around the neurodiversity paradigm. Firstly, an understanding of neurodiversity would enrich researchers' own understandings of the world and thereby feed into the discourse around literacies, in the same way that engaging with conversations around race, gender or socioeconomic background helps a researcher to understand the multiple intersecting factors that shape lives. I have drawn parallels between NLS and neurodiversity, demonstrating how these ideas can be united to address coexisting concerns. Secondly, and more directly, this is to encourage further literacy research that allows for the voices of neurodivergent people to become increasingly present. As Murray (2020) suggests, 'people have different experiences of the world, and unless we listen to them when they tell us what makes their lives difficult and what helps, we often make things worse' (p. 105). Literacy research has a history of illuminating the lives of marginalised people, helping to shift traditional perspectives. A greater focus on the lived experience of neurodivergent people in literacy research would enrich society's understanding of the value of literacies and the nature of neurodivergence. We know that texts have the power to shape lives, both positively and negatively. By focussing on the texts around neurodivergent lived experience, there is an opportunity for literacy studies to further broaden the scope of its impact.

6.7 Concluding Thoughts

This chapter has called for the expansion of literacy research to take greater account of work around neurodiversity, as well as exemplifying the value of inclusive, narrative methodological approaches. My own story, demonstrating the impact of various texts, has addressed issues around neurodivergence, non-written communication, representation, cognition, affective experience, self-expression and identity. These texts engaged with dimensions of experience that include the sensory, the spatial, movement, meaning-making, power, learning and thought. Evidently, a single autoethnography by a white, male neurodivergent academic is not enough in itself: it is necessary to take account of the culturally and socially diverse nature of the neurodivergent population. I hope that my 'opening' is a hint at the possibility for future work.

References

American Psychiatric Association. (2013). *Diagnostic and statistical manual of mental disorders (DSM-5)*. American Psychiatric Publishers.

Amiri, A. M., Peltier, N., Goldberg, C., Sun, Y., Nathan, A., Hiremath, S. V., & Mankodiya, K. (2017, March). WearSense: Detecting autism stereotypic behaviors through smartwatches. In *Healthcare* (Vol. 5, No. 1, p. 11). Multidisciplinary Digital Publishing Institute.

Bakan, M. B. (2014). The musicality of stimming: Promoting neurodiversity in the ethnomusicology of autism. *MUSICultures, 41*(2), 133–161.

Baron-Cohen, S. (2000). Theory of mind and autism: A fifteen-year review. In *Understanding other minds: Perspectives from developmental cognitive neuroscience* (Vol. 2, pp. 3–20). Oxford University Press.

Baron-Cohen, S. (2010). Empathizing, systemizing, and the extreme male brain theory of autism. In *Progress in brain research* (Vol. 186, pp. 167–175). Elsevier.

Barton, D., Hamilton, M., Ivaniúc, R., & Ivanič, R. (2000). *Situated literacies: Reading and writing in context*. Psychology Press.

Belek, B. (2019). Articulating sensory sensitivity: From bodies with autism to autistic bodies. *Medical Anthropology, 38*(1), 30–43.

Botha, M., Hanlon, J., & Williams, G. L. (2020). Does language matter? Identity-first versus person-first language use in autism research: A response to Vivanti. *Journal of Autism and Developmental Disorders*. https://doi.org/10.31219/osf.io/75n83

Bottema-Beutel, K., Kapp, S. K., Lester, J. N., Sasson, N. J., & Hand, B. N. (2020). *Avoiding ableist language: Suggestions for autism researchers*. Autism in Adulthood.

Chapman, R. (2020). Chapter 5: What kind of thing is autism? In D. Milton (Ed.), *The neurodiversity reader* (pp. 41–47). Pavilion.

Clark, A., & Chalmers, D. (1998). The extended mind. *Analysis, 58*(1), 7–19.

Davies, W. J. (2019). Autistic listening. In: *Aural diversity conference 2019*. Conference. http://usir.salford.ac.uk/id/eprint/56380/1/Davies_Autistic_Listening_paper_2019_v4.pdf. Accessed 30 Apr 2021.

Deleuze, G., & Guattari, F. (1987). *A thousand plateaus*. Bloomsbury Publishing.

Deligny, F. (2015). *The Arachnean and other texts*. Minneapoli Univocal Publishing.

Ellis, C., Adams, T. E., & Bochner, A. P. (2011). Autoethnography: An overview. *Historical Social Research/Historische sozialforschung, 36*, 273–290.

Lockwood Estrin, G., Milner, V., Spain, D., Happé, F., & Colvert, E. (2020). Barriers to autism Spectrum disorder diagnosis for young women and girls: A systematic review. *Review Journal of Autism and Developmental Disorders*, 1–17. https://doi.org/10.1007/s40489-020-00225-8

Fletcher-Watson, S., & Happé, F. (2019). *Autism: A new introduction to psychological theory and current debate*. Routledge.

Frith, S. (1996). Music and identity. In S. Hall & P. Du Gay (Eds.), *Questions of cultural identity* (pp. 108–127). Sage.

Gernsbacher, M. A. (2017). Editorial perspective: The use of person-first language in scholarly writing may accentuate stigma. *Journal of Child Psychology and Psychiatry, 58*(7), 859–861.

Grandin, T. (2006). *Thinking in pictures: And other reports from my life with autism*. Vintage.

Hayward, S. M., McVilly, K. R., & Stokes, M. A. (2018). Challenges for females with high functioning autism in the workplace: A systematic review. *Disability and Rehabilitation, 40*(3), 249–258.

Jensen, M. E., Pease, E. A., Lambert, K., Hickman, D. R., Robinson, O., McCoy, K. T., … Ramirez, J. (2013). Championing person-first language: A call to psychiatric mental health nurses. *Journal of the American Psychiatric Nurses Association, 19*(3), 146–151.

Jones, S. (2014). "How people read and write and they don't even notice": Everyday lives and literacies on a Midlands council estate. *Literacy, 48*(2), 59–65.

Jordan, C. J., & Caldwell-Harris, C. L. (2012). Understanding differences in neurotypical and autism spectrum special interests through internet forums. *Intellectual and Developmental Disabilities, 50*(5), 391–402.

Kapp, S. K. (2020). *Autistic community and the neurodiversity movement: Stories from the Frontline* (p. 330). Springer Nature.

Leander, K. M., & Ehret, C. (Eds.). (2019). *Affect in literacy learning and teaching: Pedagogies, politics and coming to know*. Routledge.

Livingston, L. A., Shah, P., Milner, V., & Happé, F. (2020). Quantifying compensatory strategies in adults with and without diagnosed autism. *Molecular Autism, 11*(1), 15.

Macari, S. L., Vernetti, A., & Chawarska, K. (2020). Attend less, fear more: Elevated distress to social threat in toddlers with autism Spectrum disorder. *Autism Research*. Online First: https://doi.org/10.1002/aur.2448

Murray, F. (2020). Chapter 10: Neurodiversity is for everyone. In D. Milton (Ed.), *The neurodiversity reader: Exploring concepts, lived experiences and implications for practice* (pp. 41–47). Shoreham by Sea, Pavilion.

Onaiwu, M. O. (2020). Morénike Giwa Onaiwu. *Autism in Adulthood, 2*(4), 270–272.

Pahl, K. (2007). Creativity in events and practices: A lens for understanding children's multimodal texts. *Literacy, 41*(2), 86–92.

Ratcliffe, A. (Ed.). (2020). *Our autistic lives: Personal accounts from autistic adults around the world aged 20 to 70+*. Jessica Kingsley Publishers.

Ribeiro, S. H., Paula, C. S. D., Bordini, D., Mari, J. J., & Caetano, S. C. (2017). Barriers to early identification of autism in Brazil. *Brazilian Journal of Psychiatry, 39*(4), 352–354.

Richards, R. (2008). Writing the othered self: Autoethnography and the problem of objectification in writing about illness and disability. *Qualitative Health Research, 18*(12), 1717–1728.

Shouse, E. (2005). Feeling, emotion, affect. *M/C Journal, 8*(6), 26.

Sinclair, J. (2013). Why I dislike "person first" language. *Autonomy, the Critical Journal of Interdisciplinary Autism Studies, 1*(2), 2–3.

Singer, J. (1999). Why Can't you be Normal for once in your life? From a problem with no name to the emergence of a new category of difference. In M. Corker (Ed.), *Disability discourse* (pp. 59–67). Open University Press.

Smith, J. (2016). The embodied becoming of autism and childhood: A storytelling methodology. *Disability & Society, 31*(2), 180–191.

Street, B. (2012). New literacy studies. In *Language, ethnography, and education: Bridging new literacy studies and Bourdieu* (pp. 27–49). Taylor & Francis Group.

Swain, D., Scarpa, A., White, S., & Laugeson, E. (2015). Emotion dysregulation and anxiety in adults with ASD: Does social motivation play a role? *Journal of Autism and Developmental Disorders, 45*(12), 3971–3977.

Travers, J., & Krezmien, M. (2018). Racial disparities in autism identification in the United States during 2014. *Exceptional Children, 84*(4), 403–419.

Tse, C. A., Pang, C. L., & Lee, P. H. (2018). Choosing an appropriate physical exercise to reduce stereotypic behavior in children with autism spectrum disorders: A non-randomized crossover study. *Journal of Autism and Developmental Disorders, 48*(5), 1666–1672.

Turner, L. (2013). The evocative autoethnographic I: The relational ethics of writing about oneself. In N. P. Short, L. Turner, & A. Grant (Eds.), *Contemporary British autoethnography* (pp. 213–229). Sense Publishers.

Tisoncik, L. A. (2020). Autistics. Org and finding our voices as an activist movement. In *Autistic community and the neurodiversity movement* (pp. 65–76). Palgrave Macmillan.

Vivanti, G. (2020). Ask the editor: What is the Most appropriate way to talk about individuals with a diagnosis of autism? *Journal of Autism and Developmental Disorders, 50*(2), 691–693.

Williams. (2020). Perceptual deviants: Understanding autistic subjectivities in a (not so) predictable world. In D. Milton (Ed.), *The neurodiversity reader: Exploring concepts, lived experiences and implications for practice* (pp. 35–40). Shoreham by Sea, Pavilion.

Wohlwend, K. E. (2009). Damsels in discourse: Girls consuming and producing identity texts through Disney princess play. *Reading Research Quarterly, 44*(1), 57–83.

Yergeau, M. (2009). Circle wars: Reshaping the typical autism essay. *Disability Studies Quarterly, 30*(1) https://dsqsds.org/article/view/1063.

Yergeau, M. R. (2018). *Authoring autism: On rhetoric and neurological queerness*. Duke University Press.

Zeman, A., Dewar, M., & Della Sala, S. (2016). Reflections on aphantasia. *Cortex, 74*, 336–337.

Zhou, M. S., Nasir, M., Farhat, L. C., Kook, M., Artukoglu, B. B., & Bloch, M. H. (2020). Meta-analysis: Pharmacologic treatment of restricted and repetitive behaviors in autism Spectrum disorders. *Journal of the American Academy of Child & Adolescent Psychiatry, 60*(1), 35–45.

Zuckerman, K. E., Sinche, B., Mejia, A., Cobian, M., Becker, T., & Nicolaidis, C. (2014). Latino parents' perspectives on barriers to autism diagnosis. *Academic Pediatrics, 14*(3), 301–308.

Chapter 7
Pop-Up Productions: Gifts Presented in Loss

Jana Boschee Ellefson and Kim Lenters

Abstract Amidst worries of the world in precarious times, like the COVID-19 pandemic, glimmers of the possible emerge in nature reclaiming space. Similarly, children's literacy practices reflect this shift. Children and the natural world are not *discussing* change; they are *doing*, *being*, and *living* it. Their unconventional approaches to activism lead us to ask: how might research of these literacies amplify a call of what might be? In animating three "literacy events" occurring during the beginning months of the COVID-19 pandemic, we explore the potential these literacy events provide. We also reflect on ethical dilemmas they present, considering how to avoid losing the data to protocol. The chapter promotes the possibilities held in enlarging the ethical scope associated with the edges of children's literacy production, challenging what is "off limits" and what is considered public domain, through presenting recollections on time, space, and children's collaborative literacy practices. We examine COVID's forced deterritorializing of literacy and the openings and blockages presented in (re)territorializing ways of being and doing for child and researcher alike—gifts presented in loss.

Keywords Children's literacy practices · Ethics · Literacy event · Pandemic literacies · Assemblage · Posthumanism · Deterritorializing literacies

7.1 Take and Give

Loss. So often we think of loss in terms of something we were once given that has now been taken away. In the beginnings of 2020, humanity saw the COVID-19 global pandemic taking. The world was thrust into a precarity in which we collectively experienced the loss of human lives, hugs and handshakes, weddings and

J. Boschee Ellefson (✉) · K. Lenters
Werklund School of Education, University of Calgary, Calgary, AB, Canada
e-mail: jana.ellefson@ucalgary.ca

© The Author(s), under exclusive license to Springer Nature Singapore Pte Ltd. 2022
C. Lee et al. (eds.), *Unsettling Literacies*, Cultural Studies and Transdisciplinarity in Education 15, https://doi.org/10.1007/978-981-16-6944-6_7

funerals, regularly scheduled business, and all we had deemed normal. But as the theory of relativity suggests, these things, these energies, cannot simply disappear; rather they transformed into something unfamiliar to most of the modern world. The world was presented with a forced leisure. Leisure, derived from Old French *licence*, points toward "freedom, liberty, power, possibility; permission" (Etymonline, n.d.). With COVID's restrictions, we were given *freedom* to stay home, *liberty* to pause, and *possibility* to reacquaint ourselves as curious new friends to what might have previously felt like drudgery—cooking, baking bread, growing food, or cleaning the nether regions of our homes. In the absence of frantic schedules and impossible expectations, children were given *permission* to explore ways of doing and being, perhaps more "normal" than ever before.

As two researchers in the area of children's literacies, COVID afforded gifts to each of us—both unexpectedly caught up in two assemblages of wildly innovating children. As a mother scholar privy to a neighbourhood assemblage of children outdoors, Jana frequently witnessed emergent and playful literacy events. Without constraints of school schedule, space, materials, or learning expectations, the activities of this "naturalistic" assemblage were intriguing. However, when viewed through the lens of our research ethics review board, the "ethics" of a mother retrospectively utilizing such information is problematic. In her neighbourhood, Kim, like many others across the world, discovered signals of hope and connection through anonymous, chalk-scrawled messages and strategically placed objects. Might standards of ethics deem these communications as accessible for academic review and research? Excited in the potential these literacy events create, we consider how to avoid losing the data to protocol.

Our purposes in this chapter are twofold. First, we want to share our observations as literacy researchers moving through the early days of the COVID pandemic to highlight what we are naming "pop-up productions" found in the everyday social and material literacies practiced by children in Jana's COVID bubble and Kim's home neighbourhood. Second, we engage with the ethical dilemmas associated with the presentation of this research, with the intention of asking questions about what we consider to be the "grey zones" of ethical protocols for social science researchers and providing responses to these dilemmas. With these two matters in mind, we frame the chapter around examining COVID's forced deterritorializing of literacy and the openings and blockages presented in (re)territorializing ways of being and doing for child and researcher alike—gifts presented in loss.

7.2 Where to Look for a Gift Horse

The dubious gift of COVID-19 avoids flashy paper wrapping or bows; rather it surrounds slinking-discrete in the air, poised to be accepted by unknowing recipients. Our blind trust in the generative emergence of hopeful possibilities thickens, branches, and breathes with offerings from posthumanist thinking. We inhale these COVID-common moments as literacy researchers who are deeply reading, discussing, and writing with and through posthumanist exploration of assemblage theory, de/reterritorialization, agency, and time. When we approach the presence and presents of coronavirus, we look at its connection to posthuman literacy theories. These ideas help articulate our excitement for the generative literacies we witness while also pushing at our ethical sensibilities in terms of what and how we research in an open system of connectivity.

Our experiences in the early weeks of the pandemic found us relating to familiar spaces, material, and people—our personal *assemblages* (Deleuze & Guattari, 1988), in changed ways. Working and learning in our homes, connecting virtually, avoiding shared physical spaces, and negotiating time differently—all forced deterritorializations—created complex groupings of human and material participants. Deleuze and Guattari identify *deterritorialization* as moves made by participants in assemblage in response to each other and the inevitable shifts in the assemblage's composition and direction those moves invoke. Though this March moment can be pointed to, the beginnings and ends of relationships in the assemblages are indecipherable. Each participant exists in both present and past, carrying memory of multiple contexts, which also become in relation with/in the assemblage (May, 2005). In this way, Deleuze, taken from Bergson, postulates time as duration rather than a linear concept. Past and present are not separate; they coexist (Deleuze & Guattari, 1988), bringing each into being. Each human and nonhuman entity existing in reference to a before-COVID and COVID-time, and even an after-COVID, brings pasts, presents, and futures into assemblage.

The assemblage within assemblage, within assemblage, shifting and moving—machines plugging into each other (Deleuze & Guattari, 1988)—is a posthumanist vision of the truth of existence in nonhierarchical relationship. Jane Bennett (2001) reminds of the primordia and void that Epicurus and Lucretius describe. All matter, alert to surrounding matter, shifting and moving, combines and recombines, not by a greater design but motivated from an inner will or "swerve" located in each atom's centre. The in-between spaces link participants in the preconscious, visceral pulls, the affective calls toward connection and transformation. And what about when these pulls connect, deterritorialize, and transform? Deleuze (1995) explains contagion as the inspiration of thought as a result of an unexpected encounter. Can this liminal energy be considered a consciousness of the group, driving decision and direction? Consciousness and contagion, in themselves, are entities with which participants are in relation (Wolfe, 2010). Deleuze contends that desire exists within a pack environment (1988). As a result of the "thing power" (Bennett, 2010) of a global pandemic, what were our local assemblages or "packs" forming, shifting, and desiring toward? Aware of the enchantment or vibrancy (Bennett, 2010) of each participant (the human, the material, the contexts, . . . viruses); we became curious about the massive shift in the ever-active flows and intensities living with/in the world. How was the entanglement of human and nonhuman producing agency in our assemblages? What communicative practices and what literacies were engaged in the being and becoming of assemblages?

In the expanded conceptualizations from research in New Literacy Studies, social, cultural, human, and nonhuman *connections* are, in fact, *literacy* (Burnett &

Merchant, 2020). We understand relationships of and to the world to create and be created via *literacy events*, a concept grown from Shirley Bryce Heath (1983) and Brian Street (2003). The shifting sense of the concept nudges at previous borders, beyond human interactions centred on written texts and the cultural power dynamics that influence them. The notion of literacy event we reference aligns with Burnett and Merchant's "literacy-as-event" (2020), including understanding of flows between time and space (Brandt & Clinton, 2002) and reconsidering event to be the *what is produced* through moments pregnant with affective possibilities that often elude perception (Ehret, 2018) and don't exist in one particular slice of time. We acknowledge the "affective encounters" (Lenters, 2016) that occur within complex contexts of continually reassembling relationships in the literacy event. Literacy events exist in the entanglements between places, people, objects, ideas, and contexts (Kuby et al., 2019) and in durations that entwine past, present, and future.

Impossible to isolate from interwoven contexts, the study of literacy necessitates methodologies that acknowledge and allow for fluidity and emergence. Posthumanist thinking recognizes the limiting potential implicated by linearly bounded research. Our lives, our everyday experiences, and the vibrancy of everything that surrounds are all data (Bennett, 2010). As researchers approaching COVID with attention to "the idiosyncratic, irrational affects that give events the very feeling to mattering" (Ehret, 2018, p. 567), we question how we might collect the data we recognized in literacy events during our first COVID lockdown and what we can ethically do with it. We attempt to gather up spilling and rising moments and capture them into a container, like a yeasty COVID sourdough starter pushing off the lid; we present three literacy events for consideration: *The Racket*, *Walking Instructions*, and *Painted Stones*.

7.3 Homeless Imagination: Freedom and Limits in the Time of COVID

My (Jana) neighbourhood is filled with children. Saturdays have often held space for them to convene in our basement, where they will pull out each and every plastic superhero, wooden block, plush animal, and glass marble from neatly labeled bins. At the end of the fun, the floor is left an overwhelming chaos of intermingled materials. An archaeologist would struggle to make sense of each child's tangents suggested by the objects, the TV show they last watched, and the play of the others. Each child develops a story through their play, occasionally linking with the others but usually only in parallel.

With the onset of COVID-19, we stopped the play entirely to protect each other's families from possible infection. Eventually, when our provincial health authority suggested it safe, we limited our interactions to front lawn visits and walks. The children adopted vocabulary and a vague understanding of "social distancing." They were permitted to ride their bikes and play in our yards. They were asked to not bring toys outside because it would be tempting to share and pass objects with their (likely grimy) hands. Without piano lessons, soccer practices, dance class, and regular school hours, the play became more frequent and longer in duration. Where ideas would have previously been sent home through assigned writing tasks or structured play centres, now children's thoughts were given opportunity to flow and mingle. A play episode from one day was easily picked up the next.

7.4 The Racket

Witnessing the adaptations to these new freedoms and limitations often distracted me from my literacy research and teaching, pulling me into the action and enhancing my thinking about the work. Without prescriptive toys and playroom walls, I mused, the children drew on collective, imaginative storytelling. Movies and plot-lines were recontextualized, characters from popular culture were hybridized, sticks became wands, car parts in the garage transformed into weapons, and a backyard racket game developed into a significant and days-long literacy event that eventually transformed into a podcast. As a researcher of literacies, I was enthralled by what I saw unfolding and began considering how this literacy event would be a fascinating addition to the literacy studies research assemblage.

Though I was very aware of the enthusiasm of their play and even had a general sense of the premise of the storyline, I was not involved in suggesting, inspiring, correcting, or even encouraging the children's creative work. One day, before passing my phone off to the podcasters, I opened the voice recording app they had been using. My hand shot to my mouth—gasp—health protocols be damned! I was delightfully surprised at the prolificacy of production—19 *titled* episodes over 10 days. As I listened, I shook my head with the familiar query of those who work with young people: "Where do they come up with these things?"

7.5 Chalk and Stone: Children Together Apart in the Time of COVID

In the time of COVID, my (Kim) personal and professional sphere radically changed. Working from home meant no walks to work in the morning and no return walks later in the day. Lunchtime rambles were the antidotes for too much time in the four walls that had become my home office. On those walks, I was delighted and moved by the ways I saw children, confined in even more restrictive ways to homes that had become home-school-playground, reaching out to each other and the wider world.

Through artwork; jokes of the day posted in sidewalk-facing windows; images of Easter eggs, hearts, and teddy bears, cleverly concealed in those same windows for neighbourhood scavenger hunts; and massive collections of hand-painted bird-houses in boulevard trees, it was as though children (and their parents) sought myriad and ingenious ways to stay connected with friends and neighbours from whom they were physically separated. Here, I elaborate on two literacy events that unfolded through material objects and across time: walking instructions and painted stones.

7.5.1 Walking Instructions

On one neighbourhood stretch, six houses long, signs began to appear at the sidewalk edge of "house one." These signs invited those passing through to engage in certain activities. The first sign, at one side of the property, proclaimed to passers-by that they were entering a song zone and were to sing aloud as they walked. At the other end of the property, a second sign told the walker they could stop singing. Over the next 2 weeks, the signs next declared the space to be a silly walk zone (complete with ideas for how to do so) and then a zombie walk zone, in each case, ending at the other side of the property with a sign directing the commencement of normal walking.

During the time of the zombie walk zone, I noticed a change in the sidewalk art at house six. Previously, this home's sidewalk was embellished with a variety of chalk images such as flowers, rainbows, and designs echoing stained glass windows. After the zombie zone had been in place a few days, the following instructions appeared:

Follow these steps
Hop 2 times
Do a dance
Sing a song
Time to shake (followed by a zig-zagged dotted walking path)
Let's hop! (followed by a 10-square hopscotch grid)
You can stop

Stretching out over the sidewalks of houses four to six, these instructions bid those traversing the space to do something other than passively move through (see Fig. 7.1). Written in a commanding voice, the font was quirky and inviting. And the instructions reminded me of those given for house one's walking zones.

While no other humans were ever around for me to observe participation in the singing-silly-zombie and walk-hop zones, I always imagined unseen children watching from their windows to see who was engaging with their games. And I wondered what they might be feeling when I didn't always join in.

Fig. 7.1   Children together apart

7.5.2   *Painted Stones*

A second literacy event unfolded simultaneously a few blocks away in the early days of COVID confinement. As with all assemblages, I don't know where it started or when. I just know when I first entered the assemblage, by noticing a small detail that attuned me to watch for more. My entry to the painted stone assemblage began with a painted rock placed on the base of a lamp post on a commercial street in my neighbourhood. Within a couple of days, I noticed a set of painted stones in the garden of a house nearby. These new stones were simply painted—some red, some blue, some green, and others purple—and suggested themselves to be the creation of a young child. Caught up by the possibility of more, I began to systematically cover the adjacent streets, streets I hadn't been walking, and came across numerous homes with painted stones, all decorated with varying degrees of sophistication. One set of garden stones proclaimed "Live Laugh Sleep", while another offered "Love", "Peace" "Dream Big" "My World" (with images of rainbow-coloured continents). And another featured owl stones. Two of these, plus another nearby, turned stones into ladybugs. I was clearly late to enter this assemblage and didn't get to watch it emerge in its early days. But what spoke to me was the strategic placement of these stones: all at the front edge of the property, bordering the sidewalk—all wanting to be noticed.

7.6   Events That Call Out, Ethical Conduct of Human Research, and Ethical Ruminations

Before addressing our entanglements in these literacy events, we explore the specific ethical conundrums they raise for us as educational researchers interested in children's everyday practices of literacy. We acknowledge the duty of care to which research ethics boards and researchers are beholden. The protocols set out by national councils and local research ethics review boards are vital for the protection of vulnerable populations. However, we find ourselves confounded by ways in which the application of these practices seems to enable and constrain particular forms of literacy research disproportionately.

Ethics protocols for research involving human participants have been developed for the protection of research participants, and yet we ask: are there situations in which they both over- and under-reach? Here, we query our three literacy events in light of ethical guidelines, first considering the question of potential overreach in Jana's situation, followed by under-reach in Kim's. As we contemplated the dilemma of stories we felt needed to be told and the ethical "no man's land" we found ourselves traversing, we reterritorialized the data, devising alternative means for addressing our situations: shifting primary focus to the researcher and nonhuman as participants in the assemblages and alternative renderings of data. We include these moves in what follows, holding these complex and contradictory ethical dilemmas in productive tension, seeking ways to discuss children's literacy practices without violating ethical protocols.

The literacy event that called out to Jana falls into the category of naturalistic study.

Naturalistic study is well-recognized in qualitative research circles and a large section in Canada's Tri-Council Policy Statement for Ethical Conduct for Research Involving Humans (TCPS 2) is dedicated to discussing it:

> Observation may be used in qualitative studies to study acts or behaviours in a natural environment. It often takes place in living, natural and complex communities or settings, in physical environments, or in virtual settings. Observational studies may be undertaken in publicly accessible spaces (e.g., a stadium, library, museum, planetarium, beach, park), in virtual settings (e.g., online groups), or in private or controlled spaces (e.g., private clubs or organizations).
>
> There are two kinds of observational research addressed in this article. In "non-participant" observational research, the researcher observes the activity, but does not intervene in any way. This is also known as "naturalistic observation." In "participant" observational research, the researcher participates in the activity in some way and also observes. (Government of Canada (2018), section B, Observational Studies sub-section)

As a parent and researcher, sheltering at home in the early days of the pandemic, Jana was a highly attuned observer of the play in which neighbourhood children were engaged. By TCPS 2 standards, the children's request for Jana to record their productions also made her a participant in the composing assemblage. As discussed earlier, these moments prompted Jana to consider what these pop-up productions might have to contribute to the research literature on literacy as a social and material practice. We (Jana and Kim) sought ethical approval from our university ethics board to discuss the ongoing literacy event. Our request was met with a categorical "no." We then asked if we might seek REB approval to invite the children to participate in a study that would document their together-apart literacy practices over the months to come. Again, this request for consideration was denied, with the rationale that because of Jana's dual role as a parent and a researcher, such a study would involve a conflict of interest and place undue pressure to participate on both her family and the neighbours.

As we consider matters of participation in naturalistic research, as identified in the TCPS 2 statement above, we note a theoretical impasse. From an assemblage perspective, the distinction presents an artificial binary: participant/nonparticipant. Within an assemblage, while their degrees of association will vary, as the assemblage evolves over time and space, all members are participants. Thinking with this idea, even as Jana began on the periphery of the literacy event, she was nonetheless a participant, along with the multiple objects and practices the children brought into the assemblage. We thus understand Jana to be a consenting participant in the assemblage and thereby someone who has permission to discuss the literacy event in a research publication. We run into difficulty, however, in considering the children's participation in the literacy event. While they may assent to the research discussion, TCPS 2, like most REBs, considers children under 18 years of age to be incapable of providing informed consent for themselves. Without the permission to even seek consent, a detailed storying of *The Racket* cannot be shared due to REB guidelines, and thus an ingenious enterprise is lost to the literacy research world.

Through the denied research moment, one that was seemingly so rich with potential, we found ourselves reflecting on what such loss means for studies of home literacy practices when parental literacy research studies can no longer be undertaken. Classic studies of children's early literacy have been conducted by researcher parents with their own children (e.g. Michael Halliday [1975, 1978], Gunther Kress [1996], Glenda Bissix [1980]), and their work has been enduringly influential in the area of literacy studies. Notwithstanding matters of parental bias, their work has withstood the test of time and informed some of our understandings of middle-class or mainstream children's literacies. If we are aiming to understand what children do when given the time and space to play with literacy, we argue that the kinds of moments parents and caregivers "happen upon" have much to contribute to understandings of children's literacy practice. If the children are able and willing to discuss those moments with a parent interested in following them, all the better. These kinds of spontaneously serendipitous findings are much harder to come by in conventionally approved "naturalistic" literacy research assemblages. However, with current REB guidelines in Canada (and possibly elsewhere), such discussion and documentation for research purposes are not possible, and the literacy research world is the poorer for it.

The chalk and stone events have us wondering about ethical under-reach. Kim's walking discoveries provide a glimpse into a different ethical conundrum—that of gathering publicly available inscriptions produced by children. Giddy with the excitement of a posthuman sociomaterial literacy scholar whose neighbourhood families offered gift after gift in their curbside renderings, Kim's initial, visceral inclination was to immediately document all that was unfolding around her. This was quickly followed by uneasiness about photographing sidewalk art so obviously created by children. And so, no photos were taken in the beginning.

As Kim continued to walk and savour the unfolding offerings, she also began to consider the ethical protocol to which Canadian researchers must adhere. With regard to publicly available data, the TCPS states:

> The assessment of whether a space is a public place must be made on a case-by-case basis. The first consideration is whether the space in question is open to the public and intended to serve the public (e.g. stadium, planetarium, beach, museums, parks, or library). The second key consideration is whether the proposed research fulfills the three conditions of the exemption in Article 2.3: a lack of researcher involvement/interaction with the individuals or groups concerned, a lack of any reasonable expectation of privacy, and the impossibility of identifying specific individuals in the dissemination of research results. (Government of Canada (2020), paragraph 4)

Together, we realized that sidewalks and the metre of front lawn that borders them are owned by the municipality and not the homeowners. The edges of private property were thus public and open to our researchers' gaze and contemplation. And this suggested that one actually could gather the empirical materials, all so publicly displayed, as they sprang up. Nonetheless, as we discussed the matter, we were left with questions. Should the children's artwork be considered public—is it like graffiti and public art installations? Connected to homes where children could potentially be identified, and created by families for purposes other than research, are children's chalk art and painted stones fair game without informed consent? With these questions in mind, we decided that there might be a chance of someone recognizing the children's homes because of the neighbouring homes in view in some of the photographs, thus contravening one of the three conditions listed above: the impossibility of identifying specific individuals in the dissemination of research results. To that end, we have opted not to include any photographs in this chapter. However, we consider the communicative assemblages documented in the photos as empirical materials with much to say regarding these children's literacy practices during the time of COVID. And so, Jana has created assemblage drawings that provide a glimpse of both the children's renderings and our analytical engagement with them.

7.7 Gifts That Keep Giving: Exploring Children's Literacies

With these ethical constraints in mind, we return to the matter of what the literacy events, these pop-up productions, offer those considering literacy studies in times of precarity. In these rare opportunities, we were able to view children's literacies in open-ended assemblages, not limited by constraints of educational institutions. We enthusiastically unpack what can be learned from these three literacy events occurring in what scientists call a naturalistic experiment—outside of the lab and the control of the researcher. Coinciding with our pop-up productions conversations, the podcast *99% Invisible* featured Michelle Fournet of Cornell University, a researcher of humpback whale sounds in Glacier Bay on the Alaskan coast (Mars, 2020). Though initially disappointed in the thought that her research would cease with the COVID-19 lockdown, she soon realized that the whales had never been listened to for an extended period of time without the constant traffic of cruise ships. She hypothesized that because of ship noise, whales need to relay concise, straightforward, and direct messages. Fournet suggested that without the noisy interruptions, the captured sounds would resemble in-depth conversations one might have with a good friend over tea—richer, more nuanced vocabulary with longer exchanges. As Fournet's speculations entered our research assemblage, we came to wonder: without the interference of standardized curricular expectations and scheduled blocks of time, did the children in our assemblages find much-needed space to leisurely engage expansive literacies, and were we, as researchers, better positioned to listen to the affective calls of children caught up in those literacies?

We read these unfolding literacy events as ways that the children sought to engage with the world, to express messages of hope, joy, imagination, and playfulness. In all three events, we see evidence of a deep-rooted "swerve," an urge to be seen and heard within a present and future assemblage. Some practices proclaimed; some invited response. The leavers of stones, chalky instructions, and audio recordings all created texts that would remain for an intended future audience. We imagine children desirous of bringing beauty into the dull gardens of early Canadian springtime and hope into the time of COVID. Children with something to say. Children affecting transformation. Children pushing outward on the borders imposed by COVID isolation.

The desiring toward be/coming part of an assemblage manifested in multiple ways, most overtly in the creation of texts—ones that fracture linear conceptions of time. Past experiences, available materials, adult anxieties, and reassurances all found their way into the assemblages, a self-(re)organizing collection without a beginning or end. In the podcasts, we recognized genres from popular culture spanning decades while utilizing a technology and genre unique to the present generation. Literacy events spanning time but held together in place kept a dialogue going when conversation seemed impossible. The invitations to follow mutual walking directions across different times and to join into an imaginary combined world allowed children to play together apart. Were the children of houses four, five, or six inspired by the ideas of the zombie family and building on them to create an extended fun walking zone? Were the painted stone children seeing themselves as part of a collective? Did the podcasters believe their recordings were accessible to others via their phones? Through these activities, we argue, the children were not just reaching out beyond the four walls of their homes; they were conversing/dialoguing/ intra-acting with seen and unseen participants in the assemblage. The creation of literacy objects—painted rocks, a podcast, chalk instructions—each invited embodied responses. In each of these literacy events, not only were the children communicating with each other; they were speaking to the passers-by in their present and the future viewer/listener, involving us in asynchronous, stretched out conversations, assemblages that unfolded through material objects and across time.

Entanglements between nonhuman and human participants, vibrating "thing-powers" (Bennet, 2010), generated agency within the assemblage. The racket drew the children into inspiration where it no longer acted as the object it had been designed to be, a participant that transformed the assemblage and became integral to the imaginative spinning of an invisible world. Jana felt the panic and upset resulting from the handful of times that the racket could not be immediately found. Its power insisted strategies be developed to honour and protect its integrity and safety, creating a special zone and sense of urgency for its care and storage. The phone's recording capacity may have shaped the dialogue reminiscent of contemporary podcasts. Caught up in the momentum of this assemblage of human and more than human, Jana was compelled to relinquish the delicate and highly smashable phone. Sidewalk offerings affected Kim, drawing her into the children's assemblages and bidding her to abandon the earbuds, podcasts, and audiobooks that had been COVID walking companions. They bid her to return, again and again, to see what would next emerge or to contemplate the perceived messages. As a researcher, she found herself continually retracing certain routes, to witness and be immersed in what she interpreted as emerging communications. In the too-quiet streets of the early days of COVID confinement, these signs of life and energy in our neighbourhoods both comforted and captivated us.

7.8   It's the Thought That Counts: Gifts Received Quietly

We marvel at the intersecting timelines between our excitement at examining the children's play and the literacy practices that spontaneously erupted from that play and the protocols for research ethics. What we thought could be a paper on agency in children's literacy assemblages and the gift of time for leisurely practice of literacy soon became a paper on research ethics and matters of "naturalistic" studies of literacy. This volume, with its focus on literacy research in precarious times, provides an opportunity for us to reflect on what we proposed, how ethics boards inadvertently circumscribe literacy research, and what may be learned from this situation, in addition to presenting recollections on time, space, and children's collaborative literacy practices. Our roles as researchers tie us to a protocol that wraps much of what we witnessed in a bundle we carry for ourselves. As quietly as we received and contemplated the pulls these literacy events offered, we may unwrap and gaze upon the moments. Though unable to be examined and announced in their entirety, these gifts of COVID will likely continue to intermingle with future assemblages of our thinking around children's literacies.

Perhaps our capacity for experiencing these memories with wonder develops from our privileged positions as scholars who did not encounter COVID first hand. However, as Bennet remarks, "if enchantment can foster an ethically laudable generosity of spirit, then the cultivation of an eye for the wonderful becomes something like an academic duty" (2001, p. 10). Amidst worries of the world in precarious times, hints of hopefulness emerge in nature reclaiming space: wild turkeys on city streets, clearer lakes, bluer skies. Similarly, children's literacy practices reflect this shift: pop-up productions of chalk drawings on neighbourhood sidewalks, objects left to find, and spontaneous performances. Youth and their assembled worlds are not *discussing* change; they are *doing*, *being*, and *living* it. Their activism speaks through their literacies and leads us to ask how research of these literacies might amplify a call for attending to what might be.

References

Bennett, J. (2001). Complexity and enchantment. In *The enchantment of modern life* (pp. 91–111). Princeton University Press.

Bennett, J. (2010). *Vibrant matter: A political ecology of things*. Duke University Press.

Bissex, G. L. (1980). *Gyns at work: A child learns to write and read*. Harvard University Press.

Brandt, D., & Clinton, K. (2002). Limits of the local: Expanding perspectives on literacy as a social practice. *Journal of Literacy Research, 34*(3), 337–356.

Burnett, C, & Merchant, G. (2020). Literacy-as-event: Accounting for relationality in literacy research. *Discourse: Studies in the Cultural Politics of Education, 41*(1), 45–56.

Deleuze, G. (1995). *Negotiations 1972–1990*. Columbia University Press.

Deleuze, G., & Guattari, F. (1988). *A Thousand plateaus: Capitalism and schizophrenia*. University of Minnesota Press.

Ehret, C. (2018). Propositions from affect theory for feeling literacy through the event. In D. E. Alvermann, N. J. Unrau, M. Sailors, & R. B. Ruddell (Eds.), *Theoretical models and processes of literacy* (pp. 563–581). Retrieved from: http://ebookcentral.proquest.com/Created from ucalgary-ebooks on 2020-06-15

Etymonline.com. (n.d.). *Online etymology dictionary* [online]. Available at: https://www.etymonline.com/word/license. Accessed 6 Dec 2020.

Government of Canada. (2018). *Tri-council statement: Ethical conduct for research involving humans—TCPS 2, Chapter 10*. Retrieved from: https://ethics.gc.ca/eng/tcps2-eptc2_2018_chapter10-chapitre10.html#a

Government of Canada. (2020). *TCPS 2 interpretations*. Retrieved from: https://ethics.gc.ca/eng/policy-politique_interpretations_scope-portee.html

Halliday, M. A. K. (1975). *Learning how to mean: Explorations in the development of language*. Edward Arnold.

Halliday, M. A. K. (1978). *Language as social semiotic: The social interpretation of language and meaning*. Edward Arnold.

Heath, S. B. (1983). *Ways with words: Language, life and work in communities and classrooms*. Cambridge University Press.

Kress, G. (1996). *Before writing: Rethinking the paths to literacy*. Taylor & Francis.

Kuby, C. R., Spector, K., & Thiel, J. J. (Eds.). (2019). *Posthumanism and literacy education: Knowing/becoming/doing literacies*. Routledge.

Lenters, K. (2016). Riding the lines and overwriting in the margins: Affect and multimodal literacy practices. *Journal of Literacy Research, 48*(3), 280–316.

May, T. (2005). *Gilles Deleuze: An introduction*. Oxford University Press.

Street, B. (2003). What's 'new' in new literacy studies? Critical approaches to literacy theory and practice. *Current Issues in Comparative Education, 5*(2), 77–91.

Wolfe, C. (2010). *What is posthumanism?* University of Minnesota Press.

Chapter 8
Engaging Parents in Inquiry Curriculum Projects with Social Media: Using Metalogue to Probe the Methodological and Ethical Dilemmas in Literacy Research

Linda-Dianne Willis and Beryl Exley

Abstract This chapter explores the dilemmas that we, two Australian researchers, faced as we worked with school communities to improve students' literacy outcomes. Our current research focuses on literacy learning and teachers engaging parents, community members, and students in curriculum inquiry, which integrates social media use. Combining a design-based research approach and social media channels, we research amidst the fray of emerging and sometimes changing policy mandates, political and cultural change in school systems, and rapidly developing digital technologies. This chapter uses the research method of metalogue as a reflexive approach to render visible the methodological and ethical dilemmas in our current research. In presenting our metalogue, we explain not only how we brokered our way through the dilemmas that arose but also how we created opportunities for innovative classroom practice and thus literacy research. We draw conclusions from our experience about the importance of doing *difficult* research and offer hope to future researchers who, like us, approach their work with bold plans to improve literacy education for all students.

Keywords Metalogue · Parent engagement · Methodological dilemmas · Ethical dilemmas · Literacy education · Inquiry curriculum · Social media

L.-D. Willis (✉) · B. Exley
Griffith University, Griffith, QLD, Australia
e-mail: l.willis@griffith.edu.au; b.exley@griffith.edu.au

© The Author(s), under exclusive license to Springer Nature Singapore Pte
Ltd. 2022
C. Lee et al. (eds.), *Unsettling Literacies*, Cultural Studies and
Transdisciplinarity in Education 15, https://doi.org/10.1007/978-981-16-6944-6_8

8.1 The Conceptual Frame of Dilemmas

We come to this chapter with decades of experience, firstly as elementary years classroom teachers in a range of urban and remote contexts covering different demographic populations and then as university academics undertaking educational research with school principals, classroom teachers, students, and their families and communities. Rather than seeing ourselves as researchers located in the metaphoric "ivory tower" (Delamont, 2005, p. 87), cut off from the realities of educational reforms, schooling, and family/community practices, we engage most heartedly in the wider social enterprise of the school-based research context. Our work contributes to the metaphor of openings in this book by exploring methodological and ethical challenges and changes we've experienced, which open up opportunities for ourselves and others to continually reimagine literacy research and practice. We use a design-based research approach (The Design-Based Collective, 2003) to work collaboratively with and alongside teachers to enhance students' literacy outcomes by identifying the potential in curricula to develop disciplinary inquiries and their pedagogical enactments with students, families, and communities through a range of social media platforms. We work across the disciplinary fields to home in on the literacies to build students' communication repertoires. We've come to call this work EPIC, an acronym that stands for *Engaging Parents*[1] *in Inquiry Curriculum* (see Exley et al., 2017; Ridgewell & Exley, 2011; Willis, 2013; Willis & Exley, 2018, 2020, 2021; Willis et al., 2020).

In an earlier version of EPIC, in 2008, Beryl (Author 2) co-taught a science curriculum inquiry with an experienced elementary years teacher, Sarah,[2] her multi-age class of 19 students (aged 7–10 years) and some of the students' parents. Beryl was intent on exploring the new digital turn in elementary schooling and drew on the "pedagogy of multiliteracies" model (The New London Group, 2000, p. 9) with its shifting pedagogic orientations to critical framing and transformed practice. A community of learners came together to participate in a situated process drama to investigate the provocation, *Microorganisms: Good or Bad?* Students then worked in small groups to take either an affirmative or negative position and to use Kahootz 3.0 (a virtual world digital construction toolset) to prepare a persuasive multimodal text to deliver at a community town hall event (Exley & Luke, 2010). To assist with communication across the community of learners, Sarah set up a system-approved online forum for a/synchronous virtual conversations. Between them, all the participants voluntarily contributed the equivalent of 49 x A4 pages of double-space typed text to this SPOC (small personal online community). As it transpired, the posts related to four topics: communication about parent visits to the classroom, dialogue about the upcoming town hall event, students discussing Kahootz 3.0, or science content discussion about microorganisms (Ridgewell & Exley, 2011). Parents with a background in science or technology were active forum participants.

---

[1] The use of the term "parents" is taken to also mean parents and carers.
[2] All participant names are pseudonyms.

This was the first time that Sarah had used a virtual world and a SPOC for school learning activities. She was in her fourth decade of teaching and was neither a technophile nor a technophobe. The hallmark of her practice was her expertise with facilitating a science curriculum inquiry. She shunned *I do*, *we do*, *you do*, explicit instruction pedagogies, instead providing the context and motivation for students to engage with each other and members of the extended learning community to develop the culminating persuasive multimodal text for the town hall audience. The 19 elementary-aged students were able to adapt to the new literacy requirements of the online forum to both receive and express science knowledge and take a position as they finalised the production of their multimodal persuasive text.

This particular version of EPIC took place in 2008, an era (apparently) devoid of some of the ethical and methodological tensions we found in the current set of EPIC projects. As researchers, we have a responsibility to provide frank accounts of the points of tension in our current work. We'll avoid calling these points of tension *problems*, as the tensions have evolved into deeper philosophical discussions about the social constructions that result from certain structural conditions and relational aspects within our research. Following Honig's (1996) conception, we'll call these points of tension "dilemmas" (p. 569). Fransson (2016) explains that dilemmas are different from problems insofar that dilemmas "emerge in situations where no obvious right or wrong way of acting exists, or when one has to choose between two or more unsatisfactory or conflicting options, values, commitments, obligations, loyalties or positions" (p. 187). In this chapter, we use the process of metalogue (Willis & Exley, 2016; Willis et al., 2018) to discuss our more recent EPIC research to render visible the dilemmas and the outcomes of our approach. Dilemmas are also different from the concept of *risk*. Risks to the research plan are still ever present and must continue to be considered at all stages. Comparing dilemmas and risks, Fransson sees dilemmas as bi/multidirectional dynamic matters that cannot be "fully solved without leaving some kind of reminder", whereas risk is a unidirectional matter that "can be fully eliminated", and any legacy is void of ongoing risk (p. 189).

Our focus on dilemmas is not to imply that we are *victims* of the structural conditions of university ethics applications or school policies and processes that give rise to methodological dilemmas but to reveal the "uncertainty, plurality, options, challenges and decision making" and "processes of power, negotiation, identity formation, positioning and manoeuvring" (Fransson, 2016, p. 185). The conceptual frame of dilemmas thus provides the permission we need to pause and ponder over the multifaceted cluster of positions in which we find ourselves as we undertake our EPIC research in precarious times.

8.2 Locating Our Research in Precarious Times

At its most general, our work in literacy education and literacy research, individually, together, and as members of other research teams, pursues the four interrelated agendas of children's pedagogic rights, pedagogy as inquiry, new literacies, and parent and community engagement. Each agenda in and of itself has been a stable research topic for decades for multiple teams of researchers, but when these agendas become entangled and situated within an era dominated by low definition curricula at the national level (Luke et al., 2012), standards-referenced assessment reforms (Klenwoski, 2013), and privacy, cyberbullying, and cybersafety issues (Bower, 2017), our current EPIC projects are being undertaken in uncertain and difficult times. None of these conditions implicated the 2008 EPIC project, but they are all entangled in our work now.

Our focus on students' pedagogic rights draws on Bernstein's (2000) initial heuristic and develops an analytical framework for looking systematically at the literacy learning possibilities made available to a range of students (Exley & Willis, 2016; Exley et al., 2017). Taken together, and following Bernstein, the three pedagogic rights emphasise (i) knowledge, in particular individuals enhancing their repertoires of knowledge, including the possibilities of knowledge boundary crossing; (ii) social, intellectual, cultural, and personal inclusion, including the right to be autonomous; and (iii) socially sanctioned political participation that positively supports the construction of a model of society. We are not so much imposing these three pedagogic rights on Australian classrooms and communities; indeed, in the Australian context from which we write, the overarching remit of the *Alice Springs (Mparntwe) Education Declaration* (Department of Education, 2019) is that students become "confident and creative individuals; successful lifelong learners; and active and informed members of the community" (p. 4). The *Alice Spring's (Mparntwe) Education Declaration* is Australia's current national education document—building on the 1989 *Hobart Declaration on Schooling* and, more recently, the 2008 *Melbourne Declaration on Educational Goals for Young Australians* (Education Council, 2014). Like its predecessors, the *Alice Spring's (Mparntwe) Education Declaration* is significant for articulating the joint commitment of State, Territory, and Commonwealth Ministers of Education to a framework for improving Australian schooling. There's alignment between Bernstein's heuristics of pedagogic rights and the education goals set out in the *Alice Spring's (Mparntwe) Education Declaration* for young Australians. Yet, our experience seems to mirror much of the research literature reporting on schooling experiences in Australia in recent years—school-based literacy education is primarily enacted to contribute to students' individual confidence and as a tool for lifelong learning to the detriment of students' creativity and their connections with the community (Woods et al., 2014).

Our explorations of a pedagogy of inquiry in a range of Australian schools have uncovered a decisive reorientation away from the rich student-centred and placed-based practices as documented by Kamler and Comber (2005), and chapters in the Boran and Comber (2001) edited collection, and many others over the last two decades. For example, in one of our more recent EPIC projects, we reported on teachers' inconsistent knowledge and understanding of curriculum inquiry (Willis & Exley, 2018). It's not that the participating teachers did not have a capacity for imagining, planning, and delivering a curriculum inquiry; rather teachers were responding to the perception that inquiry-based units and their associated pedagogies were not a priority for the Australian Curriculum, Assessment and Reporting Authority. During a semistructured interview, one experienced participating teacher, Erin, commented: "So inquiry based units I think kind of went out the window with the introduction of the Australian Curriculum because we work now to the achievement standards and they're very specific and we teach with the gradual release model" (Willis & Exley, 2018, p. 93).

Since the release of the inaugural Australian Curriculum: English in 2011, Australian elementary school English teachers have been stymied by a lack of professional development opportunities for this new curriculum (Bradfield & Exley, 2020). Research has also documented the unintended consequences and unhelpful pressures of high-stakes national literacy assessment in Australia. The priority given to the National Assessment Program—Literacy and Numeracy (NAPLAN) has caused a narrowing in curriculum focus for an already low-definition curriculum, delivery of teacher-centric pedagogy as prescribed by the state departments, a decrease in student motivation for school learning, and diminished possibilities for teacher-parent-community engagement (Cumming et al., 2016; Willis et al., 2021). This reality, we've found, is more prevalent in communities marked by diversity and/or disadvantage.

Social media platforms are often reported as being both exciting and brimming with possibilities for school-based literacy learning (see Bower, 2017) and, in turn, widening students' repertoire of literacy practices (Mills & Exley, 2014; Pandya & Golden, 2018). There are just as many accounts of the "messy realities of digital technology use in schools" (Selwyn, 2011, p. 22), where the realisation of immersive virtual learning has failed to match the rhetoric. Many schools and education systems are "caught in the headlights of the digital era" (Luke et al., 2012, p. 251), offering formalised and bounded experiences that are an "artificial facsimile" of real-world uses of digital technology (Selwyn, 2011, p. 25).

To put it briefly, whereas in 2008, it was a relatively uncomplicated affair to find schools and teachers with whom we could work to undertake an EPIC project, in the current era, we've had to work hard to find school leaders who will give their teachers permission to introduce a pedagogy of inquiry that also includes parents and community members and makes use of emerging technologies, such as those provided by social media platforms. The challenges, however, aren't limited to finding participants; changing ethics requirements and shifting policy mandates have implicated our continuing EPIC work. The next section of this chapter explains the method of metalogue, and following that, we employ this approach to render visible the dilemmas we faced during some of our more recent EPIC projects.

8.3   Metalogue as Research Method

In this chapter, we use metalogue as a research method (Willis & Exley, 2016; Willis et al., 2018) to render visible and reflect on the dilemmas we've experienced while undertaking literacy research fieldwork in precarious times. Our use of metalogue grew from dialoguing cogeneratively with teachers in EPIC as they collaboratively interrogated their usual pedagogies to open possibilities for parent and community engagement in student literacy learning through curriculum inquiries that integrated social media. Cogenerative dialogues describe interactive social spaces that enable substantive conversations about aspects of learning and teaching. The affix, *co*, in the word "cogenerative", denotes working together or jointly with others to plan and/or teach. *Generative* describes unfolding processes in developing shared understandings and fresh insights about aspects of EPIC. Cogenerative processes describe the successful formation, continuation, expansion, and transformation of communities of practice as members work together towards common goals to mutually benefit all involved (see Willis, 2013, 2016; Willis et al., 2018).

These processes are encouraged by the *purposeful* design of cogenerative dialogues. Participants (e.g. teachers, parents, researchers, students, and/or community members) willingly enter these spaces and are encouraged to adopt inclusive, respectful practices, such as attentive listening, suspending judgement, inviting one another to participate, allowing one another equal talk time, accepting all ideas as valuable, and seeing differences as opportunities to learn from others (Willis, 2016). Reaching consensus is not necessarily the aim of these dialogues but rather meaning-making leading to shared understandings about aspects of learning and teaching (Willis, 2013). These understandings benefit from the dialogic processes associated with interacting socially and connecting emotionally with others in a safe, supportive environment (see Alexander, 2017; Matusov, 2020).

Our use of metalogue resembles cogenerative dialoguing, but the dialogue is more critically framed as participants apply higher (meta)-level analysis to these conversations to deepen understandings about both the products and the processes of research. Bateson (1972) appears to have coined the term, *metalogue*, defining it as "a conversation about some problematic subject [where ideally] the structure of the conversation as a whole is also relevant to the same subject" (p. 12). Drawing on Bateson, Willis et al. (2018) liken metalogues to metanarratives, "where information, ideas and even emotions that emerge in conversation fold back into the conversation to enable the participants to reflexively consider the problem" (p. 50). The subject we considered for this chapter comprised the multiple, complex methodological and ethical dilemmas we encountered in our EPIC research. In the vein of Bateson, we structure our writing to highlight Honig's (1996) conception of dilemmas. We've chosen to describe two EPIC events. After each one, we represent the dilemmas *through* our writing, probing our goals for research, tensions that emerged, ways we managed these, reactions of those involved (real and perceived), new dilemmas that surfaced, opportunities and implications for innovative practice and research, how our experiences may inform future literacy research, and the value of metalogue.

8.4   Event 1: Parents as Social Media Participants in Learning Spaces

In 2016, Linda (Author 1) co-planned an EPIC project with a preparatory year teacher, Erin, who worked in a coeducational school on the northern outskirts of the capital city. Erin's class comprised a wide-ranging demographic, with as many families in the bottom socioeconomic quartile as in the top socioeconomic quartile. The school leadership team and classroom teachers were conscious of the children's struggles to perform on the annual national reading, writing, spelling, and grammar assessments. They were equally conscious, as observed by another teacher at the school, that the children liked their parents to see their school work.

The project planned by Erin and Linda engaged the children (aged 4–5 years), parents, and community members in exploring a geography inquiry on *place*, with a particular focus on places that are special (Willis & Exley, 2018). Erin had set up a closed SPOC on a free downloadable app called *Seesaw*. Seesaw is an icon-driven digital portfolio and social media platform (see http://web.seesaw.me/). Erin taught the students to log their learning artefacts using a range of modalities, such as written, audio, photographic, video, or emoticons. The posts could be *private* (between the child, teacher, and parent) or *public* (between all registered and approved account holders, including the whole class and the whole parent group) (Exley et al., 2017). All posts needed to be approved by Erin before being made available to the designated audience. While the item-by-item approval process created an extra task for Erin, the students could independently curate and archive their own learning artefacts and blog posts, which saved Erin time compared to the manual process of curating and archiving the students' learning in a Microsoft Office folder and sending individually crafted emails with attachments to parents (Exley et al., 2017).

Erin also invited parents to access the students' entries and post written or spoken comments or upload a photo and comments about the family's favourite holiday place. After a slow start, Erin provided a verbal reminder for parents to participate at a school parent information evening. After this second reminder, 47% of the parents had responded to the class blog site (Willis & Exley, 2018). The use of this social media site provided students with an immediate known audience for their work, provided parents with a *ping* to their phone to let them know that their child had posted, and also provided parents with an opportunity to contribute to their child's learning (Willis & Exley, 2018). Erin noted the affordances of the social media platform as putting parents "in the picture about what was happening in the classroom" and simultaneously providing "a monitoring tool" for keeping track of students' learning (Willis & Exley, 2018, p. 94).

This recount denies the many complexities of *doing* research which we negotiated along the way. In what follows, we re-present an excerpt from our transcribed audio-recorded conversation to probe the circumstances that surrounded Event 1 and show how our understanding of what happened became clearer and deeper through the use of metalogue.

8.5   Event 1: Metalogue

Linda: Beryl, do you recall our research with Erin and her colleagues and their use of Seesaw?
Beryl: The school really loved the idea of the EPIC projects; in fact, the school put their hand up to be involved. When we met with the principal and teachers, they liked the idea of inquiry and also engaging parents, but as soon as the discussion included using a social media forum as the means of communication between the children, parents, and class teacher, the school hesitated. Part of that hesitation was "What if something goes wrong? What if someone brings their outside social media practices [e.g. trolling, cyberbullying] into this learning space?"
Linda: I know you've said previously that during the ensuing conversations, it was actually Erin who made the point that managing behaviours is not something new in schools.
Beryl: She did. Her comment sent us scouring the school's policies and then system-level policies until we realised there *were* no policies that addressed the rights and responsibilities of children, parents, and community members participating in these online learning situations. So then we asked the question, "What would a social media policy look like?"
Linda: The collaborations that followed between us and the school were intense. We needed to work extensively with all of the stakeholders involved to develop the first draft of this inaugural policy.
Beryl: Yes, it meant dialoguing with the school, dialoguing with the system, to and fro, back and forth, making sure the policy aligned with the school's and system's overarching pedagogical practices and school's preferred vision for relationships with parents and the community while also ensuring the policy accorded with what we knew about social media forums. After the school was satisfied with the policy, it became what we rolled out. It also became part of our ethics application to gain research approval from the university and access approval through the system of education.
Linda: Just how crucial do you think the policy was for the success of our research at the time?
Beryl: I think if we didn't have the policy, our research wouldn't have passed smoothly through the ethics approval process because we were definitely on the cusp of—perhaps not dangerous territory—but I'd say tricky territory insofar as nobody quite knew what to do with this [our EPIC research]. We have templates for how to do an interview and protocols for what an interviewer can and can't say, but

once we started talking about this dynamic online space, one that is often reported in the mainstream media as being full of ills, we couldn't escape raising serious concerns.

This excerpt from the beginning of our metalogue highlights the "tricky footwork" (Blackmore & Hutchison, 2010, p. 499) that preceded our launch of EPIC at this school. Through focused conversation, the precariousness of doing innovative research, how roadblocks became opportunities for creative solutions, and how working together with the school, teachers, and education system forged positive relationships became clearer. The dialogue also revealed how brokering the perplexities of practice for both the school and researchers was needed throughout the development of the social media policy. These negotiations created the conditions for shared moments of realisation, dilemma, resolution, and innovation—deepening understandings and appreciation of the challenges, complexities, and complications of contemporary research for all involved. These insights also included other implications, particularly around timelines for achieving our goals. Once the project stalled, our metalogue revealed the time it took to dialogue around what sh/could be done, investigate possible solutions, and ultimately craft an entirely new policy document. Time was needed for the intellectual work involved in researching, liaising, drafting, and writing while simultaneously contextualising our response to suit the particular context in which we were working, without defeating our intended purposes. Despite the *messiness* of the research we've described, the value of metalogue included the sense-making these conversations afforded to guide our decisions at the time and thereafter to enrich understanding of our experiences as literacy researchers every time we revisit our EPIC work.

8.6   Event 2: Changing Policy Requirements About Students' Social Media Use

In 2019, we were invited to extend EPIC into another preparatory to year 12 coeducational school—this time located in a satellite city south of the capital city. Just under half of the families were in the bottom socioeconomic quartile, and another third were in the bottom-middle socioeconomic quartile. Nearly half of the students came from language backgrounds other than English, with Samoan being the most common language background, followed by Khmer (Cambodian), Hmong (Southeast Asian), Arabic, and Hindi. By all indications, the children were happy to be at school, and the parents were glad that their children were at this school. We also witnessed the parents and other younger siblings talking easily in the communal areas, greeting each other with great fondness, strolling through the school to put their child's school bag at the classroom, or making their way to the school administration building to deliver messages from home. If the school called a parent meeting to discuss an upcoming sports competition or extracurricular cultural activity, the parents flocked to attend. Yet, we heard from the school leaders and classroom teachers that the parents, out of respect for the teachers, engaged little in the curriculum or classroom work. Motivated by research (e.g. Goodall & Montgomery, 2014) attesting to the benefits of bringing the relationship between parents and their child's learning closer together, the school wanted to explore the possibilities of an EPIC project.

As is typical of our work, we bring teachers from the same school together to form a learning community. We cogenerate with them to orientate their existing units of work into inquiry questions while simultaneously exploring the pedagogical practices that give purchase to a wider repertoire of receptive and expressive literacies. We encourage teachers to talk about the resources already in their schools, including the digital hardware and software, and the human resources in the community, including parents and perhaps others in the wider community. At one meeting, the year 3 teacher, Louise, hadn't yet seen Microsoft Teams, but the year 7 teacher, Antoinette, had already started using this software with her class. A mentor-mentee relationship was born. At the same time, Antoinette explained that she'd previously been *burnt* by parent engagement and came to this EPIC project with some trepidation. The year 10 teacher, Charlize, spoke from her position as a parent of a young school child. Her son's teacher (at another school) used the Seesaw App (mentioned earlier) for parent-school communication, allowing the children to log pictures, audios, and videos that pinged to Charlize's phone. Charlize declared that Seesaw allowed her to feel like she had her son's classroom in her hands, on her phone. Louise reminded Antoinette that the parents were working hard, often managing multiple part-time and seasonal jobs to pay the modest school fees. The three teachers continued to cogenerate to flesh out their inquiry units: science and an inquiry about heat in the early years, geography and water use globally in year 7, and the *Mystery of God* in year 10. Discussion turned to the teachers' preferences for the SPOC. Despite considerable interest in Charlize's experiences with Seesaw, new dilemmas arose, which we explored in our recorded metalogue for this chapter—a transcribed excerpt of which we re-present below.

8.7   Event 2: Metalogue

Beryl: Can I just take a step back to Erin's school when we first met with the school leadership team and teachers; our meeting also included their IT (information technology) teacher. He spoke about how he used Twitter professionally, Facebook personally, Pinterest [personally in the past], and a Facebook page for the school and was involved in the active parent network group. And he was the one who recommended the Seesaw app as the social media for the EPIC project, and where did he see the Seesaw app? It was promoted at a professional development day for schools in the district in the education system in which we were working.
Linda: That's right. After weighing up many other options, you couldn't blame Erin and her colleagues after seeing Seesaw and its capabilities to assist young children's literacy learning and user-friendliness for parents for choosing it for their

EPIC project because they and the school also considered it was endorsed at system level for their use.

Beryl: But of course by 2019, a lot of water had gone under the bridge. We've [in Australia] had a great deal of conversation nationally around the e-Safety Commissioner (see Australian Government, 2020), so education systems have mobilised and sorted themselves out a bit more since the days when we needed to develop our own social media policy for Erin's school.

Linda: Yes, there's been a lot of education aimed at schools and parents around cyberbullying, online grooming, sexting, and so on as well as research and media publicity about apps like ClassDojo (see https://www.classdojo.com/), highlighting unknown risks to children, teachers, and schools around data harvesting, storage, and misuse. We of course had highlighted these aspects in speaking to representatives of the system of education in which we were working as well as in our ethics application to the university. What we encountered next was a wall at the system level and from the university ethics committee, with both entities indicating that Seesaw and similar apps could no longer be used in our research. The need for due diligence around overseas data storage was cited as the main concern.

Beryl: But what we found was that neither entity had an answer for what we *could* use. In meeting with a school system representative, we found that objections ran deeper than data storage and included issues of access to the systems in place in schools and the need at system level to institute structures to ensure when it came to the use of blogs and the parent portal, for example, that the *right* people had the *right* level of access.

Linda: This shift in approach at the system level to manage what teachers used to communicate with students and parents had implications not only for us as researchers but also for teachers and school leaders. Teachers were left confused, wondering what they could or couldn't use. School leaders were told to rein in app use by teachers especially those perceived as *loose cannons* for having created their own social media accounts to communicate with parents. We saw first-hand how apps like Seesaw could promote literacy learning at home and school by better engaging students and parents in their child's learning. Without tools to allow teachers to easily *push out* information about what students were doing in the classroom and similarly for parents to easily *push in* information about their child's learning at home, our intended goals for EPIC were somewhat thwarted.

Beryl: Agree. Despite the benefits of collaboration for professional learning reported by all three teachers in the 2019 EPIC project, their use of Microsoft Teams as the system-level preferred platform ultimately proved a very poor substitute for what we'd found in 2016. We also knew that Seesaw was still being used in other schools, including Erin's. In fact, one teacher from her school contacted me earlier that year to say their parent engagement had increased with 47,000 hits on Seesaw, and there were months yet before school finished!

Linda: The irony deepened for us when we learnt that those in leadership positions at the system level were aware of what different schools were doing in this space but left each school's principal responsible for what happened on the ground.

Beryl: I think it was because they were actually trapped; they knew what they *didn't* want, but they didn't actually have a solution for a way ahead. And then they were caught in this *quagmire*, where the policies they developed around social media use were in contradistinction to their own vision statement on the necessity to better engage parents.

Linda: Which was the reason we were doing EPIC research in these schools in the first place!

This second metalogue excerpt shows the increasingly complex ethical and methodological dilemmas we faced during our EPIC research over 3 years. Two schools (located 2 h apart) sought to satisfy system-level policy mandates about parent engagement, yet the social media integrated inquiry curriculum projects they each developed to engage parents contrasted starkly. Our own commitment to conduct ethical research meant that issues we'd raised with the education system and university about social media apps between doing research at the first and the second school affected our ability to achieve our stated research goals. Although we managed the tensions which arose in 2019—embracing opportunities to explore the use of a new platform (i.e. Microsoft Teams) for student and parent engagement—our findings showed limited impact on literacy learning and teaching through strengthened home-school connections (see Willis et al., 2020). The need to comply with changing policy mandates restricted our repertoire of choice methodologically. There was, however, evidence of the value of collaboration not only among the teachers but also among their students. This gives weight to the benefits of cogenerative dialoguing approaches, which appear to have encouraged more "substantive conversations" (student-to-student; student-to-teacher) in their classrooms (Willis et al., 2020, p. 43). Our use of metalogue also showed the value of this method for providing not *off-the-shelf* solutions to the dilemmas we described but rather an approach which recognises our views "[are] always provisional, are unpredictable and can lead in many directions" (Matusov, 2020, p. 17). Indeed, metalogue provided time and space to think aloud together and through *purposeful* talk enabled us to begin to disentangle the story threads—deepening understanding of our research and providing a more coherent narrative from which others might learn.

8.8   Concluding Thoughts

This chapter points to the need for researchers in contemporary contexts not to take the ease of opening the metaphoric gate to research in schools for granted. At the same time, it highlights the need to be agile in response to inevitable dilemmas and willing to work collaboratively with participants as these emerge. We commend the value of deliberative reflexive methods and hope our journey encourages others to avoid portraying methods as always seamless and uncomplicated. Our tale is timely for literacy researchers and educators alike, who must anticipate future waves of change as mass virtual technologies gain momentum and as global events, such as the COVID-19 pandemic, unfold with unpredictable impacts. As we prepare literacy learners for the realities, opportunities, and uncertainties of their worlds, we, like Bernstein (2000), must surely continue to emphasise their pedagogic rights (along with their parents' rights) to enhance repertoires of knowledge; inclusion socially, culturally, and personally; and positive participation in the construction of a better society.

References

Alexander, R. J. (2017). *Towards dialogical teaching: Rethinking classroom talk* (5th ed.). Dialogos.

Australian Government. (2020). *eSafety Commissioner: Helping Australians have safer, more positive experiences online*. Retrieved from https://www.esafety.gov.au/

Bateson, G. (1972). *Steps to an ecology of mind*. Ballantine Books.

Bernstein, B. (2000). *Pedagogy, symbolic control and identity: Theory, research, critique*. Rowman & Littlefield.

Blackmore, J., & Hutchison, K. (2010). Ambivalent relations: The 'tricky footwork' of parental involvement in school communities. *International Journal of Inclusive Education, 14*(5), 499–515. https://doi.org/10.1080/13603110802657685

Boran, S., & Comber, B. (Eds.). (2001). *Critiquing whole language and classroom inquiry*. National Council of Teachers of English.

Bower, M. (2017). *Design of technology-enhanced learning: Integrating research and practice*. Emerald.

Bradfield, K., & Exley, B. (2020). Teachers' accounts of their curriculum use: External contextual influences during times of curriculum reform. *Curriculum Journal, 31*(4), 757–774.

Cumming, J. J., Wyatt-Smith, C., & Colbert, P. (2016). Students at risk and NAPLAN: The collateral damage. In B. Lingard, G. Thompson, & S. Sellar (Eds.), *National testing in schools: An Australian assessment* (pp. 126–138). Routledge.

Delamont, S. (2005). Four great gates: Dilemmas, directions and distractions in educational research. *Research Papers in Education, 20*(1), 85–100. https://doi.org/10.1080/0267152052000341345

Department of Education. (2019). *Alice Springs (Mparntwe) education declaration*. Retrieved from https://docs.education.gov.au/documents/alice-springs-mparntwe-education-declaration

Education Council. (2014). *The Hobart declaration on schooling (1989)*. Retrieved from http://www.educationcouncil.edu.au/EC-Publications/EC-Publications-archive/EC-The-Hobart-Declaration-on-Schooling-1989.aspx

Exley, B., & Luke, A. (2010). Uncritical framing: Lesson and knowledge structure in school science. In D. Cole & D. L. Pullen (Eds.), *Multiliteracies in motion: Current theory and practice* (pp. 17–41). Routledge.

Exley, B., & Willis, L.-D. (2016). Children's pedagogic rights in the web 2.0 era: A case study of a child's open access interactive travel blog. *Global Studies of Childhood, 6*(4), 400–413. https://doi.org/10.1177/2043610616676026

Exley, B., Willis, L.-D., & McCosker, M. (2017). Children as advocates—The potential of using social media in the early years of schooling. *Practical Literacy: The Early and Primary Years, 22*(2), 9–12.

Fransson, G. (2016). Manoeuvring in a digital dilemmatic space: Making sense of a digitised society. *Nordic Journal of Digital Literacy, 11*(3), 185–201.

Goodall, J., & Montgomery, C. (2014). Parental involvement to parental engagement: A continuum. *Educational Review, 66*(4), 399–410.

Honig, B. (1996). Difference, dilemmas, and the politics of home. In S. Benhabib (Ed.), *Democracy and difference. Contesting the boundaries of the political* (pp. 257–277). Princeton University Press.

Kamler, B., & Comber, B. (2005). Turn-around pedagogies: Improving the education of at-risk students. *Improving Schools, 8*(2), 121–131. https://doi.org/10.1177/1365480205057702

Klenowski, V. (2013). Sustaining teacher professionalism in the context of standards referenced assessment reform. In A. Luke, A. Woods, & K. Weir (Eds.), *Curriculum, syllabus design and equity: A primer and model* (pp. 88–102). Routledge.

Luke, A., Wood, A., & Weir, K. (2012). *Curriculum, syllabus design and equity*. Routledge.

Matusov, E. (2020). Pattern-recognition, intersubjectivity, and dialogic meaning-making in education. *Dialogic Pedagogy, 8*, 1–24. https://doi.org/10.5195/dpj.2020.314

Mills, K. A., & Exley, B. (2014). Time, space and text in the elementary school digital writing classroom. *Written Communication, 31*(4), 434–469.

Pandya, J. Z., & Golden, N. A. (2018). Fostering impossible possible through critical media literacies. In K. Mills, A. Stornaiuolo, A. Smith, & J. Z. Pandya (Eds.), *Handbook of writing, literacies and education in digital cultures* (pp. 50–60). Routledge.

Ridgewell, J., & Exley, B. (2011). The potentials of student initiated netspeak in a middle primary science-inspired multiliteracies project. *Research in Science Education, 41*(5), 635–649.

Selwyn, N. (2011). *Schools and schooling in the digital age: A critical analysis*. Routledge.

The Design-Based Collective. (2003). Design-based research: An emerging paradigm for educational inquiry. *Educational Researcher, 32*(1), 5–8.

The New London Group. (2000). A pedagogy of multiliteracies: Designing social futures. In B. Cope & M. Kalantzis (Eds.), *Multiliteracies: Literacy learning and the design of social futures*. Macmillan Publishers.

Willis, L.-D. (2013). *Parent-teacher engagement: A coteaching and cogenerative dialoguing approach*. (Unpublished doctoral dissertation), Queensland University of Technology, Brisbane, Australia.

Willis, L.-D. (2016). Exploring cogenerativity for developing a coteaching community of practice in a parent-teacher engagement project. *International Journal of Educational Research, 80*, 124–133. https://doi.org/10.1016/j.ijer.2016.08.009

Willis, L.-D., & Exley, B. (2016). Language variation and change in the Australian Curriculum English: Integrating sub-strands through a pedagogy of metalogue. *English in Australia, 51*(2), 74–84.

Willis, L.-D., & Exley, B. (2018). Using an online social media space to engage parents in student learning in the early-years: Enablers and impediments. *Digital Education Review, 33*, 87–104.

Willis, L.-D., & Exley, B. (2020). *Engaging parents in their child's learning and wellbeing – Change, continuity and COVID-19*. Our schools – Our Future issues paper. Published by Independent Schools Queensland. Retrieved from https://rms.isq.qld.edu.au/files/Weblive_OSOF/Engaging_Parents_Issues_Paper.pdf

Willis, L.-D., & Exley, B. (2021). Spotlight on parent engagement: Practice and research. Ways to engage parents in their child's learning and wellbeing: Lessons from lockdown. *Practical Literacy: The Early and Primary Years, 26*(1), 40–41.

Willis, L.-D., Grimmett, H., & Heck, D. (2018). Exploring cogenerativity in initial teacher education school-university partnerships using the methodology of metalogue. In J. Kriewaldt, A. Ambrosetti, D. Rorrison, & R. Capeness (Eds.), *Educating future teachers: Innovative perspectives in professional experience* (pp. 49–69). Springer Nature. https://doi.org/10.1007/978-981-10-5484-6_4

Willis, L.-D., Exley, B., & Clancy, S. (2020). Spotlight on parent engagement: Practice and research. Using science inquiry to engage parents in student language and literacy learning. *Practical Literacy: The Early and Primary Years, 25*(2), 42–43.

Willis, L.-D., Povey, J., Hodges, J., & Carroll, A. (2021). *Principal leadership for parent engagement in disadvantaged schools: What qualities and strategies distinguish effective principals?* Springer Nature. https://doi.org/10.1007/978-981-16-1264-0

Woods, A., Dooley, K., Luke, A., & Exley, B. (2014). School leadership, literacy and social justice: The place of local school curriculum planning and reform. In I. Bogotch & C. Shields (Eds.), *International handbook of educational leadership and social (in)justice: Springer international handbooks of education volume 29* (pp. 509–520). Springer Publishing.

Part III
Disruptings

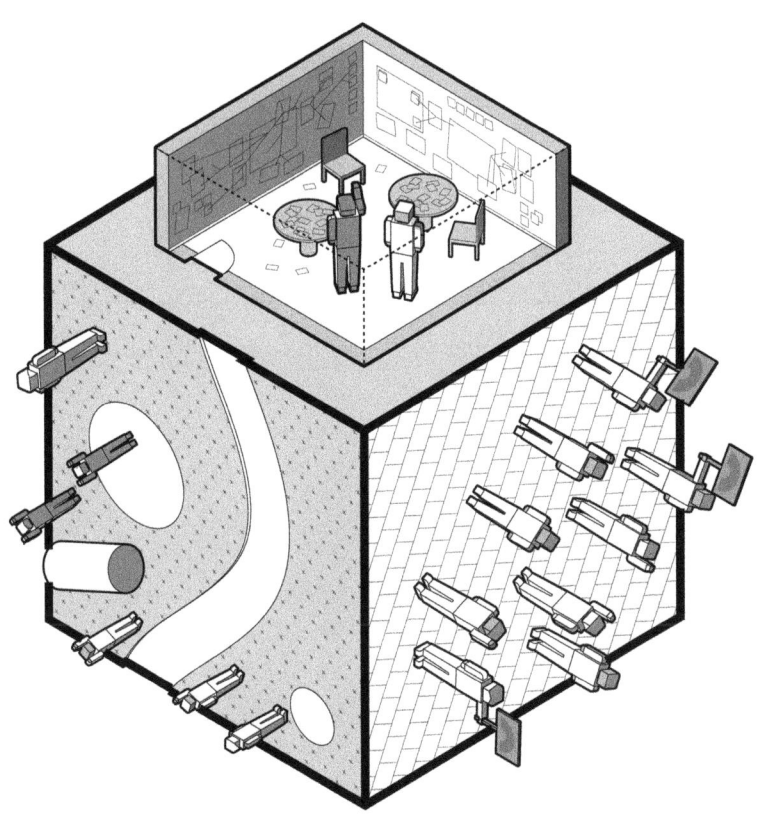

Chapter 9
Literacies Yet to Come: Young Children's Emergent, Provisional and Speculative Literacies for Precarious Futures

Abigail Hackett

Abstract In response to increasing global environmental precarity, this chapter considers what kinds of literacies will be most relevant for young children, for the future they are likely to inherit. Setting out the problematics of human exceptionalism and "time as progress" that education in general and literacy in particular tend to get caught up in, I propose understandings of interdependency between human and planetary well-being as a starting point for considering the emergence of literacies in new ways. Drawing on 3 years of ethnographic research with young children and families in community spaces, I present examples of literacies as emergent, provisional and both actual and virtual. I argue that noticing such "literacies yet to come" has important lessons to teach us about interdependency between human meaning-making and the more-than-human world. Such a stance prompts literacy scholarship to extend beyond empirical research and fine-grained accounts of what seemed to (truly) unfold in the moment, in order to explore other modes of thinking that might gesture towards the multiple immanent possibilities. For this reason, literacy scholarship needs to continue to ask: *What ways of being in the world might enable children to thrive in the future, and what role might literacies play in enacting, valuing or making available these ways of being?*

Keywords Future · Time · Human exceptionalism · Entanglement · Precarity · Emergent literacies · Young children · Families · More-than-human

Events such as pandemics and climate crises, more-than-human phenomena to which humans have contributed but cannot control, require dramatic changes to how we organise everyday life. At the same time, such events might offer possibilities for rethinking society along more just lines (Roy, 2020). In this sense, global

A. Hackett (✉)
Manchester Metropolitan University, Manchester, UK
e-mail: A.Hackett@mmu.ac.uk

© The Author(s), under exclusive license to Springer Nature Singapore Pte
Ltd. 2022
C. Lee et al. (eds.), *Unsettling Literacies*, Cultural Studies and
Transdisciplinarity in Education 15, https://doi.org/10.1007/978-981-16-6944-6_9

131

shifts create both precarity and new openings; in this chapter, I consider what this might mean for our work as literacy researchers and educators.

At a national and a global scale, impacts of the COVID-19 pandemic on education, community and environment, family life, health and even survival have impacted the least powerful the most (Best Beginnings et al., 2020; Marmot, 2020; Power et al., 2020). Describing the pandemic as a portal, Roy (2020) makes the point that whilst COVID-19 has brought inequalities such as these into sharp relief, historically "pandemics have forced humans to break with the past and imagine their world anew." Stanley Robinson (2020) suggests that COVID-19 might have implications for conceptualisations of time in particular and for how we imagine the future. In relation to climate change, he suggests our inability to empathise with the humans of the future is behind our failure to act; that "the fact that these problems will occur in the future lets us take a magical view of them." Both COVID-19 and climate change require changes in behaviour now to benefit future lives. However, in the case of COVID-19, "we are the future people" (Stanley Robinson, 2020); that is, our own lives will be benefited in the future by changing our behaviour now. Perhaps then, thinking with the shifting and uncertain experience of living during the COVID-19 pandemic, now is a good time to consider young children's literacy practices in relation to living well in the future.

Young children today are growing up towards an uncertain future, likely to be characterised by increasing environmental precarity. As Somerville and Powell (2018) write, twenty-first-century children are growing up with a different sense of urgency in relation to the environment; they are growing up in a world "already out of control". COVID-19, as a zoonotic disease, stems from humans' encroachment on the habitats of other species and so itself reframes questions about the relationship between humans and the environment (Van Dooren, 2020). Thus, the rise of further zoonotic diseases, possible ongoing or fluctuating physical distancing measures, environmental disasters and countless other interventions into daily life that humans are unable to predict ahead of time form the backdrop to the question: *What kinds of literacies will be useful or relevant to young children as they grow up in this changing world?*

Young children's literacies have, for many years (in western thought at least), sat near the beating heart of anxieties about the "proper" development of young children, believed by many to evidence children's ability to rationalise, problem-solve, make abstract connections, empathise with others or hold their own views. The emphasis on, for example, acquiring as many words as early as possible and the rarefication of specific middle class western child socialisation practices as essential or natural (Avineri et al., 2015; Viruru, 2001) all speak of the deep and historic entangling of "language" and "literacies" with the supposedly special nature of the human species (Finnegan, 2002). Over 20 years ago, in his work on young children's meaning-making, Kress (1997) asked the question: How to educate children for a digital and globalised future that adults have not themselves experienced? This question seems even more pertinent today. However, as I will go on to argue, the way we frame and answer this question *now* might need to shift to better account for the interdependency of the success of human life and planetary well-being. Young children's futures may well involve or require different kinds of literacy practices compared to those of present-day adults. In this chapter, I mobilise the notion of "literacies yet to come" to consider the future of early childhood literacies in a globalised yet environmentally precarious world.

9.1 Unsettling Literacies in Contexts of Precarity

Conceptualisations of time as "progress" are tightly plaited into the notion of human life as special and distinct from other life (Springgay & Truman, 2019; Tsing, 2015). In particular, a kind of forward-looking, cumulative, predictable and linear version of time seems to be an important component of a rhetoric that:

> humans are different from the rest of the living world because we look forward—while other species, which live day to day, are thus dependent on us. (Tsing, 2015, p. 21)

"Time as progress", then, is important for upholding the myth of human exceptionalism (as a species). Also, as noted above, notions of time as progress and humans as masterful seem to stutter in the current context, in which it becomes increasingly apparent that some things are getting worse, not better (for humans at least; see Schrader, 2012). More-than-human aspects of, for example, climate change or zoonotic disease are able to intervene dramatically into human orderings of the world. As Tsing (2015) reminds us, progress has stopped making sense. She urges us to seek out narratives that exist beyond, or in spite of progress, in order to identify modes or accounts of future "more-than-human liveability" (Tsing, 2015). What might the implications be, then, for literacy education? The emphasis on time as progress towards a predictable future (a future that education is assumed to enhance) is also notable within the field of literacy, for example, in the equation of "time on task" and efficient use of time with increased and faster learning (Compton-Lilly, 2016, Jones et al., 2016; Pacini-Ketchabaw, 2012). We see this during the COVID-19 pandemic (in the UK at least), through a policy rhetoric about children "falling behind" and needing to "catch up" with their learning. In this sense, early childhood literacies, like much of early childhood education, are partly a forward-looking-to-the-future endeavour, in which actions now are intended to benefit individuals later.

For feminist scholars, precarity is a political and ontological position, grounded in "indeterminacy, vulnerability, and responsibility" (Powell, 2019, p. 193). For Butler, "Precarity exposes our sociality, the fragile and necessary dimensions of our interdependency" (2012, p. 148). Drawing on Butler, Powell (2019) gives us a useful distinction between precarity and precariousness:

> Precarity names the political condition of neoliberal capitalism as that which thrives on instability, on the ways in which the precariousness of life is exploited through the social and economic conditions of disparity and inequality that capitalism creates. (Powell, 2019, p. 193)

Thus, precarity is both inherent to the human condition and political, in that "it is a vulnerability that is differentially distributed and relational" (p. 193). Within this ambivalence, we glimpse the "tactical distribution of precarity" (Butler, 2012, p. 148), in which some life is considered worth protecting over others. As Zembylas (2019) proposes, an account of precarity needs to acknowledge the universality of precarity (and the pointlessness of "the idealization of invulnerability" (p. 99), a state living beings can never achieve), without losing sight of the specificity of experiences of precarity and its unequal distribution. Thus, there are inherent tensions in considering how literacy educators and researchers might respond to an unpredictable future characterised by precarity. In part, education's role might be to prepare children to succeed in precarious futures (resilience? particular skill sets? information? empowerment?). This is a stance that might cohere with the idea of time as progress, or with a belief that time on task will pay off in terms of increased individual success, or invulnerability. Yet at the same time, precarity requires foregrounding the unequal effects of environmental precarity (including, of course, impacts of climate change) on communities and children. In doing so, it demands that we recognise the politics of deeming some life more grievable than others (Butler, 2012). It requires then, thinking collectively, beyond individual competencies or skill sets.

In a report commissioned as part of UNESCO's inquiry into the future of education, the Common Worlds Research Collective (2020) have argued that planetary and human well-being are indivisible and that "education needs to play a pivotal role in radically reconfiguring our place and agency within this interdependent world" (p. 2). Many of the recommendations in this report speak to the dilemmas of thinking beyond "progress" and responding to some of the questions about precarity I outlined above. For example, the authors critique education's logic of "perpetual economic growth in the guise of human advancement" and the tendency of education to act as a "vehicle for promulgating human exceptionalism" (Common Worlds Research Collective, 2020). Instead, they argue for the need to understand humans as ecological beings, entangled in a more-than-human world, and to shift from individual developmental frameworks to focus on the collective and convivial.

It is possible to see similar debates playing out within the COVID crisis itself: for example, questions about which lives are most important to protect, the unequal distribution of precarity and the need to think about vulnerabilities and the consequences of our choices at a collective rather than an individual scale. Indeed, increasingly, scientists are drawing connections between the COVID pandemic and climate change, suggesting the most likely causes of the rise in zoonotic diseases in human populations in recent years lie in climate change (Beyer et al., 2021), habitat encroachment and intensified food production practices (van Dooren, 2020). As it becomes increasingly apparent how little we know about these connections or the consequences of human action, researchers and educators today can only speculate about the kinds of worlds young children will live in and with when they are adults. However, if (as literacy scholars have contended) literacies are important or powerful partly because they render the world differentially meaningful, it seems pertinent to ask: What role might literacies play in the reconfiguring of human relationships with place and other animals required for future survival (Common Worlds Collective, 2020) and planetary well-being (Somerville and Muris, forthcoming)? Notions of human interdependency and more-than-human entanglement, then, may offer some starting points for the question of literacies for future planetary well-being (Somerville & Murris, forthcoming).

9.2   Mastery, Entanglement and the Need to Rethink Early Childhood Literacy

Kuby et al. (2019) make the case for a more expansive view of what "counts" as literacies, as a counter to the hierarchies that narrow definitions of literacy can create. The conflation of literacies with human exceptionalism has played an important role in "civilising" projects of white colonial powers (Tarc, 2015; Viruru, 2001), setting up hierarchies of the human which exclude certain groups on grounds of race, indigeneity, religion and so on (Braidotti, 2013; McKittrick, 2015; Truman, 2019). It is also important to note that the connection between language and human exceptionality is specific to western culture; in many non-western cultures, understandings of other animals and the land itself as possessing language are well-established (Abram 1996; Sundberg, 2014; Todd, 2016). Thus, the insistence on a view of language and other semiotic practices (what we might call multimodal meaning-making) as the exclusive preserve of humans also acts as a form of cultural erasure and epistemic violence.

In considering the future of early childhood literacies, we need a way of considering human survival on the planet as a whole, *without* erasing the unequal way in which threats to survival fall on the marginalised and less powerful. In addition, a consideration of global inequality cannot be separated from the history and ongoing present of colonial violence and exploitation. One "way in" to thinking about all of these factors in relation to education in general, or to literacies in particular, is Singh's (2018) invitation to *Unthinking Mastery*. For Singh, "mastery" in education, that is, individualised human competencies that give students control over a world perceived to be less animate, less "in control" and, importantly, separable from the student, has much in common with more insidious and toxic forms of mastery within colonialism. "Mastery invariably and relentlessly reaches toward the indiscriminate control over something—whether human or inhuman, animate or inanimate" (Singh, 2018, pp. 9–10). Pointing out that western humanity's goal of mastery has "fractured the Earth to the point of threatening destruction of its environment and itself" (p. 19), Singh (2018) warns that ultimately "human practices of mastery fold over onto themselves and collapse" (p. 19). In other words, a goal of mastery creates an illusion that it is possible to deny the dependency of the one who considers themselves master on (more-than-human) others.

This returns us to the problematic of the tendency for western "environmental sustainability" discourses to promise that few lifestyle compromises and no redistributions of power will be required because, it is believed, "Man's" exceptional ingenuity will invent some sort of technological solution (Alaimo, 2016; Somerville & Powell, 2018). It returns us, also, to the historic conflation of literacies with human exceptionalism and the propensity of western child socialisation practices in relation to language and literacy to emphasise "progress", fixed meanings and a separation between object and subject (MacLure, 2016). Early childhood literacy practices could/can, for example, emphasise or erase humanities' interconnectedness with and dependency on the more-than-human world (MacLure, 2016), reproduce or disrupt racialised hierarchical categories of human life (Truman, 2019) or offer (trans)language as a fluid experimentation rather than a bounded object closely connected to nationhood (Gurney & Demuro, 2019). If the question of more-than-human entanglement and understanding humanity's interdependency with the planet (Common Worlds Research Collective, 2020) is an important starting point for living well in an environmentally precarious future, a key question for future literacies might be:

> *what kinds of literacies might promote or obstruct children's deep understandings of interdependency between human and planetary survival that are likely to be essential in the future?*

Through the rest of this chapter, I will explore this question with reference to empirical examples of how literacies unfold within more-than-human assemblages in which children, like all of us, are entangled.

9.3   Literacies Yet to Come

The title of this chapter, "Literacies Yet to Come", is intended to act as a heuristic to consider these knotty problems of uncertain futures, the precarity of life and young children's literacies. I find the phrase useful because it can hold multiple meanings simultaneously. In this section, I explore these meanings in conversation with small vignettes drawn from a recent research project "The Emergence of Literacy in Very Young Children". Funded by the British Academy, the study was a 3-year-long ethnography located in two close-by urban communities in northern England (Hackett, forthcoming). The following vignettes are drawn from the resulting substantial dataset of fieldnotes, still images and video footage that investigated the literacy and language practices of children aged between 12 and 36 months, with a particular interest in what, beyond humans, might be involved in their emergence. The following examples have been specifically selected to enable the reader to consider literacies beyond a progress narrative (Tsing, 2015), in that they describe practices that are obscure, are difficult to pin down as "literacies" and seem to resist the application of rational or functional explanations.

9.3.1 Emergent Literacies Yet to Come

At playgroup, Z fetches the grumpy-looking plastic baby doll. She loves that baby doll; pushes it in pushchair, washes it in the water tray, places it in a high chair, (left over from snack time) in the sun to dry off. P and H want to play with the baby too, try to pick it up and take it somewhere else, but Z is firm—baby needs to dry. The high chair is right near the chalks, and H hovers with a chalk, eventually drawing a single line of blue on baby's head. Gradually, all three children begin to colour the baby doll, first using different coloured chalks on the baby's head, then working down over the baby's whole body. As she watches all this, Z tells her reassuringly "we can just wash baby", and she agrees, "yes, it is fine we can wash her".

Young children are frequently seen as practisers of emergent literacies, as filled with yet-to-be-fulfilled potential. The project to recognise young children's emergent literacies as something more than "inadequate manifestations of adult literacy" (Kress, 1997) has been powerfully taken up by the field of New Literacy Studies and multimodal literacies. Writing about the presence of literacy practices in homes and communities, Gillen and Hall (2013) note "young children are from birth witnesses to and participants in such practices" (p. 7). Taking this proposition further, Flewitt (2013) proposes "early literacy is viewed as beginning at birth and unfolding in babies' everyday experiences" (p. 4). In identifying meaning-making as multimodal and these processes as taking place in complex ways long before children can read or write, Kress' (1997) theory of multimodal literacies opens up possibilities for thinking about young children's literacy practices beyond their observation of and participation in the literacy practices of adults. However, in Kress' descriptions of young children navigating a complex, fast moving, digital (and thoroughly human-dominated) world, navigating, thriving and understanding, he proposes, are achieved by semiotic meaning-making as motivated, intentional design, conveying messages to other humans "as transparent as is possible" (p. 14, emphasis added). In other words, through multimodal meaning-making, Kress argues, young children can achieve the same kinds of mastery, rational ordering and control that older children and adults do through written and spoken language.

An overemphasis on function, competency and predesign in accounts of children's meaning-making risks overlooking the way in which, when young children entangle with objects or spaces with little adult input, these are often the moments of most intense engagement, creativity and spark. Drawing on Stern's work, Boldt (2020) has argued for the importance of "what happens or is being learned that we cannot so easily put into words but matters nonetheless" (p. 12). These vitalities both shape the energy of a space, such as a classroom or playgroup, but also transcend that space, making connections across geographies and temporalities (Boldt, 2020). Often young children's multimodal literacies occur in relation to, and in response to, places and things (Hackett, forthcoming) in ways that seem to exceed rational choices being made in order to march in a predictable fashion towards mastery of certain adult skills (Kuby et al., 2015). For example, accounts of the emergence of young children's literacies from a more-than-human context have described a tablet *emerging* as a text within "serendipitous concurrences" (Burnett et al., 2020,

p. 175) and the way in which "language and story emerge and disappear simultaneously" during play and movement (Hackett & Somerville, 2017, p. 386). These observations have important implications for how we think about the emergence of literacies; Burnett et al. (2020) describe literacies as emerging from a "steadily unfolding mix" (p. 174) of things, movements, atmospheres and bodies. Taking as an example the vignette above, of the children mark-making on the baby doll (Fig. 9.1), we might wonder: Is it literacies? Was it predesigned? Is it about separating form from meaning and conveying ideas transparently? Or is it only useful because it holds the potential (as a mark making activity) to evolve in that direction? I am reminded here of Rautio's (2013) provocation that, in considering children's autotelic practices with things, "were we to ask why children carry stones….. Explanations would surely surface and lend themselves to be neatly categorized (p. 395)". In other words, the insistence on multimodal literacies as *always* being about predesigned signification and human mastery risks becoming its own self-fulfilling prophecy. By committing to value what unfolds in incidents, such as the one above, between children, chalks and plastic baby, perhaps we might yield new and fruitful lines of enquiry about the nature of emergent literacies and future precarity.

Within emergent systems theory, emergence is understood as a process that operates beyond the individual (Burnett et al., 2020) and relies on interdependency, as heterogeneous components come together in unpredictable ways (Dalke et al., 2007). Writing about posthuman literacies, Rautio (2019) describes emergence as "the growing of a system in a way that the system doesn't depend on the individual parts" (p. 231). Thus, randomness is the defining feature of an emergent system; there can be no leader, and "there can be no precise recipe either" (p. 232). In other words, the seeming randomness and unpredictability of young children's literacies,

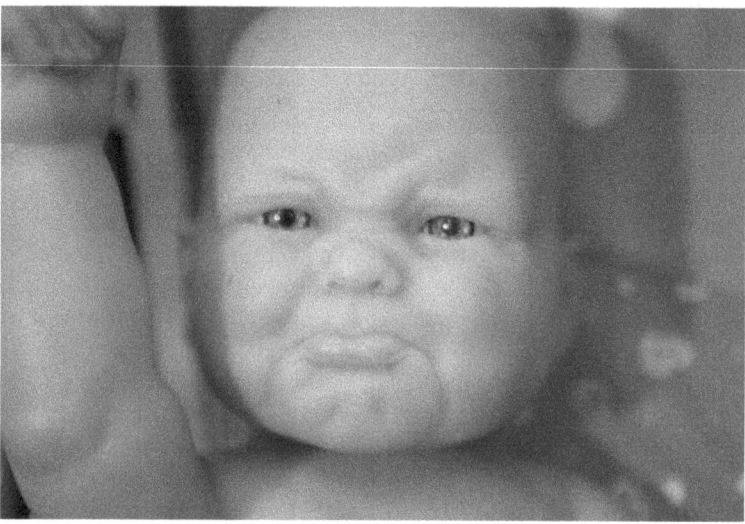

Fig. 9.1 Grumpy baby doll. (Image credit Steve Pool)

the way in which intended meanings-to-be-signified seem to be slippery and constantly on the borderline of what might "count" as literacies, are important for their emergence (Hackett, forthcoming). Like any emergent system, emergent literacies require "a degree of randomness and autonomy, not control, to function" (Rautio, 2019, p. 232). Perhaps we need to pay more attention to these more-than-human entanglements, with all their intensity and vitality, if we would like to understand more about what drives young children's literacy and language practices and how these things emerge. A better understanding of processes of emergence might help us to reconceptualise literacies as interdependent with a more-than-human world, rather than exclusively a human preserve indicative of our species' exceptionalism.

9.3.2   Provisional Literacies Yet to Come

She stands with H in the outside space next to a pop up tunnel. It is a warm day so the playgroup has moved outside. The ground here is sloped, and the play tunnels have been slowly rolling away down the little hill and needing to be fetched back all afternoon. H pushes the play tunnel and as it rolls back towards him, as says "oh oh". H and the tunnel repeat this several times, as the adults nearby observe and giggle.

In this vignette, H happens to push the tunnel and it seems to roll back towards him. He exclaims at the indignity of the wind/tunnel and pushes it up the slope again. With this tiny serendipitous action, an exclamation, a watching audience, the tunnel somehow transforms into a cheeky, boundary-pushing character, teasing H in its defiance to stay where it is placed (Fig. 9.2). In this way, a tiny multimodal story seems to emerge through the repetition of movement and reaction between H, the slope, the breeze, the tunnel and the audience ("I push the cheeky tunnel away, it rolls back towards me…."), and everyone present, it seems, shares a sense of the humour in the narrative. Like the term "literacies yet to come", young children's

Fig. 9.2 H and the tunnel

gestures, body movements, arrangements of objects or vocalisations and the stuff of multimodal literacy practices can be more or less "transparent" (Kress, 1997); they can be multiple, provisional or unfixed or have meanings that are dependent on how they seem to work in the moment.

My fieldwork with young children in communities is replete with accounts such as H and the tunnel. These are stories in which meanings seem shared amongst a group in the moment, yet when I try to recount them to you on these pages, they seem much less convincing, barely anything at all, certainly not compelling examples of multimodal meanings that can be effectively abstracted from one context and presented in another. In relation to conceptualising literacies yet to come, perhaps this situatedness, in a given moment, a place or a certain point of view, is important for understanding literacies beyond abstract meanings and human exceptionalism. The provisional and place-specific nature of such meaning-making reflects its more-than-human nature, in which "language and story emerge *and disappear* simultaneously when we consider movement as a world-forming communicative practice" (Hackett & Somerville, 2017, p. 386 (emphasis added)).

Perhaps what we have to learn here is to question the assumption that transparent and abstractable meanings are always superior, desirable or the intended end goal of young children's literacy practices (Hackett, forthcoming; Viruru, 2001). Paying attention more widely to entanglements and intensities between children and the world, the way in which meanings can seem provisional or multiple or rely on context and place in order to make sense, is one more starting point for thinking about literacies yet to come.

9.4   Actual/Virtual Literacies Yet to Come

W walks to the plastic hoops that lie in the grass near the tunnel, looks at them, half steps on one with her foot, is unbalanced slightly. W tries again to stand on the hoop, but leg catches and W falls over on the soft grass. W on her hands and knees, feet and hands sinking deep into the grass and clumps of slightly dry grass cuttings, as the wind whips up pink blossom petals from a nearby tree, so that they blow across the lawn. There is the sound of a man in the house just over the way drilling a window frame.

Burnett and Merchant (2020) draw on the Deleuzian notion of the event, in order to think about the multiple potentialities in any literacy event, including those that remain unrealised. Emphasising the way in which literacies are bound up in liveliness and fluidity and emerge relationally and in the moment, they describe literacy as event as containing "not just…what happened, but for what might have been, and in doing so accounts for potentialities" (p. 49). In the previous section, I described the rolling tunnel as an example of a multimodal story, albeit a tiny, easily overlooked one, which emerged between the tunnel, the wind, H, his surprise and his audience. In the vignette above, W's manipulation of the plastic hoops could perhaps have tipped into a similar kind of story. Yet somehow, this time, it did not. Burnett and Merchant's (2020) argument that literacies always exceed what it is possible to perceive enables a reconsideration of how "meanings get generated and settle" (p. 51). If representation or signification relies on the perception/interpretation of another, literacies are not only provisional in that they rely on in-the-moment emergence of gesture, vocalisation and so on (as described above) but also because they rely on the partial, situated and unsteady perception/interpretation of what meanings may or may not be bound up in these soundings and movements.

As I argue elsewhere (Hackett, forthcoming), "not literacies", that is, the things that remain provisional, that are not named and that do not tip into anything that can be read as multimodal meaning-making, need to remain closely involved in analysis of young children's language and literacy practices. Pahl and Rowsell (2020) have described this as the "not-yet of literacy" (p. 67), and Burnett and Merchant (2020) recommend "sensitising ourselves to potentialities" in order that we might "grasp not just what has happened but also what might happen" (p. 52). Each of these positions gestures towards a speculative mode of articulating literacy practices as more-than-human, emergent, fluid and provisional. In the final part of this chapter, I will take up this invitation, as I return to the opening provocation: the question of literacies for young children responding to and living well within an environmentally precarious and interdependent future.

9.5   Telling Speculative Stories About Literacies Yet to Come

Literacies yet to come are emergent, provisional and both actual and virtual, deeply entangled with the more-than-human world, and, as such, can teach us much needed lessons about interdependency of human and planetary survival (Common Worlds Research Collective, 2020). Such shifts in conceptualisations of interdependent survival, unthinking mastery and the role of literacy itself prompt literacy scholarship to extend beyond empirical research and fine-grained accounts of what seemed to (truly) unfold in the moment, in order to explore other modes of thinking that might gesture towards the multiple immanent possibilities for literacies yet to come. Scholars across the social sciences have explored speculative storytelling as a mode that allows us to "suspend disbelief about change" (Stirling et al., 2019) by disorientating or reframing our ideas about what is true (de Freitas & Truman, 2020). In the interests of unsettling literacies in order to respond to precarious futures, I argue that a speculative mode offers rich possibilities for future thinking.

One piece of writing that might work to formulate different questions about the future of young children's literacies is Le Guin's (1989) *The Carrier Bag Theory of Fiction*. Le Guin (1989) proposes that human's first tool was likely not the spear but "the carrier bag, the sling, the shell or the gourd" (p. 166), something to carry, share and distribute rather than conquer and kill. Showing how theories of human evolution (like theories of literacies) are entangled with colonialism, mastery and patriarchy, Le Guin critiques a "hero narrative" of hunter and spear, in which domination, individual success and "winning" are placed at the heart of the story of human survival (Leddy, 2019). Leddy (2019) points out "We have come to embrace the idea that a succession of one thing defeating another literally is history." Understandings of young children as developmental projects filled with potential for future success also rely on this narrative. Seductive and exciting as a story of "winning" is, it offers only a very partial account of what is involved in living well and thriving in and with the world. Moreover, it is an account plaited in with narratives of progress (Tsing, 2015), colonialism (Singh, 2018) and meritocracy.

However, there are also the messy, conflicted stories about how things unfold in the moment and the other ways of being that survive *in spite of* progress (Tsing, 2015). Harder to describe in words and without a clear purpose or logic, they might leave us adults, as supposed "educators", "professionals" or "experts", exposed and vulnerable. In addition, they might, like Roy's portal (2020), work to bring into sharp relief the way in which early literacy practices sit within the (unequally felt and distributed) logics and material conditions of young children's lives. *What would a carrier bag account of young children's language and literacy practices look like?* The increasing attention the field of literacy research has paid in recent years to those aspects of literacies that flicker provisionally in and out of view, emerging from more-than-human assemblages that do not rely on human mastery or predesigned outcomes, offers hopeful possibilities for the role literacy scholarship might play in liveable future worlds. Rebecca Solnit (2020) writes that, for those of us who are not sick or suffering, and not on the front line, our task is to try to understand this moment and what it might make possible. She offers us this metaphor, which might guide our hopes for literacy scholarship in the coming years:

> When a storm subsides, the air is washed clean of whatever particulate matter has been obscuring the view, and you can often see farther and more sharply than at any other time. When this storm clears, we may, as do people who have survived a serious illness or accident, see where we were and where we should go in a new light. (para. 16)

9.6   Coda

Young children's literacies are not always transparent, definite or easily abstractable from place, and perhaps this is not a bad thing. Such interdependent literacies indicate that the best response to living in an environmentally precarious future might not be a predesigned solution, or a challenge to be "won", but instead speak of the entanglement of human and planetary well-being across numerous scales (Common Worlds Collective, 2020). Thus, I have argued that paying attention differently to young children's literacy practices has important lessons to teach us about interdependency between human meaning-making and the more-than-human world.

For literacy educators and researchers, then, the question is not so much how to accelerate children's literacies as quickly as possible along a linear trajectory but to ask ourselves what mode of being in the world we wish to convey to young children and involve them in. I mentioned at the start of the chapter anxieties around children "falling behind" and "catching up" their learning as a result of COVID-19 and school closures. Perhaps, whilst the children of 2020 may be a little behind in relation to their school readiness and standardised test scores, this generation has learnt a much more valuable lesson. They have lived through and experienced, in an intense and embodied way, the way in which humans are not masters of their destiny. This lesson has not been easily learnt, and the price paid has fallen much too heavily on the shoulders of the most vulnerable children, in the form of physical harm and abuse, financial hardship, stress and bereavement (e.g. Marmot, 2020). As with many other examples of the impacts of environmental precarity and human/planetary interdependence, the most vulnerable and marginalised have suffered the most and paid the highest price. Attending to the unequal distribution and impact of precarity during, for example, COVID-19, and asking what we might learn from this about collective ways to live well with each other and the world might be a better use of educators' time and energies than continuing a commitment to a "catch up curriculum", revolving around the mastery of certain skills.

Looking towards a precarious future, in which inequalities will be brought into increasingly sharp relief and, yet at the same time, opportunities may present themselves to organise human life differently, along more socially just and less environmentally destructive lines, literacy scholarship needs to continue to ask:

1. *What ways of being in the world might enable children to thrive in "pockets of more-than-human livability?" (Tsing, 2015)*
2. *And what role might literacies play in enacting, valuing or making available, these ways of being?*

References

Abram, D. (1996). *The spell of the sensuous*. Vintage Books.

Alaimo, S. (2016). *Exposed. Environmental politics and pleasures in posthuman times*. University of Minnesota Press.

Avineri, N., Johnson, E., Heath, S., McCarty, T., Ochs, E., Kremer-Sadlik, T., Blum, S., et al. (2015). Invited forum: Bridging the "language gap". *Journal of Linguistic Anthropology, 25*(1), 66–86.

Best Beginnings, Home-Start UK, and the Parent-Infant Foundation, UK. (2020). *Babies in lockdown: Listening to parents to build back better*. Available: https://babiesinlockdown.info/download-our-report/

Beyer, R. M., Manica, A., & Mora, C. (2021). Shifts in global bat diversity suggest a possible role of climate change in theemergence of SARS-CoV-1 and SARS-CoV-2. *Science of the Total Environment*. https://doi.org/10.1016/j.scitotenv.2021.145413

Boldt, G. (2020). Theorizing vitality in the literacy classroom. *Reading Research Quarterly*. Online First.

Braidotti, R. (2013). *The posthuman*. Polity Press.

Burnett, C., & Merchant, G. (2020). Literacy-as-event: Accounting for relationality in literacy research. *Discourse: Studies in the Cultural Politics of Education, 41*(1), 45–56.

Burnett, C., Merchant, G., & Neumann, M. (2020). The appearance of literacy in new communicative practices: Interrogating the politics of noticing. *Cambridge Journal of Education, 50*(2), 167–183.

Butler, J. (2012). Precarious life, vulnerability, and the ethics of cohabitation. *Journal of Speculative Philosophy, 26*(2), 134–151.

Common Worlds Research Collective. (2020). *Learning to become with the world: Education for future survival.* Paper commissioned for the UNESCO Futures of Education report.

Compton-Lilly, C. (2016). Time in education: Intertwined dimensions and theoretical possibilities. *Time & Society, 25*(3), 575–593.

Dalke, A., Cassidy, F., Grobstein, K., & Blank, D. (2007). Emergent pedagogy: Learning to enjoy the uncontrollable—And make it productive. *Journal of Educational Change, 8*(2), 111–130.

De Freitas, E., & Truman, S. (2020). New empiricisms in the anthropocene: Thinking with speculative fiction about science and social inquiry. *Qualitative Inquiry.* Online first.

Finnegan, R. (2002). *Communicating. The multiple modes of human interconnection.* Routledge.

Flewitt, R. (2013). *Early literacy: A broader vision.* TACTYC occasional paper.

Gillen, J., & Hall, N. (2013). The emergence of early childhood literacy. In N. Hall, J. Larson, & J. A. Marsh (Eds.), *Handbook of early childhood literacy* (pp. 3–17). Sage.

Gurney, L., & Demuro, E. (2019). Tracing new ground, from language to languaging, and from languaging to assemblages: Rethinking languaging through the multilingual and ontological turns. *International Journal of Multilingualism.* Online first.

Hackett, A. (forthcoming). *More-than-human literacies in early childhood.* Bloomsbury.

Hackett, A., & Somerville, M. (2017). Posthuman literacies: Young children moving in time, place and more-than-human worlds. *Journal of Early Childhood Literacy, 17*(3), 374–391.

Jones, S., Thiel, J., Da'vila, D., Pittard, E., Woglom, J., Zhou, X., Brown, T., & Snow, M. (2016). Childhood geographies and spatial justice: Making sense of place and space-making as political acts in education. *American Educational Research Journal, 53*(4), 1126–1158.

Kress, G. (1997). *Before writing: Rethinking the paths to literacy.* Routledge.

Kuby, C. R., Gutshall Rucker, T., & Kirchhofer, J. M. (2015). 'Go Be a Writer!': Intra-activity with materials, time and space in literacy learning. *Journal of Early Childhood Literacy, 15*(3), 394–419.

Kuby, C., Thiel, J., & Spector, K. (Eds.). (2019). *Posthumanism and literacy education. Knowing/becoming/doing literacies.* Routledge.

Le Guin, U. (1989). *The carrier bag theory of fiction. In dancing at the edge of the world.* Grove Press.

Leddy, S. (2019). *We should all be reading more Ursula le Guin.* https://theoutline.com/post/7886/ursula-le-guin-carrier-bag-theory

MacLure, M. (2016). The refrain of the A-grammatical child: Finding another language in/for qualitative research. *Cultural Studies – Critical Methodologies, 16*(2), 173–182.

Marmot, M. (2020). Health equity in England: The Marmot review ten years on. *British Medical Journal, 368,* m693.

McKittrick, K. (2015). Yours in the intellectual struggle. In K. McKittrick (Ed.), *Sylvia Winter. On being human as praxis.* Duke University Press.

Pacini-Ketchabaw, V. (2012). Acting with the clock: Clocking practices in early childhood. *Contemporary Issues in Early Childhood, 13*(2), 154–160.

Pahl, K., & Rowsell, J. (2020). *Living literacies. Literacy for social change.* The MIT Press.

Powell, K. (2019). Walking as precarious public pedagogy. *Journal of Public Pedagogies*, Number 4. Guest Edited by WalkingLab.

Power, M. Page, G. Garthwaite, K., & Patrick, R. (2020). *COVID realities: Experiences of social security for families on a low income during the pandemic.* Centre for Household Assets and Savings Management, University of Birmingham, Briefing Paper BP15/2020. Available https://www.birmingham.ac.uk/documents/college-social-sciences/social-policy/chasm/briefing-papers/covid19/chasm-bp15-2020.pdf

Rautio, P. (2013). Children who carry stones in their pockets: On autotelic material practices in everyday life. *Children's Geographies, 11*(4), 394–408.

Rautio, P. (2019). Theory that cats have about swift louseflies: A distractive response. In C. Kuby, K. Spector, & J. Thiel (Eds.), *Posthumanism and literacy education. Knowing/becoming/doing literacies* (pp. 228–134). Routledge.

Roy, A. (2020). The pandemic is a portal. *Financial Times*. 3 April. Available online: https://www.ft.com/content/10d8f5e8-74eb-11ea-95fe-fcd274e920ca. Accessed 16 Oct 2020.

Schrader, A. (2012). The time of slime: Anthropocentrism in harmful algal research. *Environmental Philosophy, 9*(1), 71–94.

Singh, J. (2018). *Unthinking mastery. Dehumanism and decolonial entanglements.* Duke University Press.

Solnit, R. (2020). What Coronavirus can teach us about hope. *The Guardian.* 7 April. Available online: https://www.theguardian.com/world/2020/apr/07/what-coronavirus-can-teach-us-about-hope-rebecca-solnit

Somerville, M., & Murris, K. (forthcoming). Planetary literacies for the Anthropocene. In J. Z. Pandya, R. A. Mora, J. Alford, N. A. Golden, & R. S. deRoock (Eds.) (under contract, 2019). *The critical literacies handbook.* Routledge.

Somerville, M., & Powell, S. (2018). Thinking posthuman with mud: And children of the Anthropocene. *Journal of Educational Philosophy and Theory, 51*(8), 829–840.

Springgay, S., & Truman, S. E. (2019). Counterfuturisms and speculative temporalities: Walking research-creation in school. *International Journal of Qualitative Studies in Education, 32*(6), 547–559.

Stanley Robinson, K. (2020). The Coronavirus is rewriting our imaginations. *The New Yorker.* 1 May 2020. Available at https://www.newyorker.com/culture/annals-of-inquiry/the-coronavirus-and-our-future?utm_source=facebook&fbclid=IwAR2uQEmAbT-vL9iSctXoHaToIc0lmmSw1pcj28jQr-ykynzPYeeDmEXUtcM

Stirling, E., Billau, S., Batty, S., & Vallance, R. (2019). Textual interface: A design fiction. In G. Brooks, H. Harriss, & K. Walker (Eds.), *Interior futures.* Crucible Press.

Sundberg, J. (2014). Decolonizing posthumanist geographies. *Cultural Geographies, 21*(1), 33–47.

Tarc, A. (2015). Literacy of the other; The inner life of literacy. *Journal of Early Childhood Literacy, 15*(1), 119–140.

Todd, Z. (2016). An indigenous feminist's take on the ontological turn: 'Ontology' is just another word for colonialism. *Journal of Historical Sociology, 29*(1), 4–22.

Truman, S. (2019). Inhuman literacies and affective refusals: Thinking with Sylvia Wynter and secondary school English. *Curriculum Inquiry, 49*(1), 110–128.

Tsing, A. (2015). *The mushroom at the end of the World. On the possibility of life in capitalist ruins.* Princeton University Press.

Van Dooren, T. (2020). Pangolins and pandemics: The real source of this crisis is human, not animal. *NewMatilda.com.* 22 March. Available at https://newmatilda.com/2020/03/22/pangolins-and-pandemics-the-real-source-of-this-crisis-is-human-not-animal/?utm_campaign=shareaholic&utm_medium=facebook&utm_source=socialnetwork&fbclid=IwAR0zUIhZdM7wQ0qMfYI7aeci0NhaNdfm__H4WRLGlJrTyhAqVH8XyAMuCIk. Accessed 16 Oct 2020.

Viruru, R. (2001). Colonized through language: The case of early childhood education. *Contemporary Issues in Early Childhood, 2*(1), 31–47.

Zembylas, M. (2019). The ethics and politics of precarity: Risks and productive possibilities of a critical pedagogy for precarity. *Studies in Philosophy and Education, 38*(1), 95–111.

Chapter 10
Perplexities and Possibilities in Literacy Curriculum and Pedagogical Change: A Research Partnership and Experiment in Materialist Methodologies

Michelle A. Honeyford, Shelley Warkentin, and Karla Ferreira da Costa

Abstract Across the body of rich, ethnographic research in New Literacy Studies, there is a consistent and insistent call: for curriculum, pedagogy, and policy to substantiate the plurality and complexity of young people's everyday literacy practices and identities. As youth have shared access to their sociomaterial, digital, and transcultural worlds, literacy researchers have documented the highly sophisticated, inventive, participatory, and activist practices through which youth create, connect, disrupt, interrogate, and change—often outside of school and in rapidly evolving, elusive, or ephemeral ways. And while research has struggled to keep pace, educational systems have been particularly ill-equipped and slow to respond. So what happens when policy-makers attempt to shift literacy pedagogy and practice through a new K-12 English Language Arts curriculum framework that embraces a critical, multiliteracy approach? What research partnerships and methodological designs have the potential to be responsive to the entanglements and encounters of literacy curriculum, pedagogy, and practice across geographically, demographically, and ideologically diverse places and spaces and in the midst of unprecedented uncertainty and change? Through a multiyear research partnership including government, university researchers, school leaders, and practitioners, we explore the conceptual and methodological perplexities and possibilities that have emerged in experimenting with a materialist methodology and ontology (Fox & Alldred, 2015; Burnett & Merchant, 2018). With data collected through interviews, online surveys, and

M. A. Honeyford (✉) · K. Ferreira da Costa
University of Manitoba, Oxford, UK
e-mail: michelle.honeyford@umanitoba.ca

S. Warkentin
Seven Oaks School Division, Oxford, UK

© The Author(s), under exclusive license to Springer Nature Singapore Pte
Ltd. 2022
C. Lee et al. (eds.), *Unsettling Literacies*, Cultural Studies and
Transdisciplinarity in Education 15, https://doi.org/10.1007/978-981-16-6944-6_10

147

embedded focus groups, we describe the processes of diffractive inquiry and analysis (Barad, 2007; Murris & Bozalek, 2019) that have opened up new theoretical thresholds (Jackson & Mazzei, 2012) of inquiry in new literacy curriculum and pedagogy. We consider the material, embodied, and non-human forces that are caught up in the phenomena of curricular and pedagogical change, and we explore the tensions of "researching in the making"—the precarity of emplacing literacy research and pedagogy in a future open and undecided (Ellsworth, 2005).

Keywords Curriculum renewal · Diffractive methodology · Language arts pedagogy · Literacy practices · Professional knowledge · Collaborative research · Relational assemblage · Curricular positioning

Disrupting: "Projects Designed to Disrupt Normative Ideas About Literacy" (co-editors)

"to break apart, to rupture, to throw into disorder; to interrupt the normal course or unity" ("Disrupt", Merriam-Webster Online Dictionary, 2020)

We *(a team that has, over time, included curriculum writers, university professors and teacher educators, an international doctoral candidate, and two undergraduate researchers)*

designed *(a SSHRC grant proposal, drafts with track changes, ethics applications, interview questions, online surveys, processes of collaborative analysis)*

this *(abstract, research questions, consent letters, participant invitations, methods tables)*

project *(title and acronym, university and government logos, grant number, calendar dates, recurring Zoom meetings, CV line item)*

to *(purpose statement, rationale, progress reports, outcomes, research training plan)*

(explore, learn, better understand, examine)

disrupt *(not knowing what might happen)*

normative *(assumed values, deeply embedded, persistently stubborn, unquestioned, standardized, told, exclusive)*

ideas *(beliefs, programs, models, practices, assessments, schedules, budgets, priorities, evidence, improvement plans)*

about *(perspective, positioning, relationship, epistemologies)*

literacy *(which is when this exercise prompted me to write something else):*

Disrupting Literacy, This Project Designs

This writing and thinking experiment, on a Saturday morning, was fueled by three espressos/trips to the kitchen and a longing to be, not alone at my desk, but in the cozy local coffee shop, having snagged the best (and most worn) black pleather seats in the house, right next to the stone fireplace, as we would have done in pre-COVID days. Now, with the city in code red (the province's highest "critical level"), I was writing in/with a Google Doc alongside my notes from our last Zoom meeting. While not there with me physically, my colleagues and collaborators' voices, collected in wisps/fragments/utterances during our virtual conversation, became present with me—conjured as if turning the radio dial. The partiality of the written word only hinted at the narrative possibilities that, like everything with this project, defied easy/efficient/singular/predetermined structures/forms. "This curriculum has always been about disrupting," Shelley had said. "Yes!" I agreed, "but I don't think that story has been told; do you?"

A haptic buzz draws my attention to my wrist. Is it time to stand? Get a drink of water? I ignore it and then, in the next instant, give in to the second insistent pulse, pulling back my sleeve. The *New York Times* logo appears and fades, and then, when I tap, it alerts me in tiny white print to the breaking news: that Joe Biden has just been declared the winner of the presidential election in the United States. I am disrupted. This project of writing this chapter on a quiet morning is disrupted. Power has been unsettled through the democratic processes of an election—enacted, embodied, and questioned, in long lines of voters, days of counting, insolent threats and challenges, protests, and calls for patience. This, too, is curriculum, is pedagogy, and is method: is *ideas about literacy*.

Upon returning to this draft of a chapter, the brief narrative that has emerged on the screen, I wonder how I should proceed: Should I write about dancing in my living room, moved by a palpable sense of relief? How my eyes, exhausted from another week in front of the computer, welled up with the words of a tweet from a president-elect so different in tone from his predecessor? How I was moved again when I watched Kamala Harris, the first woman, the first Black American, and the first South Asian American to be elected vice president—disrupted in the midst of a Saturday morning run in the park—congratulating her political partner, smiling, affirming that they did it, that he will be the next president of the United States? Do I explore the network news commentators talking about the politics of a divided nation, the potential unrest from challenges to a winner being pronounced by media that for 4 years has been labeled as "fake news" and positioned as the enemy of the people? Do I attempt to somehow articulate, as I listen to those comparing this president and this election to others in history, all that is significant about this particular moment as I watch people donning face masks and coming together in Black Lives Matter Plaza?

"Forces/moving/acting and being acted upon." I come back to this phrase that I had written an hour earlier. It is still relevant; it is still helpful to think with. But it means something else now, something *more*. It produces and evokes new images, words, emotions, and moments. "Forces moving/acting" now includes people in the streets, electoral college numbers, and Twitter posts congratulating a president elect and firing an ousted leader. Power has shifted. Things are always on the move.

Disrupting Literacy, This Project Designs

Throughout this project, we have made a concerted effort to acknowledge the dynamic, constantly moving and changing nature of this research. We have resisted (maybe too insistently at times) the lure to theme/categorize, to reduce/condense, and to conclude, determine, or "find." This has slowed down our work, a project originally defined by the timelines of a 1-year grant. But we have been moved by different verbs: to probe, interrogate, question, unravel, complicate, follow, test/try out, play with, and wonder.

This was the commitment of our partners in the process of writing the ELA curriculum: that the renewing of the curriculum was about more than the writing of a document but about changing beliefs and practices about literacy and learning. Thus, time and space were allocated in the process for engaging with literacy research; multiple opportunities were created for participation, reflection, collaboration, and consultation; the format/contents of the curriculum grew from this process (not limited or constrained by predetermined forms); "implementation" was reimagined and supported through sustained, 3-year professional learning cohorts with geographical clusters of school divisions across the province; and the curriculum framework was not to be "done", finalized, printed, and delivered only to be quickly outdated again. It was developed in an interactive digital format, available online—a living document, designed to be revisited and updated over time.

That same commitment to open-ended process and possibility has been evident in our collaborative research practice. We have continued to work together, in some different iterations, as schedules allowed, over time. We have felt the pressure and temptation of an end date—to conclude, wrap up, report, and move on. The data we collected in the early days through interviews and focused research conversations during cohort sessions felt a little stale/dated/predictable at times, in part because of the deep understandings gained through the pilot project and consultations. It was tempting to summarize and represent what we thought we knew—the concerns, questions, understandings, and tensions at any point in time—and to declare the work "done"—ready to present, publish, and share with stakeholders and to inform the writing of the next grant application.

But like the curriculum itself, we knew such research would be quickly outdated. And there was a nagging awareness that what would be reflected in such research would be only what we could easily see, notice, anticipate, recognize, and know because we were already familiar with its shape and form. What was more interesting, alluring, challenging, defying, and potentially transformative was what was in the shadows—blurred, obscured, at the edges, only hinted at, or completely unknown. So we embraced a diffractive methodology (Barad, 2007; Mazzei, 2014; Murris & Bozalek, 2019), exploring and experimenting together with the data in different ways and over time, attentive to what would emerge (Burnett, Merchant, Neuman, 2020), and open to how it might surprise or confront us, lead us in new directions, or change us. We eschewed themes and embraced phenomena—complex, messy, and organic assemblages of literacy curriculum/pedagogy/research. We let go of clear results, outcomes, and products, and we became open to process, emergence, and newness.

Disrupting literacy—through exploring language arts curriculum, pedagogy, and research—*this project designs*. It has opened us to new possibilities, differences, discomforts, and unknowns. We were aware when we began that the curriculum, and our research, could be challenged by the results of a looming provincial election. An emerging curriculum could be easily revoked or revised unrecognizably, or its older/safer predecessor could be restored. We were also hearing rumors of plans to conduct an external review of the K-12 school system, the outcomes of which could include recommendations for significant organizational, budgetary, and assessment changes. We didn't anticipate that this work—and time—would see us through shifts in our employment/roles, would make possible an opportunity to collaboratively co-design and teach a university course, or would shape our interests and epistemologies as practitioners and researchers.

And of course, we could not fathom the depth and breadth and significant personal, professional, and systemic disruptions and loss of a pandemic, shutting down schools; launching us into emergency remote teaching and learning; making immense and intense demands on educators, administrators, and families; and highlighting again the disparities and inequities in our communities. We could not have predicted the global sweep and impact of the Black Lives Matter movement, the protests and strikes galvanizing students, communities, and educators in fighting anti-Black racism, anti-Indigenous racism, and all forms of systemic oppression in policy, policing, and practice. We did not know how schools would reopen, reallocating every inch of space by carefully measuring; marking with stickers, tape, and signs; rescheduling days to limit the number of students on campus, in the hallways, or at recess at any one time; redesigning highly social and interactive learning experiences with a goal of keeping safe distance and separation; reorganizing into cohorts to limit contact and allow for tracing; and rethinking how to engage students—both in person and online—while trying to build community and connections. We could not have foreseen the level of exhaustion, stress, and concern, nor the imaginative and creative responses of educators, parents, schools, and students.

In the context of these (and other) living/forces, it has become clear that while a curriculum is about creating something, it is always more. It is about becoming and doing something, finding ways to live out curriculum, pedagogy, and research in/with/against larger and, yes, often unknown, unpredictable, and unprecedented forces and flows. This project is, and simultaneously, is not about a document, a set of practices, or a list of findings. It is about finding how we wish to live, act, and be individually and together in our local and global contexts.

Disrupting Literacy, This Project Designs Even in writing this chapter, this project designs. In what follows, we are open to that design: the agency of curriculum, pedagogy, and research to disrupt what things "should" look like, be, or do and to write about what has happened when we have been open to the various ways that curriculum, pedagogy, and research have moved us.

10.1 Disrupting Curriculum: An Origin Story

An early Monday morning meeting request dinged on my phone late Sunday night after a busy weekend trip away. "We are going to adopt another jurisdiction's curriculum. You will need to decide which one." I wept. How easily the words seemed to roll off their tongues. The statement seemed so callous and uncaring. Others wondered why I took it so "personally," and it took some time for me to understand my emotional response to this request. Curriculum, to me, had to embody our lives, our identities, and our beings. It had to be a lived experience. It had to be ours. How could a curriculum, understood at that meeting as a document to be delivered, embrace the diverse voices, histories, stories, and experiences of our province?

Despite its inauspicious beginnings, this curriculum story became a story of collaboration, reimagining, and agency. That initial meeting launched our inquiry into what we really meant by curriculum; what its purpose, function, and audience were; and who decided. Previous curriculum journeys understood development and implementation as distinct processes, where a small number of educators engaged deeply and collaboratively in a design process and the majority of educators attended workshops to learn how to implement the new curriculum. We wondered how we might engage all educators more deeply in networked, reflective, and sustained processes and how we might learn from students, parents, and community members. Rather than "imposing already fully understood principles to specific examples", how might we encourage "specific examples, locales, communities of work and cultural realities to question, shape, and supplement (Gadamer, 1989, p. 39) those principles and to make them "fitting" for the circumstances of their application" (Jardine & Friesen, 2013, p. 5)?

Rather than working with a static group of people over time, this messier model drew in individuals and groups from across the province at different times and for different purposes. Each encounter provided new and unique perspectives, questions, and ways of thinking about curriculum, teaching, learning, and literacy. The conceptual framework that would guide our ongoing work emerged from these initial encounters. I recall one particular discussion about what was really at the center of our work in education. Myriads of frameworks, documents, and professional learning had imprinted a student-centered philosophy in Manitoba. This remained a strongly held belief, but questions arose about whether the student was truly alone at this center. Maybe it was community? Although placing community at the center of the framework seemed a small change, it was pivotal in helping us truly embrace Gadamer's notions while also expanding our understandings of what counts as literacy and who decides.

Another space was abuzz with educator talk about what it looks and sounds like when students are active members of communities of practice. Educators from northern, rural, and urban contexts, from Hutterite and independent schools, and from diverse linguistic and cultural backgrounds gathered to share snapshots from their lived experiences. These snapshots and ensuing discussions led us to explore concepts like social practices, literacy practices in land-based learning, leveraging plurilingualism in classroom contexts, multiple ways of knowing and seeing the world, and multiliteracies. Various groups continued these conversations with their own networks and noticed the idea of practice in their everyday lives, their communities, and their schools.

By examining what we really meant by curriculum, by placing community at the center of our framework, and by drawing from our own stories of practice, we began to shift our language and understandings. How might a curriculum embrace this idea of social practice? Could a focus on practice provide a richer, deeper, more holistic representation of literacies? How might this shift (away from objectives, outcomes, and standards and toward practices) affect how we talk about learning? About teaching? About assessment? Further inquiry with a range of educators helped build initial guiding principles. Rather than a set of rules to be followed, these principles were co-created and revised over time as we learned about how they lived and were shared in communities of practice. The guiding principles were designed to underpin learning design and support critical reflection and decision-making.

My colleague and I were sitting in a small windowless resource room that we called "the bunker." Chart paper hung from doors, shelves, and walls, covered with sticky notes and marked by arrows, circles, underlines, and colors to provide traces of thinking. Articles and books covered the tables. Teams of educators from various school divisions (teachers, principals, divisional consultants/coaches, and others) had been playing with the now named English language arts practices: *Language as Sense-Making*, *Language as System*, *Language as Exploration and Design*, and *Language as Power and Agency*. The teams had been co-designing rich learning experiences for students to meaningfully enact all four practices. Based on their close observations in the context of these experiences, teams had documented their questions, design decisions, noticings, and wonderings. Their critical reflections as curriculum-makers were now the focus of our days in the bunker, noticing, wondering, and analyzing their in-practice notes, turning to the current literature in curriculum, language, and literacies. We talked about the "what ifs" or the possibilities that may have yet been unseen. This in-practice curriculum work was emergent; it did not begin with a set of expectations (that could have limited imagination and possibility). Rather, descriptions of practice emerged from experiences. Initially, educators felt a lot of uncertainty ("How are we supposed to know what to do? How do we know if we are doing the right thing?"). Assessment (reporting, really) provided the biggest hurdle. We held fast to the slow, intentional, open-ended process despite our own trepidations and the pressure mounting to "provide the answers." Collaborative inquiry with groups in sustained, 3-year learning cycles allowed space to explore assessment, focusing on how students' literacy practices grow, deepen, and transform over time and across contexts. The teams we were supporting provided rich participatory ground for curriculum inquiry and design, as well as an openness to disrupt and deepen practice. Collective and dialogic, this work invited educators into experiential processes and flows of professional knowledge- and practice-in-the-making, evident in what we observed and heard in these days together.

Educators from various school divisions and very different contexts are listening intently to one another's processes for designing rich learning experiences (from initial conception to post-experience reflections). Diverse artifacts are strewn across the round tables, including in-action video clips on screens, teachers' notebooks of reflections, written plans, student work, anecdotal observations, and curated and annotated photo albums. Educators are noting powerful intentional and responsive design moves and juxtaposing these alongside evidence of student learning (i.e., observations, conversations, products, and processes). At one table, a teacher from a northern isolated community and a teacher from a suburban neighborhood at the southern edge of Winnipeg are in deep discussion about the ways that their designs centralize community and meaningful contexts. They are noticing and documenting the multiple ways that their learners enacted the practices in layered and authentic ways. At another table, a school principal is documenting a lively conversation about assessment, where teachers are working to articulate how they examine a body of evidence of learning in order to draw professional judgment. Yet another group is mapping out the intentional scaffolding decisions they made to support language and literacy development in the context of a rich learning experience. This is the work of curriculum-making: educators working together to theorize, interrogate, co-design, and reflect deeply on teaching and learning.

We continue to believe that "English language arts in Manitoba is conceived as a learning landscape that represents a space for pedagogical possibility" (Manitoba Education, 2019, p. 21). Curriculum design remains a living process as opposed to a stale document, enacted by cohorts of educators, inquiry groups, practicum partnerships, university courses, and research groups who continue to engage in envisioning, reimagining, and unsettling curriculum and literacies.

10.2   Disrupting Methodology: An Experiment

We designed several methods of data collection in various phases of this project: questions about literacy, curriculum, student learning, pedagogy, professional engagement, and assessment that we asked of educators through online surveys, embedded focus groups, and interviews. These are detailed in Appendix A. But the data and analysis we have engaged in/with have also encompassed *narratives* from our own teaching and learning experiences; *places*, like the too-cold gyms or too-warm church halls where we circulated among tables at cohort meetings or the outdoor learning center where we read transcripts in front of a roaring fire (at what became our last in-person "data analysis party"); *people*, like the educators who shared powerful teaching stories documented with videos, images, transcripts, and other evidence of student learning and engagement; *materials*, like the large bags that attended all our analysis meetings, stuffed with printed transcripts, highlighters, scissors, yarn, post-its, markers, and tape; *histories* of curriculum and literacy teaching experience shared in consultations by those whose names grace the inside cover of more than one provincial curriculum document; *digital artifacts*, like the project's Dedoose site, our many shared Google docs, or the provincial online ELA wiki, each with a rich and messy audit trail of collaborative interactions/changes/revisions that have contributed to this work over time; and the *affective* dimensions of this project, the anticipation of a morning devoted to collaborative conversation and analysis, the appreciation for the difference in insights and perspectives that would push us in our individual and collective understandings, and the anxiety felt at times when the project seemed to grow too large and unwieldy. These are all just part of what has become the research assemblage of this project.

In taking up a diffractive methodology (Barad, 2007; Mazzei, 2014; Murris & Bozalek, 2019), we embraced uncertainty, which, for government and school partners, was risky. This demanded time (it was not efficient); it was unconventional (and thus, perhaps, somewhat "suspect"); it would not guarantee a particular (predictable) outcome. Yet, such an approach aligned with the focus on process that had been important in the writing of the curriculum and in its ongoing implementation—a process that welcomed play, made time for reading literacy research and theory, made room for messiness and complexity, and valued relational engagement with difference, understanding the vastly different contexts in which/where curriculum intra-acts: stark contrasts in geography, demographics, socioeconomics, epistemologies, values about school, learning, language, and literacy.

Such an ethos was critical. It contributed to creating the conditions for us as a team to read about, engage with, and take up what felt like a radically new-yet-already-inherently-known-and-necessary material orientation to literacy, curriculum, and practice as emerging in activity across spatiotemporal scales (Canagarajah, 2018). Our strategic and ongoing attunement to the data encompassed the agents and resources of our—and our participants'—space/matter/environments, producing research assemblages (Fox & Alldred, 2015; Coleman & Ringrose, 2013; Masny, 2013) comprised of "the bodies, things and abstractions that get caught up in social inquiry, including the events that are studied, the tools, models and precepts of research, and the researchers" (Fox & Alldred, 2015, p. 400). The methodological ethos of the research assemblage was also always (a) highly collaborative, (b) theoretically relational, and (c) attentive to what it produced—interconnected qualities which have generated and sustained our wonder (MacLure, 2013) in the unfolding encounters with the data and our engagement with curricular and pedagogical change over time and which have continuously disrupted any predilection for predictable patterns in data analysis.

A highly collaborative ethos in this project was generated through shared purpose, established relationships, trust, and an appreciative stance for what happened when we—and our sociospatial repertoires, both human and material (Canagarajah, 2018)—came together. With research being a part-time and/or (for some of us) a voluntary endeavor, sustaining a highly collaborative ethos has not been easy nor altogether successful. The ethos has thrived when this project has been the focus of our time and attention, generally in spurts and particularly over the summer. But even when dormant—our research activities temporarily suspended or slowed down—it has been present in its connections to our everyday practices as educators, learners, and researchers. Our collaboration—in this project and in our other related and interconnected relationships as colleagues, co-teachers, invited speakers, professor/graduate student, and advisor/student—has brought us together in different configurations and purposes over time, and that work, even if not directly connected, has added epistemological, ontological, and ethical layers and nuances to our relations with one another and with this project.

The work of analyzing data, for instance, was the focus of designated days we all fiercely guarded on our calendars and looked forward to—gathering in different places as we took turns hosting one another. But these meetings were supported by data analysis engaged in by groups within the team: for example, the sustained and ongoing dialogue of doctoral and undergraduate researchers working together in Dedoose, connecting (via Zoom, more recently) to read/engage/think with data in half-day sessions twice a week and in weekly extended meetings with the PI. And, as that was happening, our government and school division partners were facilitating professional learning, supporting teams in curriculum inquiry, or, in other instances, hosting consultation meetings to review curriculum pieces in development (with some of us around the table). The various positions and roles we have taken up with the curriculum, data, and one another have sparked ongoing reengagement with the project—layered in the textures of different experiences, narratives, and examples that have added depth and complexity to what has emerged (in the curriculum, in practice, and in this research). This has not been without its challenges: we enter (and reenter) this work at any one time from disparate places/spaces and with divergent priorities or concerns. At times, the differences in our positionalities and experiences—with the curriculum, as researchers, as teachers in K-12 classrooms, or as theorists, or in our understandings of diverse Manitoban communities—have prompted questions that could have been easily dismissed as irrelevant to, or potentially derailing the work, sidetracking the group's goals or hijacking precious time from the days we valued so highly. But the team consistently engaged and probed these ruptures, and it was often in the sharing of stories, experiences, concepts, theories, or histories—and their unexpectedness in those conversations, sometimes—that we also grew to appreciate the complexity of the work and the diversity of perspectives encountered through it, both in the room and in the data.

The methodological ethos of this project has been relational, then, not only in our practices of reading data with theoretical "texts in hand" (as crucial as that has been) but also as a product of grappling with the data together. Our collective entanglement with theories and beliefs encompassed our diverse personal and professional networks (in urban, rural, and northern communities in the province, as well as several international contexts), drew upon our different cultural and linguistic ways of knowing, and produced divergent responses, depending upon what resonated with or challenged our intersectional identities and experiences.

Our working spaces have also made room for the relational work of sharing and respecting the personal and professional concerns that enter into such spaces over time—caregiving of parents and children, navigating the competing needs and expectations of complex roles, and responding to the problems and issues of the day that sometimes wrested our attention somewhere else. Even in—and sometimes because of—the constant change and uncertainty of these times, this work has continued to call us to (at)tend to it because it is relevant, necessary, and important. It captures our pedagogical imaginations with possibilities of what could be. It is insistent and incessant in its calls for systemic change, equity, and epistemological justice. It has been at work changing us, our ways of thinking about teaching and learning, power, and agency.

And for all these reasons, it has been important to pay attention to and document what is being produced. Our intentions in this research project have always been about being open to possibility, difference, and newness. We have not wanted, nor been able, to predict/know/see in advance what might be relevant, what might move us, or where this could go. That is not to say that we have not given considerable time, thought, and attention to research design but that we have been intentional in our methodological stance and commitments to the "what else": What else happens? What else appears? What else is made possible? What else is negated or excluded as a result? What else needs to be considered? A "what else" stance encompasses the relationality in literacy research that is theorized so well in Burnett and Merchant's (2018) reconceptualization of "literacy as event" as:

> a generative heuristic to work with. Rather than using event to explore the social situated-ness of literacy as located in time and space, our conceptualisation of literacy-as-event rests on three related ideas: (1) event is generated as people and things come into relation; (2) what happens always exceeds what can be conceived and perceived; and (3) implicit in the event are multiple potentialities, including multiple possibilities for what might materialise as well as what does not. (p. 49)

In approaching literacy research as relationally generative, as excessive beyond what we can conceive and perceive, and as inherently multiple in potential and possibility, we have been pushed over and over again to the "threshold between knowing and unknowing" (MacLure, 2013, p. 228). At times, this has been the most frustrating facet of this work—recognizing that there is always more beyond our knowledge and reach and that we may not ever be any closer to naming or knowing it—but it has also been the most rewarding aspect of engaging in this work collectively, in the ways that the excessive multiplicity continues to push us beyond what we already know, think, and believe. This has been a generative space for producing new questions, playing with new ideas, and discovering new tools and environments that afford both tentative and more sustained creative and collaborative activity. In these coming-togethers, more has been produced: analytic memos encompassing multiple forms (digital files, notebooks, post-its, index cards, Google Docs), audio and video recordings of meetings and conversations, and physical and digital folders of artifacts and photos—of drawings, annotated data, poetry, material creations, etc. and always, more questions.

Disrupting Literacy, This Project Designs

Our struggle then was what to do with what had been generated: What would "move the experiment forward" (Murris & Bozalek, 2019, p. 1505) into dialogue in other spaces, with other audiences, and into pedagogy and practice? How could our work, and that of our participants, stay relevant, oriented "towards what things do, rather than what they 'are'; towards processes and flows rather than structures and stable forms; to matters of power and resistance; and to interactions that draw small and large relations into assemblage" (Fox & Alldred, 2015, p. 407)?

Figure 10.1 is one attempt to move the experiment forward, a visual prompt to consider the processes and flows, power and resistance, and the small and large relations of materials, bodies, places, and abstractions that come together to create

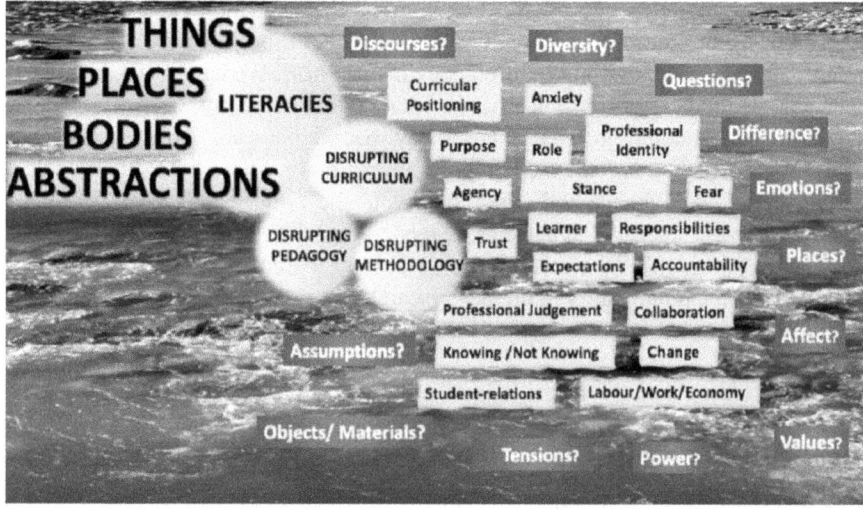

Fig. 10.1 An experiment: prompting relational assemblage analysis

phenomena related to curricular and pedagogical change in literacy and language arts. In exploring these phenomena in our data, Feely's (2020) questions have been helpful:

1. What disparate components, forces, or relations make up the phenomenon?
2. What semiotic/discursive flows, material flows, and social flows can be mapped? How do assemblages enable or constrain flows in certain directions?
3. What processes regulate and normalize/stabilize and maintain order? What processes enable subversion and new relations/destabilize and allow for change, creativity, and novelty?

This inquiry process has generated questions (notated with question marks in Fig. 10.1) both emerging from and applied to the components, forces, and relations making up these phenomena; the mapping of semiotic/discursive, material, and social flows; and exploration of the processes that territorialize/deterritorialize. In relation to the visual, the flow of water through/over/against/around rock emphasizes the dynamic movement of phenomena, the coming together of the material, human, nonhuman, concepts, and places in literacy curriculum, practice, and research in different ways, always producing something new.

10.3   Disrupting Practice: An Example

The ELA curriculum framework document begins by stating its purposes, which are to:

- "support, nurture, and inspire the learning growth of all learners."
- "provide direction for learning design and assessment."
- "set out the philosophical and pedagogical foundations for English language arts learning."
- "present the four English language arts *practices* and their characterizing *elements*."
- "describe the multiple ways that students engage in practices at various points in learning"; and to "encourage educators and learners 'to engage in vital, rigorous, and venturous forms of pedagogy'. (Jardine and Friesen 4)" (Manitoba Education, 2019, p. 1)

The introduction concludes by emphasizing that "shifts in curriculum design and growing knowledge related to changing educator practice" require "networked, connected, and emergent processes" of professional learning and change "that engage educators deeply and in sustained ways in conversation, reflection, and action" (p. 2). As noted in the curriculum narrative told earlier, the writers resisted the industrial model of implementing change by unilaterally imposing "already fully understood principles" but encouraged and expected that sites, "locales, communities of work and cultural realities" would "question, shape, and supplement (Gadamer, 1989, p. 39) those principles" in and for their contexts (p. 2).

Thus, right from the beginning, the ELA curriculum framework positions teachers as "called upon to interpret and live out curriculum" (Manitoba Education, 2019, p. 6), for example, by engaging in ongoing professional inquiry into their teaching and learning, by designing meaningful and venturous forms of pedagogy with their students, and by critically questioning, shaping, and contributing to the curriculum informed by their epistemic knowledge of students, families, and communities. Curricular positioning, then, encompasses a host of things, places, bodies, and abstractions that come together in relation to interpreting and living out curriculum. These include individual and shared histories and experiences with language and literacy across lifetimes and generations, inclusive of the memories and emotions connected to literacy agency and identity (Williams, 2018) as readers and writers, speakers and listeners, viewers, and representers (in English and in other languages, semiotic systems, and modalities). How curriculum is interpreted and lived out is shaped by biographical narratives of literacy, language, and learning in and outside of school; by experiences that have affirmed, questioned, or negated students' and communities' linguistic and cultural identities; and by the extent to which students and communities have seen themselves and their knowledge reflected in, distorted by, or missing from texts, classrooms, and curriculum.

In this project, curricular positioning references the "institutional, geopolitical and social relations in which we are [all] embedded" (Mukherjee, 2017, p. 292): those that shape our interpretations and enactment of curriculum as researchers and the relations of all those referenced in this work (e.g., teachers, consultants, literacy coaches, students, administrators, parents, policy-makers). All are situated (Haraway, 1991) by curriculum "within particular socio-spatial dynamics of domination and subordination" (Mukherjee, 2017, p. 292); all "embody a particular politics of location (Rich 1986)...always already multiply constituted by their specific place, cultural and social roles, and experiences" (Mukherjee, 2017, p. 292).

Thus, in this project, we find ourselves "troubling positionality", theorizing and analyzing curricular positioning as a complex phenomenon of disparate components, forces, and relations, heeding Mukherjee's (2017) call to restructuring "conventional analysis of positionality" through more "highly contingent" and "relational understandings" (p. 292). As we pose questions about curricular positioning in relationship to interpreting and living out curriculum, we have seen the "manner in which these multiple and shifting positionalities emerge at particular points" but also how they "cannot be predicted" (Mukherjee, 2017, p. 293). In this work, positionality, too, is open to being disrupted by discursive, material, and social flows, by engaging with things, places, bodies, and abstractions of curriculum that make it possible to see teaching and learning as "relational and unstable process[es]" (Mukherjee, 2017, p. 296). In our research, then, we have been interested in curricular positioning as a phenomenon that can draw our attention to processes that maintain and stabilize particular curricular positions, for example, as a consequence of "a superiority of knowledge" that "preempts" pedagogies "for knowledge in the making" (Ellsworth, 2005, p. 94) but also to positionings that disrupt epistemic certainties and superiorities, affording literacy pedagogies where new relations are possible.

Disrupting Literacy, This Project Designs
Taking a critical material and ontological view of curricular positioning opens up possibilities "to gain new understandings and insights as to who we can become" (Kincheloe, 2006, p. 182). What, then, we might ask, is produced in the process of breaking "up closed circuits of exchange of ideas, identities, and practices inside education" (Ellsworth, 2005, p. 97)? What is disrupted and unsettled? What new intensities and potentialities emerge? This project has constantly reminded us as practitioners and researchers to "ask questions about ethics, morality, politics, emotion, and gut feelings, seeking not precise steps to reshape our subjectivit[ies]" (Kincheloe, 2006, p. 182) but new relations in and through which to engage the full, messy, and real material, social, and discursive perplexities and possibilities of literacy curriculum, pedagogy, and research.

10.4   Coda

> Instead of trying to manage and control a relation that is uncontrollable, we might ask: What might we learn from ways of teaching that are predicated, paradoxically, on the impossibility of teaching? (Ellsworth, 1997, p. 9)

We have shared a story, an experiment, and an example. These are incomplete and unfinished; there is always more. As this project and the process of writing this chapter have reminded us, "Literacy in the making matters" (Ehret, Hollett, & Jocius, 2016, p. 372). Burnett and Merchant (2018) point out that such a perspective "invites literacy research to focus more on the relations mediated through the process of making meaning" (p. 52). In focusing on the relations and what they produce while looking at literacy curriculum, pedagogy, and research, as a team, we tried to engage making meanings (plural), with a growing appreciation—and expectation—that those meanings "can and often do [did] turn out in unexpected ways" (Burnett & Merchant, 2018, p. 52). As we dove in "what else" we could see/understand/discuss/read/reflect about/do, unexpected ways of understanding and doing curriculum, pedagogy, and research emerged.

That has also been part of our experience here, in the writing of this chapter: in exploring the disruptive production of curriculum, methodology, and pedagogy, new forces have been felt and become visible, forces "ontologically prior to curriculum", forces "out of which curriculum itself emerges", and forces that put up "something new to thought" (Rajchman, 2000a, p. 44, as cited in Ellsworth, 2005, p. 12). Such disruption and unsettling prompts different ways of knowing and being, learning that is made possible when "curriculum/teaching theory and practice" are no longer "divided into 'separate domains'" (Ellsworth, 2007, p. 81) but where learning and research are open to uncertainty, to "falling into relation with the world and others," where "collaborative research and collaborative yearnings" would be generated and "processes of change, exchange, invention, and relationality would rise to the top of things to become very curious about as researchers" (Ellsworth, 2007, p. 81).

As this project continues to design and disrupt, we engage with curiosity in inquiries related to the possibilities, vulnerabilities, and unpredictabilities of practices in the making, in questions "whose answers can only be put together in emergent practices—in vulnerable, on-the-ground work" (Haraway, 2003, p. 3). This necessitates a shift in expectations in the everyday "doing" of practice and its goals. It requires getting in the mud, seeing how things look from unexpected angles, and sniffing out a wide range of possible directions. "On-the-ground" practice is deeply relational and locational, rhizomatically rooted in community and place, revealing the interconnectedness and interdependence of all things, always moving and growing, never complete. As practices-in-the-making, literacy curriculum and pedagogy are simultaneously grounded in our being and becoming in the midst of particular times, places, ideas, and events but also always reaching beyond where we are (Greene, 1995, p. 93) through practice "that cobbles together nonharmonious agencies and ways of living that are accountable both to their disparate histories and to their barely possible but absolutely necessary joint futures" (Haraway, 2003, p. 3).

Disrupting literacy (*complacency, certainty, control*), this project designs (*imagines, invites, includes, affects*). The complexities of teaching and learning literacies in a world marked by constant and profound changes in the ways we communicate, interact, and relate to each other continually unsettle literacy practices. Elections, movements, and pandemics serve to illustrate that "no vision, narrative, or plan can anticipate or perform the work of remaking knowledge in the moment" (Ellsworth, 2005, p. 149). Now more than ever, we are uncertain about the future of things, nature, and people. Our communities and world continue to be challenged by racism and oppression of all kinds, by poverty and inequity, and by the ongoing effects of climate change. As our questions become more complex, there is a need for curriculum, research, and pedagogy that envision and welcome contingencies, perplexities, and possibilities, which are open to the incompleteness of educational projects that encompass the always unfinished and relational work of learning and living.

Funding Information This Research in Renewing Literacies project is supported in part by funding from the Social Sciences and Humanities Research Council.

This research (Research in Renewing Literacies, Protocol **#E2018:041 (HS21759)** was approved by a University of Manitoba Research Ethics Board (REB). The Research Ethics Boards are consituted and operate in accordance with the current Tri-Council Policy.

Statement: Ethical Conduct for Research Involving Humans.

Expiry: May 7, 2022

Appendix: Data Sources

Phase 1	Phase 3	Phase 3
Online surveys	Interviews and focus groups	Online surveys
Educators across the province were invited to participate in the online surveys, designed to better understand educators' relationship with curriculum in their understandings of literacy and language arts and in their pedagogical decision making, and intended to gauge teachers' familiarity and use of the new ELA curriculum framework document. Due to a government media black-out period in advance of an unanticipated provincial election, the survey was delayed until late in the school year, so we conducted the survey twice: once in line and again in early Fall Invitations to participate m the survey were extended through the wiki. listservs, and at both provincial ELA conferences. While the number of respondents was relatively small (81), the data was representative of the province geographically (urban, rural northern), and of school and professional demographics (school levels, teaching experience).	One hour, open ended interviews were conducted with those who volunteered through the online survey and those who had participated in piloting the new curriculum. The interviews (8) were held with literacy leaders as schools/divisions around the province, with a range of participation/ experience with the new curriculum. The focus groups were embedded in day-long professional learning sessions with teams from school divisions across the province who were participating in three year sustained professional learning cycles with the new curriculum. Throughout the day, table groups participated in timed, recorded conversations in response to questions about curriculum, student learning and assessment, instructional decision-making and professional learning. About 170 participated in these conversations, representing a range of schools and divisions	In our roles as researchers—and as a school division administrator, faculty advisor (to teacher candidates in practicum placements), as parents, curriculum specialists, and pre- and in-service teacher educators—we were interested in how educators were making pedagogical decisions: What were their goals/motives/hopes for students' learning and engagement? Had any of their thinking about the curriculum changed? Since this was an unplanned research activity, we applied for an amendment to our ethics application for an online survey, sent out to educators through the provincial ELA wiki and listservs. Survey responses were collected from 64 educators.

References

Barad, K. (2007). *Meeting the universe halfway: Quantum physics and the entanglement of matter and meaning*. Duke University Press.

Burnett, C., & Merchant, G. (2018). Literacy-as-event: Accounting for relationality in literacy research. *Discourse: Studies in the Cultural Politics of Education, 41*(1), 45–56.

Burnett, C., Merchant, G., & Neumann, M. (2020). The appearance of literacy in new communicative practices: Interrogating the politics of noticing. *Cambridge Journal of Education, 50*(2), 167–183.

Canagarajah, S. (2018). Materializing 'competence': Perspectives from international STEM scholars. *The Modern Language Journal, 102*(2), 268–291.

Coleman, R., & Ringrose, J. (2013). Introduction. In R. Coleman & J. Ringrose (Eds.), *Deleuze and research methodologies* (pp. 1–22). Edinburgh University Press.

Ehret, C., Hollett, T., & Jocius, R. (2016). The matter of new media making. *Journal of Literacy Research, 48*(3), 346–377.

Ellsworth, E. (1997). *Teaching positions: Difference, pedagogy, and the power of address*. Teachers College Press.

Ellsworth, E. (2005). *Places of learning: Media, architecture, pedagogy*. Routledge.

Ellsworth, E. (2007). "What might become?" What might become thinkable and do-able if we stop treating curriculum/teaching theory and practice as separate domains of academic research? *Journal of Curriculum and Pedagogy, 4*(1), 80–83.

Feely, M. (2020). Assemblage analysis: An experimental new-materialist method for analyzing narrative data. *Qualitative Research, 20*(2), 174–193.

Fox, N., & Alldred, P. (2015). New materialist social inquiry: Designs, methods and the research-assemblage. *International Journal of Social Research Methodology, 18*(4), 399–414.

Greene, M. (1995). *Releasing the imagination: Essays on education, the arts, and social change*. Jossey-Bass.

Haraway, D. (1991). *Simians, cyborgs, and women: The reinvention of nature*. Routledge.

Haraway, D. (2003). *The companion species manifesto: Dogs, people, and significant otherness*. Prickly Paradigm Press.

Jackson, A. Y., & Mazzei, L. A. (2012). *Thinking with theory in qualitative research: Viewing data across multiple perspectives*. Routledge.

Jardine, D. W., Clifford, P., & Friesen, S. (2006). *Curriculum in abundance*. Lawrence Erlbaum.

Kincheloe, J. (2006). Critical ontology and indigenous ways of being: Forging a postcolonial curriculum. In *Curriculum as cultural practice* (pp. 181–202). University of Toronto Press.

MacLure, M. (2013). Researching without representation? Language and materiality in post-qualitative methodology. *International Journal of Qualitative Studies in Education, 26*(6), 658–667.

Manitoba Education. (2019, October). *English language arts curriculum framework: A living document*. Manitoba Education.

Masny, D. (2013). Rhizoanalytic pathways in qualitative research. *Qualitative Inquiry, 19*, 339–348.

Mazzei, L. A. (2014). Beyond an easy sense: A diffractive analysis. *Qualitative Inquiry, 20*(6), 742–746.

Merriam-Webster. (n.d.). Disrupt. In *Merriam-Webster.com dictionary*. Retrieved November 30, 2020, from https://www.merriam-webster.com/dictionary/disrupt

Mukherjee, S. (2017). Troubling positionality: Politics of "studying up" in transnational contexts. *The Professional Geographer, 69*(2), 291–298.

Murris, K., & Bozalek, V. (2019). Diffracting diffractive readings of texts as methodology: Some propositions. *Educational Philosophy and Theory, 51*(14), 1504–1517.

Williams, B. (2018). *Literacy practices and perceptions of agency: Composing identities*. Routledge.

Chapter 11
Engaging DIY Media-Making to Explore Uncertain and Dystopic Conditions with 2SLGBTQ+ Youth and Allies in New Brunswick, Canada

Casey Burkholder, Funké Aladejebi, and Jennifer Thompson

Abstract Dystopias—societies organized around deep inequalities—have existed in the context of Atlantic Canada since colonization. In this article, we seek to center the concept of dystopia as an important sphere of inquiry through participatory visual research with six 2SLGBTQ+ young people (14–17) in Fredericton, New Brunswick, Canada. Using an intersectional lens (Crenshaw, 1989), we consider how intersecting power structures—gender, race, class, and disability—produce unequal impacts in relation to social and reproductive justice issues in Atlantic Canadian contexts. In this paper, we highlight DIY media-making—as a multiliteracy practice—with 2SLGBTQ+ youth to explore social and reproductive justice. As early as 1994, Julian Sefton-Green and David Buckingham wrote about the importance of acknowledging the situated nature of people's local literacy practices and of examining the ways that people make meaning through multiple texts in order to instigate social change. Other scholars working within a multiliteracy framework (see, e.g., Barton and Hamilton, Literacy practices. In Barton D, Hamilton M, Ivanic R (eds) Situated literacies: theorizing reading and writing in context. Routledge, pp 25–32, 2005; Rowsell J and Pahl, The Routledge handbook of literacy studies. Routledge, 2015) argue that an understanding of multiliteracies includes modes of processing, producing, analyzing, and meaning-making. Centering 2SLGBTQ+ youth agency, we position DIY media-making as a multiliteracy practice through stencil production and drawing. Through a close reading of three youth-produced images, and an interdisciplinary inquiry into dystopias present and future, we seek to make visual an ethical place of belonging among the dystopic.

C. Burkholder (✉)
Faculty of Education, University of New Brunswick, Fredericton, NB, Canada
e-mail: casey.burkholder@unb.ca

F. Aladejebi
Department of History, University of Toronto, Toronto, ON, Canada

J. Thompson
Center for Public Health CReSP, University of Montréal, Montreal, QC, Canada

© The Author(s), under exclusive license to Springer Nature Singapore Pte Ltd. 2022
165
C. Lee et al. (eds.), *Unsettling Literacies*, Cultural Studies and Transdisciplinarity in Education 15, https://doi.org/10.1007/978-981-16-6944-6_11

Keywords 2SLGBTQ+ · DIY · Dystopia · Participatory visual research · New Brunswick · Youth

11.1 Introduction

> I did watch the world burn. Say nothing to me of innocent bystanders, unearned suffering, heartless vengeance…Well, some worlds are built on a fault line of pain, held up by nightmares. Don't lament when those worlds fall. Rage that they were built doomed in the first place (Jemison, 2017, p. 6)

Dystopias—societies organized around deep inequalities—exist in the context of Atlantic Canada as a reflection of ongoing processes of colonization. Interested in thinking about dystopia as a way to challenge deep-rooted inequalities, in this chapter, we take up Jemison's call not to be bystanders and to activate around the injustices we are witnessing and experiencing, even as the futures we work toward are uncertain. Current research paradigms for studying dystopia are often founded upon and limited by values and assumptions from the past and present and limited by the supposed certainty of the neoliberal status quo. As Godhe and Goode (2017) explained, "our capacity to imagine alternative futures has seemingly atrophied over more than two decades of neoliberal hegemony: 'capitalist realism' (Fisher, 2009) has meant persuading citizens that there is no alternative to the onward march of globalized markets, finance capitalism, deregulation and environmental degradation" (p. 3). In some ways, we know for certain that existing conditions are dystopic, and yet, this very condition creates disproportionate uncertainties and precarities for certain people and groups. We see a tension in thinking through dystopia as it seems simultaneously tied to both certainty and uncertainty. In this context, and with the need to find ways to disrupt this atrophy and imagine alternative futures, we turn to the social justice possibilities around literacies as creative and political acts (Freire & Macedo, 1987) amidst uncertainty. We suggest that expanded ideas around literacy and literacies, such as The New London Group's (1996) pedagogy of multiliteracies, offer transformative paradigms for studying dystopia in ways that acknowledge the multitextual, multimodal, and multilingual environments in which we learn and enact change. We explore dystopia as an important sphere of opening up inquiry in order to dismantle what seems normal, accepted, and inevitable.

In particular, we take up participatory visual methodologies to unsettle the concept of dystopia with 2SLGBTQ+—two spirit, lesbian, gay, bisexual, transgender, queer, and the plus refers to the gender identities and sexualities that are not represented by the terms "2SLGBTQ"—youth and ally-preservice teachers in Fredericton, New Brunswick, Canada. With the ongoing structural oppression of 2SLGBTQ+ folks, the past experiences, present concerns, and imagined and uncertain futures of 2SLGBTQ+ youth matter for dystopic inquiry and create openings within and around existing precarities. We propose that responding to dystopic conditions through participatory visual research, described in this chapter as drawing and stencil production, with 2SLGBTQ+ youth and allies, offers a type of DIY (do it yourself) multiliteracy media-making practice for social change (Mitchell & Burkholder, 2015; Stuart & Mitchell, 2013). Working within a research for social change framework (Mitchell et al., 2017) and through DIY media production, we seek ways not just to study phenomena but also to actively transform what we are studying and living.

We write together as three early career female scholars—one Black (Funké) and two White[1] (Casey and Jen)—who have been working together to think through the ways in which systems and structures reflect dystopic conditions that have long been in place in New Brunswick, Canada—unceded and unsurrendered Wolastoqiyik, Mi'kmaq, and Passamaquoddy territory. Our larger project, *Exploring Dystopia with Youth: Confronting Unsustainable Futures Through Participatory Visual Inquiry into the Past and Present*, explores dystopic conditions in Atlantic Canada, past, present, and future, with a focus on how DIY multiliteracies and participatory visual research methods might be harnessed to explore intersections between various forms of injustice across categories of race, gender, and reproductive health and environment. Attending to the embeddedness of historic and ongoing legacies of slavery and colonialism, alongside exploitative and extractive practices of late-stage capitalism (Preston, 2017), we explore dystopias through DIY media-making, with a focus on power and how youth navigate existing dystopic structures. Contributing to the areas of education and Canadian youth studies (Chen et al. 2017), we are interested in how the concept of dystopia is enacted in access to reproductive and health care and how dystopic conditions already exist and create disproportionate uncertainties and precarities for racialized, gendered, and economically marginalized bodies and communities.

We focus our inquiry in this chapter on a DIY stencil and drawing production workshop with three queer, trans, and nonbinary youth and three youth allies (aged 14–25) in Fredericton, New Brunswick Canada, which sought to address dystopic conditions in education and healthcare systems for queer, trans, and nonbinary people. Julian Sefton-Green and David Buckingham (1994) wrote about the importance of acknowledging the situated nature of people's local literacy practices and examining the ways that people make meaning through multiple texts in order to instigate social change or take action (see also The New London Group, 1996). Other scholars working within a multiliteracy framework (see, e.g., Barton & Hamilton, 2005; Rowsell & Pahl, 2015) argue that an understanding of multiliteracies includes multiple modes of processing, producing, analyzing, and meaning-making.

Centering youth agency, we disrupt the notion that young people are disengaged consumers of media and position youth as knowledge producers through participatory visual and DIY methods of inquiry, including stencil production (Burkholder & Thorpe, 2019) and drawing (Literat, 2013). In this chapter, we highlight the

---

[1] Drawing on the activism and scholarship of Eve Ewing (2020), we explicitly capitalize Black and White as the "seeming invisibility [of Whiteness] permits White people to move through the World without ever considering the fact of their Whiteness…White people get to be only normal, neutral, or without any race at all" (para. 8).

importance of DIY stencil production practices with youth as openings to imagine alternative ways to create community and belonging in ways that embrace gender-inclusive youth resistance to reproductive injustice in New Brunswick, Canada. To address these objectives, we ask two sets of research questions: (1) When faced with uncertain and dystopic conditions in relation to gender-affirming health care, how do young people respond through stencil production and drawings? Here, we understand gender-affirming care as "the processes through which a healthcare system cares for and supports an individual, while recognizing and acknowledging their gender identity and expression" (BC Nurses' Union, 2016, p. 2). How might engaging in media production with young people and sharing these productions in digital communities work to counter dominant forms of apathy and denial and support youth to claim a stake in creating solidarities, belonging, and community-making in contexts of uncertainty? With 2SLGBTQ+ youth and allies, through an inquiry into dystopias past and present, we seek to make visual an ethical place of belonging amidst dystopic precarities, to define our understanding of stencil production as a DIY multiliteracy practice for social change, and to imagine our work in solidarity in the face of unsustainable and uncertain reproductive and gender-inclusive health-care futures.

11.2   Context

The workshop we highlight in the chapter took place in September 2019 in Fredericton, New Brunswick, Canada.[2] Our work first considers how the colonization of the Wabanaki Confederacy—Atlantic Canada—disrupted and outlawed existing structures of gender and sexual diversity as a strategy to oppress and colonize existing nations and peoples within this territory (Reid, 2019). This colonization is extensive and ongoing, enacted through state structures that replicate inequitable, uncertain, and uneven access to education and health care; these challenges stand at the intersection of gendered, racialized, and Indigenous identities. For many, privilege renders these structures invisible, and yet there is also a growing public acknowledgment of the need to heed Indigenous, Black, and 2SLGBTQ+ calls for change to address the dystopic and precarious conditions that are already there. In a poem published on November 3, 2020, Black, queer, and Muslim-American poet, Devyn Springer, wrote:

the apocalypse was already here,
it has been here, striking in plain sight,

---

[2] Our context, Fredericton, New Brunswick, is situated on the unsurrendered and unceded traditional lands of the Wolastoqiyik peoples. Signed in 1725, the Peace and Friendship Treaties established Mi'kmaq and Wolastoqiyik title over these lands and provided rules for ongoing relations between nations. We acknowledge the land and the unhonored Treaty of Peace and Friendship, as an example of the existing dystopic conditions that exist within this territory. New Brunswick was founded on stolen land and provides the geographical and societal context for our inquiry.

it is not a thief in the night we must watch for,
nor an impending catastrophe we must manage,
but an infestation so large, so vast in sheer numbers,
so incalculable in the lives it's collected,
and audacious in the histories it's stolen,
that we think it has yet to arrive.

Our work also takes place during the ongoing struggle to fund Clinic 554—a Fredericton-based family medical practice that centers gender affirming health care, including abortion (Clinic 554, 2020). The chronic underfunding of Clinic 554 by the New Brunswick provincial government led to its recent closure in October 2020, leaving a gaping hole in access for trans people seeking health care and any person seeking an abortion in the geographic region of Fredericton. Currently, only two cities in New Brunswick, Bathurst and Moncton, offer surgical abortions—both 2-h drives from Fredericton and Saint John (Bell, 2020). The impending closure of Clinic 554[3] was the impetus for the September 2019 workshop we describe in this chapter, where 2SLGBTQ+ youth and allies created drawings and stencils to be shared broadly online. We sought to provide youth input on the crisis and amplify their calls for reproductive justice and gender inclusive health care. The eventual closure of Clinic 554 in October 2020 intensifies reproductive injustice and the dearth, and therefore precarity, of gender inclusive health care in New Brunswick—clearly dystopic conditions.

11.3   Positioning Ourselves in Relation to the Study

We came together to do this work in 2018—long before the current coronavirus pandemic—when we began to think about the ways that we might work with young people to explore dystopic conditions from the past, in the present, and in the future. We write together as people who have commitments to educational and social reform in the context of Atlantic Canada. Casey is an Associate Professor who teaches and researches in the area of gender, sexuality, participatory visual research, and Social Studies education. She is increasingly disappointed in the affronts on queer, trans, nonbinary people, as well as cisgender women, in relation to schooling and health services provided in New Brunswick. Her commitments to educational and social change are drawn from her embodied and internalized experiences of homophobia from her own educational experiences. She writes and works in solidarity with the youth and preservice teachers enrolled at her university. While Casey led the workshop we describe in this chapter, Funké and Jen have collaborated as "critical friend[s]" (Costa & Kalick, 1994, p. 49), who have brought analytical frameworks and visual analyses to the data in order to make sense of the

---

[3] Rumors of the Clinic's impending closure began in August 2019. The Clinic was put up for sale in June 2020 and effectively closed in September 2020 (Bell, 2020).

participant-produced stencils and drawings as examples of DIY multiliteracy practices for social action.

Funké is an Assistant Professor of Black Canadian history deeply invested in the bridging of academic and community knowledges. Her early research in Fredericton recognizes the long-standing history of Black communities in New Brunswick but also considers gaps in educational access and knowledge about these histories. By emphasizing the necessity of participatory research and a recognition of community-based knowledges, largely through oral histories, Funké considers the important avenues by which we can understand and situate advocacy work for persons of African descent in New Brunswick.

Jen is a postdoctoral researcher currently working in the area of youth knowledge mobilization in Quebec. Centering questions about how participatory visual methodologies offer ways to expand and transform research processes, Jen's research has explored gender relations within education, as well as in relation to environmental issues. Jen collaborated with Casey on a 2SLGBTQ+ youth workshop with some of the participants in a July 2019 embroidery and patch-making workshop while she was a Summer Scholar in the Faculty of Education at the University of New Brunswick.

Taking our collective interest in praxis and research for social change, we put our work in conversation with youth-produced stencils and drawings as DIY media for reproductive justice and a multiliteracy practice for social action. We turn now to the theoretical framework for the chapter: intersectional feminism.

11.4   Intersectionality as Theory and Method

While we theorize dystopias as purposely unsettling, our study brings together methods and approaches that also seek to unsettle dominant discourses that situate dystopia as a futured experience. Black feminism (Jacobs, 2019; King, 2016; Pellow, 2016) and critical future studies (Godhe & Goode, 2017) anchor our research. Using an intersectional lens (Crenshaw, 1989), we consider how intersecting power structures—gender, race, class, and disability—produce unequal impacts in relation to race, gender, reproductive health, and environmental issues in Atlantic Canadian contexts. Intersectionality as method works to dismantle interlocking systems of oppression as it compels a type of praxis to disrupt systemic oppressions (Cho et al., 2013). We consider the situated, specific, and relational nature of social power and also consider how social relations shape and are shaped by environmental factors (Sturgeon, 2016; Thompson, 2016), including access to gender-affirming reproductive care.

We also seek to ground this intersectional framework within the context of Canada (Aladejebi, 2015). Black Canadian feminists call attention to intersections of race, culture, geography, national origin, sexuality, and gender, which transform and situate diverse minority populations—especially Black Canadian communities (Wane et al., 2002). This framework shifts our understandings from theory to practice in order to place youth (and their intersectional experiences) at the center of analyses but also to position their voices as active creators and writers of their own stories. We explore the ways in which this approach can provide mechanisms for activism by privileging the experiences of those affected by intersecting forms of oppression (Wane et al., 2002).

We draw on the work of participatory media scholar Henry Jenkins (2006) in the area of convergence or DIY culture to center young peoples' active roles as knowledge, cultural, and media producers. We also draw on the work of Gillian Rose (2014), who highlights the affordances of visual research methods, including the generative nature of conversations between researchers and participants as visuals are produced, and the ways that visual production has the ability to "reveal what is hidden in the inner mechanisms of the ordinary and the taken for granted" (Knowles and Sweetman as cited in Rose, 2014, p. 28). Rose suggests that the collaborative nature of visual methods supports participants' ownership over the visuals they create and the knowledge they produce, such that participants are positioned as "experts…as they explain their images to the researcher" (p. 29). We adopt Rose's approach to visual analysis and apply it to the drawings and stencils produced in our collaborative project.

11.5   The Workshops: *Where Are Our Histories?*

In December 2018, Casey—with PhD candidate and collaborator Amelia Thorpe—began a series of monthly arts-based workshops with queer, trans, and nonbinary youth (aged 13–17) in Fredericton (Thorpe, 2020) in order to investigate the erasures of queer histories from New Brunswick Social Studies curricula and classrooms. As the initiative evolved, it grew to encompass young people's school and social experiences more broadly. The first workshop in December 2018 centered on stencil and cellphilm production (cellphone + filmmaking; see MacEntee et al., 2016) that responded to the prompt, "Where are our [queer] histories?" One of the results of this first workshop was that the young people wanted to keep meeting and making art together. In theorizing youth stencil production as a posthuman multiliteracy practice, Casey and Amelia argued that stencils were:

> nestled within other materialities in the workshop and as actors within the research space—[which] prompted reflection on the participants' experiences as queer, trans, and non-binary youth who inhabit school spaces…about the ways that gender and sexuality are experienced and often erased as landscapes within school spaces. (Burkholder & Thorpe, 2019, p. 299)

Our present chapter takes this theorizing and turns it toward the production of two stencils and two drawings produced by 2SLGBTQ+ youth and allies that centered their concerns over the impending closure of Clinic 554 and offered a call for action amidst dystopic conditions in relation to gender and reproductive injustice.

11.5.1 Save Clinic 554 Drawing and Stencil Production Workshop

From January 2019 until February 2020, Casey, Amelia, and the *Where Are Our Histories* 2SLGBTQ+ youth met in monthly DIY media production-based workshops, where the membership fluctuated between three and seven members. In October 2019, we—three 2SLGBTQ+ youth, three youth who identify as 2SLGBTQ+ allies, and Casey—met and produced drawings and stencils that took up the prompt "what matters to you in your community?" Together, through a discussion about pressing issues in Fredericton, we decided to highlight our responses to the significance of Clinic 554, our fears about its precarious financial state, and what that meant for gender-affirming and gender-inclusive reproductive health care in the province.

11.5.2 Drawing and Stencils as DIY Multiliteracies for Social Action

In what follows, we engage in Gillian Rose's (2012) framework for critical visual analysis—which highlights the production of the image, the image itself, and the audiencing of the image—in order to present a reading of four creative productions: two participant-produced drawings by Raven and Kristy, one participant-produced stencil by Scott, and one researcher-produced stencil by Casey.[4]

Raven is a 15-year-old 2SLGBTQ+ artist, activist, and collaborator in the *Where Are Our Histories* project. Raven and Casey first began working together in December 2018, when we collaborated on several cellphilms about queer erasure in social studies curricula and in New Brunswick schools in general.[5] Raven's drawing (see Fig. 11.1) uses marker, pen, and bright colors. Three people are depicted, including a self-portrait of the artist. The person on the left holds up an agender[6] flag, and the person in the center holds a sign reading CLINIC 554. The third person's shirt reads, "Save my family doctor." At the top of the image, a rainbow extends horizontally across the image. Behind the figures, a number of images, patterns, and words are repeated. The text looks like doodles and graffiti, and each phrase is intentional. Words featured include "equality," "recycle stuff," and "Jenica A"—in reference to the Green Party MP for Fredericton. Other statements featured in the graffiti highlight things that are important to Raven, from "pineapple belongs

---

[4] Kristy and Scott are pseudonyms. Raven is a participant-chosen pseudonym. Casey is non-anonymized.

[5] See our work from our Queer Cellphilms NB project, https://www.youtube.com/channel/UCXORsJs60OVKJ7TSDnEl6xg

[6] Agender is a nonbinary gender identity that means that a person is without gender (Pulice-Farrow et al., 2020).

Fig. 11.1 Kristy's 554 and Raven's Save Clinic 554

on pizza" to "Clinic 554 is very important" to "Pokémon, gotta catch them all." In talking about the piece, Raven shared that they "just wanted to show that Clinic 554 is really important for the LGBTQ community, and not just like, for what people think it is for [abortion services], but like for counseling and healthcare, and I just think it is a big part of the community. It will be sad if it closes." We see this point to be worth noting because there is a clear awareness demonstrated here that abortion is still thought of as negative, as Raven discursively constructs abortion as a service that is separate and distinctive from the other reproductive and gender-affirming care that people receive within Clinic 554. Even within gender-diverse communities, there is an awareness of popular media and conservatism within the province of New Brunswick (e.g., Quon, 2020), which creates negative assumptions about access to care that are so much more than "just" abortion.

Kristy, who attends university and identifies as a 2SLGBTQ+ ally, produced a drawing, "554" (Fig. 11.1) that combines text, pastel, pen, and drawing and that makes visual the multiple services that Clinic 554 provides. Kristy attended the workshop as a volunteer preservice teacher participant who wanted to interact with youth in an out-of-school setting and who sought to learn more about arts-based approaches to activism with youth. For example, within the outline of the first number 5, Kristy wrote the terms "safe abortions," "pediatrics," "family doctor," "safe hormone injections," "HIV care," and "trans health," effectively naming the specific types of care services offered by the clinic. When Clinic 554 is discussed in local media (see, e.g., Quon, 2020), it is often described only as a "private abortion clinic" (Bissett, 2020, para. 1). However, as Kristy and other sources (see, e.g., Hansen & Harnish, 2020) make clear, the Clinic provides gender-affirming care in a family practice setting. One of the services that Clinic 554 provides is abortion care, and this is the site of its defunding by the provincial government (Clinic 554, 2020). By producing this drawing and consenting to its dissemination online on Casey's Twitter (Fig. 11.3), Kristy is engaging in a DIY multiliteracy practice for social action: seeking to inform larger public audiences about the services that Clinic 554 provides for community members and disrupting broader mainstream narratives that simplify its diverse meanings and supports for people.

Scott is a university student in the field of education who also identified as a 2SLGBTQ+ ally. Scott is a preservice teacher-activist who wanted to collaborate in the youth workshops to practice art-informed pedagogy and learn about 2SLGBTQ+ youth activism outside of school contexts. Scott wanted to create a stencil that could communicate his thoughts in French for Francophone communities, who have long-standing histories in New Brunswick. Here, Scott engages with a multiliteracy framework by acknowledging the limitations of monolingualism and recognizing how people are often engaging in and producing meanings around texts across multiple languages (Rowsell & Pahl, 2015). We note that a multiliteracy framework means acknowledging that the monolingual and autonomous model of literacy is a false and homogenizing thing (Rowsell & Pahl, 2015). Scott created his stencil by layering tape over a black piece of cardstock (see Fig. 11.2). Then, he used a paintbrush to splash pink, mauve, and white paint over the top of the tape, creating a marbled aesthetic. Settling on the message, "Sauvons Clinique 554" (Save Clinic 554), Scott's piece seeks to engage Francophone communities, who also access the clinic but whose perspectives are largely removed from the ways that saving Clinic 554 is discussed in the media (Bell, 2020). Because the art we were producing was meant to be public facing—and shared in social media and real-life contexts (including on Casey's office door)—Scott's choice to highlight the need to "Sauvons la Clinique 554" speaks back to the erasure of Francophone advocacy for the Clinic within local activist circles and popular media.[7]

As a practice that first began when she was a classroom teacher and continues in her current research practice, Casey always produces DIY media alongside participants, taking up the prompt in her own way. With collaborative research methodologies in mind, Casey is cognizant that her interpretations might influence the modes

Fig. 11.2 Scott's *Sauvons la Clinique 554* [Save Clinic 554] and Casey's trauma-informed care

[7] See exceptions, including an August 2020 Radio Canada, Ici Nouveau-Brunswick interview with Monique Brideau: https://ici.radio-canada.ca/nouvelle/1728657/clinique-avortement-chirurgical-nouveau-brunswick-lections-recours-collectif

that participants take up, but she feels that crafting alongside participants is an example of engaged practice, of showing her own interpretation, and of being vulnerable with participants—who have varying degrees of comfort with the notion of media production. In her stencil, Casey decided to use cursive writing to amplify a phrase that she found on Clinic 554's website that highlighted its goals for providing care for community members within Fredericton (see Fig. 11.2). Casey decided not just to quote the website's statement about services but to reframe the quote as a call for action. Her stencil reads, "All we want is 'feminist, trauma-informed, harm reduction anti-racist care in Fredericton.'" Casey wanted to highlight antiracism within the project—as racism is a dystopic condition well entwined with reproductive injustice. The picture of Casey's stencil depicts a moment mid-production before she had finished cutting. With this picture, Casey wanted to show how stencils are often drafty and allow space for mistakes and how stencil production offers an example of the political nature of DIY itself. Casey's call for action through her stencil was intentional as she thought about ways that the images might later be disseminated—especially through online communities.

After we produced both the stencils and drawings, we photographed them using our cellphones and disseminated them across our personal social media networks. Kristy, Raven, and Scott also consented to sharing their work publicly through Casey's professional social media network (Fig. 11.3), and Raven also shared their image with a teacher in their school. Although their drawings and stencils were produced within the confines of a 3-h workshop, they have had a life and impact outside of the workshop space. We see this dissemination of these powerful visuals as one of the methodological contributions of DIY multiliteracies that center dystopia as a sphere of inquiry in order to both document resistance and provoke transformative change.

11.6 Taking the Pieces Together

By producing drawings and stencils to address the impending closure of Clinic 554 and sharing these pieces online, we suggest that this practice might be conceptualized as DIY multiliteracy practices for social action. Our research both disrupts autonomous notions of literacy (Street, 2006) and positions youth-produced drawings and stencils as a DIY literacy practice that acknowledges dystopic and uncertain conditions and speaks back to these conditions. Although our interventions—the production of stencils and drawings and sharing these online—did not change the outcome of the closure of Clinic 554, they did create new openings and communities of inquiry and activist practice. The images also align with broader social critiques about conservative news and media reporting and contest these messages. The pieces reflect youth awareness of the potential of DIY media in making and effecting change, by identifying opportunities for naming and acting on injustices. The awareness that something can be done (even if it does not work out) is a radical practice for mobilization and consciousness-raising. Multilayered communities

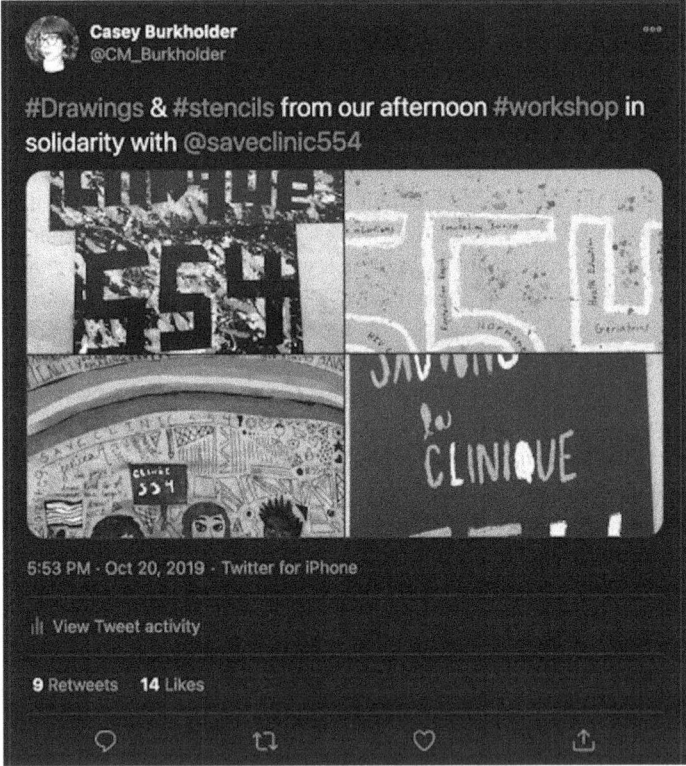

Fig. 11.3 Sharing the pieces with online networks

were developed in the workshop, between 2SLGBTQ+ youth, ally youth, and a researcher, and also between the community of producers and online communities. While we did not stop the closure of Clinic 554, we did share what the clinic meant to us. This effort has led to other collaborations, including the production in Summer 2020 of a cellphilm[8] and two lesson plans[9] that could bring the notion of gender-affirming care to Grade 7 Social Studies classrooms.

Our stencils and drawings also inspired art production in a knowledge mobilization project called *Pride/Swell*[10]: *Art & Activism with 2SLGBTQ+ Atlantic Canadian Youth*, where Raven's drawing became a recruitment tool for participants. Later, as a part of *Pride/Swell* and in the context of the COVID-19 pandemic, Casey created

---

[8] See Araujo, N. and Burkholder, C. (2020). Gender affirming care: Save Clinic 554. [cellphilm]. https://www.youtube.com/watch?v=91MRZVNe5OI

[9] See Chase, A. and Burkholder, C. (2020). Lesson plans. *Queer histories matter: Queering Social Studies in New Brunswick.* [website]. https://www.queerhistoriesmatter.org/lessonplans

[10] Pride/Swell is an art, activism, and archiving project Casey is engaging in with 2SLGBTQ+ youth and collaborators Dr. Katie MacEntee, Dr. April Mandrona, and Amelia Thorpe.

both a DIY facemask[11] that read "Save Clinic 554" in response to the prompt "staying safe, but never silent," as well as a doll holding an embroidered protest sign reading "Save Clinic 554"[12] in response to the prompt "embodying future selves." At a time when the precarity of the future seems accentuated by the uncertain and dystopic conditions created by the pandemic, we seek to highlight the complex ways that injustices are playing out and understood. For youth participants of this study, the urgency of access to health care and the potential closure of Clinic 554 brought the reality of dystopia to the ongoing present rather than a future coming. Participants remained aware of the disparate and precarious locales of access to care available to 2SLGBTQ+ communities and joined in ongoing struggles to voice their concerns. Not finding these platforms in mainstream media outlets, participants used DIY media-making to expand their access to public audiences. They participated in practices of consciousness-raising that considered the more nuanced ways that Clinic 554 provided necessary services for their communities. This is the makings of radical practice work and resistance. The October 2019 workshop and the production of media within it continues to affect research and activist communities in the context of Fredericton—a form of social action.

While DIY media-making within this project largely considers the intersections of gender and sexuality, there are limitations in the ways in which race, reproductive, and environmental justice are engaged within these spaces. We acknowledge that in this part of the project exploring reproductive and health-based dystopias with 2SLGBTQ+ youth and allies, the majority of our research population is White—which we see as a limitation to our work. Stronger considerations must be given to explore how racialized communities are excluded from access to services, which are connected, but not limited, to health care within the province. For example, African-Canadian community consultations in Saint John, New Brunswick, revealed learning gaps around access to resources and information within the province (Canadian Council on Learning, 2008). In addition, community members reported that various institutions within the province lacked people who understood the needs of African-Canadians. The more recent treatment of Dr. Ngola—a Black physician in New Brunswick whose medical privacy was denied as his COVID-status was disclosed at a press conference by the premier, Blaine Higgs—also reflects deep-rooted elements of systemic racism, harassment, and violence directed at persons of African descent within the province.[13] To date, there has been no comprehensive assessment outlining the experiences of racialized populations despite ongoing calls to action around this issue (Metallic, 2020). These are avenues not fully explored within this discussion but remain intimately connected to the

---

[11] See Casey's selfie and facemask at https://www.instagram.com/p/CGpT0EYD01E/

[12] See Casey's doll and tiny protest sign at https://www.instagram.com/p/CG42K4rjchznTPYthZ9gTGZPcd1d57Idau3SRo0/

[13] See Dryden, O. (2020). Racist responses to Covid-19 place us all at greater risk. *The Chronicle Herald*, September 3. [Viewed December 15, 2020]. Available from https://www.thechroniclehe-rald.ca/opinion/local-perspectives/omisoore-dryden-racist-responses-to-covid-19-place-us-all-at-greater-risk-492256/

intersecting experiences and multiple understandings of how dystopia and precarity are experienced in the past and present.

11.7 How Can We Move Forward with DIY Solidarities and Collective Resistance?

While the range of complex issues related to social change certainly cannot be resolved in this study, we seek to find ways forward to create new openings and communities that can work together to make space for beauty, for resistance, and for collaboration in the face of increasing disparities in gender-affirming reproductive health care, certainly since the closure of Clinic 554. Moving forward, our study contributes to disrupting conventional thinking about literacies and engaging in research for social action with and by youth. Young people in particular have specific and important stakes in questions about uncertainty and precarity in dystopic pasts, presents, and futures and are already engaging in resistance and activism in Atlantic Canadian contexts. For example, Kendra Levi-Paul advocates for equitable access to health and education in New Brunswick. Also in New Brunswick, Husoni Raymond and Felomena Degratsias have played central roles in building Black Lives Matter—Fredericton in response to systemic racism within the province. In Nova Scotia, Kyturea Jones, Payton Ashe, and Donntayia Jones build community through resisting gentrification of their Halifax neighborhood, and Tina Yeonju Oh's climate activism has garnered international recognition. Prince Edward Island's Queer Youth Collective offers the only community-based youth group specifically for 2SLGBTQ+ youth on the island. These projects reflect an awareness among young people that dystopia is indeed in process and that bridging across solidarities offers important moments for collective resistance and coalition building. DIY multiliteracies for social action, as demonstrated throughout this chapter, offer important methodological and theoretical frameworks for looking at uncertain and dystopic conditions, past, present, and future. Working with dystopia as a sphere of inquiry for imagining alternative futures, we hope to build on these moments to investigate the ways in which issues of justice, racism, dispossession, uncertainty, gentrification and progress, and access to reproductive health services shape communities and community members in different ways. We see stencil production as one method of DIY multiliteracy practice for social action, as it has the potential for participants and the research team to share their works broadly in multiple spaces, both online and offline. Providing a gender and race focus to the future community building and media-making workshops will encourage those communities most impacted by reproductive injustice to imagine their place in resisting unsustainable and uncertain futures together through DIY multiliteracy practices for social change.

Acknowledgments We would like to send our heartfelt thanks to the participants in the workshop and the collaboration of Amelia Thorpe, a PhD Candidate at the University of New Brunswick and a co-facilitator to many of the 2SLGBTQ+ youth workshops. The research described in this paper was supported by the University of New Brunswick's Young Scholar Award (2019), a SSHRC Insight Development Grant (2018–2020), and a New Brunswick Innovation Fund Emerging Projects Grant (2019–2020).

References

Aladejebi, F. (2015). Black female educators and resistive pedagogies, 1960s–1980s. *Ontario History, 107*(1), 111–129.

Barton, D., & Hamilton, M. (2005). Literacy practices. In D. Barton, M. Hamilton & R. Ivanic (Eds.), Situated literacies: Theorizing reading and writing in context, (pp. 25–32). Routledge.

BC Nurse's Union. (2016). *Gender affirming care: Position statement.* [Viewed December 15, 2020]. Available from: https://www.bcnu.org/AboutBcnu/Documents/position-statement-gender-affirming-care.pdf

Bell, M. (2020). The closing of Clinic 554. *The Brunswickan.* [online]. [Viewed December 15, 2020]. Available from: https://www.thebruns.ca/articles/the-closing-of-clinic-554

Bissett, K. (2020). Demonstration in Fredericton as private abortion clinic to lose its doctor. *CTV News.*[online]. [Viewed December 15, 2020]. Available from: https://atlantic.ctvnews.ca/demonstration-in-fredericton-as-private-abortion-clinic-to-lose-its-doctor-1.5121665

Buckingham, D., & Sefton-Green, J. (1994). *Cultural studies goes to school: Reading and teaching popular media.* Taylor & Francis.

Burkholder, C., & Thorpe, A. (2019). Cellphilm production as posthumanist research method to explore injustice with queer youth in New Brunswick, Canada. *Reconceptualizing Educational Research Methodology, 10*(2–3), 292–309. [Viewed December 15, 2020]. Available from: https://doi.org/10.7577/rerm.3680

Canadian Council on Learning. (2008). *African Canadian knowledge exchange community outreach.* [Report]. [Viewed December 15, 2020]. Available from: http://en.copian.ca/library/research/ccl/african/african.pdf.

Chen, X., Raby, R., & Albanese, P. (Eds.). (2017). *The sociology of childhood and youth in Canada.* Canadian Scholars.

Cho, S., Crenshaw, K. W., & McCall, L. (2013). Toward a field of intersectionality studies: Theory, application, and praxis. *Signs, 38*(4), 785–810. [Viewed December 15, 2020]. Available from: https://doi.org/10.1086/669608

Clinic 554. (2020). "About". [online]. [Viewed December 15, 2020]. Available from: http://www.clinic554.ca/about.html

Costa, A., & Kalick, B. (1994). *Assessment in the learning organization: Shifting the paradigm.* Association for Supervision and Curriculum Development.

Crenshaw, K. (1989). Demarginalizing the intersection of race and sex: A black feminist critique of antidiscrimination doctrine, feminist theory and antiracist politics. *University of Chicago Legal Forum, 19,* 139–168.

Ewing, E. (2020). I'm a Black scholar who studies race. Here's why I capitalize 'White.' *Zora.* July 2. [Viewed December 15, 2020]. Available from: https://zora.medium.com/im-a-black-scholar-who-studies-race-here-s-why-i-capitalize-white-f94883aa2dd3

Fisher, M. (2009). *Capitalist realism: Is there no alternative?.* John Hunt Publishing.

Friere, P., & Macedo, D. (1987). *Literacy: Reading the word and the world.* Bergin & Garvey Publishers.

Godhe, M., & Goode, L. (2017). Beyond capitalist realism: Why we need critical future studies. *Culture Unbound. Journal of Current Cultural Research, 9*(1), 1–22.

Hansen, J., & Harnish, S. (2020). Myth # 1: Clinic 554 is a "private abortion clinic." *NB Media Co-op.* April 14. [Viewed December 15, 2020]. Available from: https://nbmediacoop.org/2020/04/14/myth-1-clinic-554-is-a-private-abortion-clinic/

180 C. Burkholder et al.

Jacobs, F. (2019). Black feminism and radical planning: New directions for disaster planning research. *Planning Theory, 18*(1), 24–39.

Jemison, N. K. (2017). *The stone sky*. Orbit Books.

Jenkins, H. (2006). *Convergence culture: Where old and new media collide*. New York University Press.

King, D. K. (2016). Multiple jeopardy, multiple consciousness: The context of a Black feminist ideology. In S. Jackson (Ed.), *Routledge handbook of race, class and gender* (pp. 36–57). Routledge.

Literat, I. (2013). "A pencil for your thoughts": Participatory drawing as a visual research method with children and youth. *International Journal of Qualitative Methods, 12*(1), 84–98.

MacEntee, K., Burkholder, C., & Schwab-Cartas, J. (Eds.). (2016). *What's a cellphilm?: Integrating mobile phone technology into participatory visual research and activism*. Brill/Sense.

Metallic, N. (2020). New Brunswick needs a public inquiry into systemic racism in the justice system: Nova Scotia shows why, *12*(1), 1–8. [Viewed December 15, 2020]. Available from: https://digitalcommons.schulichlaw.dal.ca/scholarly_works/496

Mitchell, C., & Burkholder, C. (2015). Chapter 43: Literacies and research as social change. In J. Rowsell & K. Pahl (Eds.), *Routledge handbook of literacy studies* (pp. 649–662). Routledge.

Mitchell, C., De Lange, N., & Moletsane, R. (2017). *Participatory visual methodologies: Social change, community and policy*. Sage.

Pellow, D. N. (2016). Toward a critical environmental justice studies: Black Lives Matter as an environmental justice challenge. *Du Bois Review: Social Science Research on Race, 13*(2), 221–236.

Preston, J. (2017). Racial extractivism and white settler colonialism: An examination of the Canadian Tar Sands mega-projects. *Cultural Studies, 31*(2–3), 353–375.

Pulice-Farrow, L., McNary, S. B., & Galupo, M. P. (2020). "Bigender is just a Tumblr thing": Microaggressions in the romantic relationships of gender non-conforming and agender transgender individuals. *Sexual and Relationship Therapy, 35*(3), 362–381.

Quon, A. (2020). Higgs says funding Clinic 554 would be a 'slippery slope.' *Global News*, September 28. [Viewed December 15, 2020]. Available from: https://globalnews.ca/news/7365089/blaine-higgs-clinic-554-slippery-slope/

Reid, A. E. (2019). *Our healing starts with our women* Master's thesis, University of New Brunswick. [Viewed December 10, 2020]. Available from: https://unbscholar.lib.unb.ca/islandora/object/unbscholar%3A9874/datastream/PDF/view

Rose, G. (2012). *Visual methodologies* (3rd ed.). Sage.

Rose, G. (2014). On the relation between 'visual research methods' and contemporary visual culture. *The Sociological Review, 62*(1), 24–46. https://doi.org/10.1111/1467-954X.12109

Rowsell, J., & Pahl, K. (Eds.). (2015). *The Routledge handbook of literacy studies*. Routledge.

Street, B. (2006). Autonomous and ideological models of literacy: Approaches from new literacy studies. *Media Anthropology Network, 17*, 1–15.

Stuart, J., & Mitchell, C. (2013). Media, participation, and social change: Working within a "youth as knowledge producers" framework. In D. Lemish (Ed.), *The Routledge international handbook of children, adolescents and media* (pp. 385–392). Routledge.

Sturgeon, N. (2016). *Ecofeminist natures: Race, gender, feminist theory and political action*. Routledge.

The New London Group. (1996). A pedagogy of multiliteracies: Designing social futures. *Harvard Educational Review, 66*(1), 60–92.

Thompson, J. A. (2016). Intersectionality and water: How social relations intersect with ecological difference. *Gender, Place & Culture, 23*(9), 1286–1301.

Thorpe, A. (2020). Queering fieldnote practice with queer, trans, and non-binary populations. In C. Burkholder & J. Thompson (Eds.), *Fieldnotes in qualitative education and social science research* (pp. 277–287). Routledge.

Wane, N. N., Deliovsky, K., & Lawson, E. (Eds.). (2002). *Back to the drawing board: African Canadian feminisms*. Canadian Scholars Press.

Chapter 12
Uncertain Springs of Activism: Walking with Hoggart

Julian McDougall, Pete Bennett, and John Potter

Abstract This chapter, in presenting adapted extracts from a book length project, revisits Richard Hoggart's *The Uses of Literacy* (1957) and argues for a theoretical, sociomaterial reclaiming of *media* literacy, a now established strand of the new literacies, through a return to Hoggart's concerns and his connecting of literacy to personal, community and cultural lives.

Hoggart was writing about the transition between literacies experienced at a time of great **uncertainty** by, in his words, the working classes. From their perspective, and through his own lived experience of this uncertainty, he sought to write about the benefits of 'mass literacy' for education and mobility, as well as about the dangers of persuasion and cultural debasement and the uncertainty of identity experienced by those 'moving up' through their uses of literacy.

Revisiting what we see as Hoggart's contribution to the project of 'drawing attention to the discursive frames that shape everyday lives and the literacy practices that are a part of them' (Jones, 2018) serves both to **unsettle** the seemingly neutral, competence and skills-based framings of media literacy and to consider the extent to which the uses of media **unsettle literacies**. Whilst there is much to challenge in Hoggart's observations, we argue that going beyond the focus on class to 'walk with' an intersectional, dynamic 'take' on the socio-material approach taken in Hoggart's *Uses* has much to offer research in our current times that seeks to better understand the lived experiences of the benefits and risks of digital, media literacies as well as the **precarity** of digital inequalities (Helsper, The digital disconnect: the social causes and consequences of digital inequalities. Sage, 2021).

J. McDougall (✉)
Centre for Excellence in Media Practice, Bournemouth University, Poole, UK
e-mail: jmcdougall@bournemouth.ac.uk

P. Bennett
University of Wolverhampton, Wolverhampton, UK

J. Potter
Institute of Education Knowledge Lab, University College London, London, UK

© The Author(s), under exclusive license to Springer Nature Singapore Pte Ltd. 2022
C. Lee et al. (eds.), *Unsettling Literacies*, Cultural Studies and Transdisciplinarity in Education 15, https://doi.org/10.1007/978-981-16-6944-6_12

Keywords Media · Literacies · Inequalities · Precarity · Ethnography

This chapter, in presenting adapted extracts from a book length project, revisits Richard Hoggart's *The Uses of Literacy* (1957) and argues for a theoretical, socio-material reclaiming of *media* literacy, a now established strand of the new literacies, through a return to Hoggart's concerns and his connecting of literacy to personal, community and cultural lives.

Hoggart was writing about the transition between literacies experienced at a time of great **uncertainty** by, in his words, the working classes. From their perspective, and through his own lived experience of this uncertainty, he sought to write about the benefits of 'mass literacy' for education and mobility, as well as about the dangers of persuasion and cultural debasement and the uncertainty of identity experienced by those 'moving up' through their uses of literacy. The precarious transition point at which Hoggart made his contribution is similar to now—from literacy to mass literacy then and into media literacy now—with another set of appeals and encouraged attitudes. As Rancière observes, 'the things that matter for theory turn up at crossover points where the different jurisdictions disappear' (Rancière, 2016: 32).

Revisiting what we see as Hoggart's contribution to the project of 'drawing attention to the discursive frames that shape everyday lives and the literacy practices that are a part of them' (Jones, 2018) serves both to **unsettle** the seemingly neutral, competence and skills-based framings of media literacy and to consider the extent to which the uses of media **unsettle literacies**. Whilst there is much to challenge in Hoggart's observations, we argue that going beyond the focus on class to 'walk with' an intersectional, dynamic 'take' on the sociomaterial approach taken in Hoggart's *The Uses of Literacy* has much to offer research in our current times that seeks to better understand the lived experiences of the benefits and risks of digital, media literacies as well as the **precarity** of digital inequalities (Helsper, 2021).

In *The Uses of Literacy* (1957), Hoggart set out 'questions of approach', concerned with avoiding a romantic or sentimental view of the past when assessing the 'debased condition' of working-class culture at his time of writing. His 'rough definition' was born of the necessity to find a focus and to justify his experiential approach, his situated and 'bodily' investigation. His interest in the thick description of 'less tangible features'—manners of speaking, clothes, habits and aspects of the social practices of community—has since been celebrated as a methodology, a form of autoethnography. *The Uses of Literacy* has been described as 'more lived, more partial and more felt than the many academic books in the tradition of the New Literacy Studies' (Pahl et al., 2020: 132).

12.1 Unsettling Landscapes

Looking at the contested uses of media literacy obliges a focus on what we mean by media, class and culture 60+ years on from Hoggart's ethnography. 'Doing Hoggart' on media literacy, or reviewing 'The Uses of Hoggart' for media literacy, makes progress towards some recommendations for how media literacy can and *should* reclaim its own (contemporary) class consciousness, away from deficit models and protectionism towards an intersectional critical pedagogy which has too often been lacking. As Hoggart says, 'A great deal has been written about the effect on the working-classes of the modern "mass media of communication"' (1990:27).

Hoggart was concerned about massification's impact on 'the common speech' and 'on oral and local tradition', which he saw as weakening but still possessing 'remarkable life', but rather than addressing this local tradition contemporaneously, Hoggart relied largely on the Hunslet of his childhood for his benchmarks (1990:27). As much ethnographic work continues to show, working-class experience is not a 'Landscape with Figures' but rather a collection of semantic ecosystems, teeming with life. Here are communities legitimising the work they are doing among themselves, fulfilling Peim's desire for 'a multi-directional thing, a mobile theory of texts, language, the subject, subjectivity' (Peim, 1993: 3).

Repeatedly questioning Hoggart's evidence and methodology, critics like David Buckingham see Hoggart's methods as problematic, particularly given the widescale impact *The Uses of Literacy* has had: 'Hoggart seems to have reached his conclusions merely from superficial observation…' (Buckingham, 2018: 2). This critique is borne out across *The Uses of Literacy*, largely by Hoggart's honest accounts of data collection; for example, the evidence bases for his analysis of the local oral tradition somewhat lack precision: 'These examples were all collected in a deliberately short time…from a …Waiting room of a children's clinic.' (1990:27). Opportunistic, certainly.

Hoggart's anxieties about the age of massification proved largely unfounded: if anything, the late 1950s, 1960s and early 1970s proved an unprecedented period of working-class credibility and creativity. However, in our time, the transition from the age of massification to something more fluid, globalised and digital, in the absence of requisite radical political settlement, has indeed precipitated a crisis. Media literacy education is entering a maturation phase, characterised by exploration of the social practices of media education and the complexity of human engagements both with media and with ways of being literate in the mediated social world. In response, the research field is beginning to acknowledge the complexity of 'dynamic literacies' and experiment with pedagogies that combine and/or cross boundaries between spaces and roles—the classroom and the extended 'third space', teachers and students working in partnership to co-create learning and professional development in hybrid combinations of physical and virtual networks. This *dynamic* approach to media literacy (Potter & McDougall, 2017) puts the influence of Hoggart and Cultural Studies, together with the methodologies of new literacy studies (Gee, 2015; Street, 2003; Kress, 2003), more actively into media education research to offer a more agile, responsive and inclusive, intersectional way of seeing media literacy and its uses.

12.2 People

Thinking about the *uses* of media literacy makes a pitch for a shift in (or to) *method*, towards, put simply, ways of seeing literacy better in the networked, digital, social media and data age (Potter & McDougall, 2017; Williamson, 2016; Cannon, 2018; Livingstone & Blum-Ross, 2020; Helsper, 2021). Using Hoggart to explore the difference media makes to literacy and asking how education should respond to this requires a departure from his frames of reference to consider how the uses of media literacy relate to feminism, critical race theory, social class, postcolonial, intersectional approaches and posthumanism and how these perspectives, political objectives and international contexts can 'decenter' the field of media literacy education. Like Kate Pahl, we see Hoggart's 'legacy', albeit flawed, as an 'imaginative sensibility, which could be understood as a complex response to lived life and its potentialities and emergence… a way of being and knowing that was not entirely academic but drew from experience' (2014: 5). Media literacy has not done enough of this kind of work, so far.

And yet it must be acknowledged that the field of media literacy is itself another other.

Hoggart's 'Them' are constructed as the other by a working-class 'group sense' of threat from a 'shadowy but numerous and powerful group, affecting their lives at every point' (Hoggart, 1957, p53). Hoggart avoids the term 'community', concerned not to obscure the tensions inherent to the collective and ambiguous views of social mobility enabled by literacy. The literacy 'ladder' was, for example, for Raymond Williams, a prime symbol of a meritocracy, which 'weakens community and the task of common betterment' and 'sweetens the poison of hierarchy' (Williams, in Littler, 2013: 54). The 'other' are the subject of mistrust, rather than fear, an attitude which is less prevalent among youth. A particular anxiety pervades around the imposed obligation for a 'double eye' (p. 57), a plural 'way of seeing' oneself as both an individual and a citizen in democracy, both of which come with duties which may conflict or at least pose complications.

Today, trust in the mainstream media 'Them' is, arguably, in crisis. But on the other hand, the algorithmic insulation of group sense adds a new layer of ideological closure, a new mode of conservation. Now, the construction of the 'Liberal Elite' is provided as a 'Them' by another 'Them'—a complex, double layering of the mass persuaders, whereby the media literacy of the group is used to offer a credible pre-prepared 'Them'. The shadowy group is thereby displaced and hidden, as a more visible, life-affecting other is located as the problem. In the mobilisation of this persuasion, 'The Media' is set up as complicit in this 'world of Them'. In Hoggart's understanding, such a process would not happen organically, from within the group; the desire to conserve, resist change, close in and avoid internal disruption would make this kind of sudden uprising against the political class and journalists unlikely. Both of these domains would be the subject of benign scepticism in favour of 'putting up with' or even sustained enthusiasm as the development of the digital (mass) mediascape is simply an ongoing transition to the 'uses of media literacy'.[1]

> In Hoggart's reading, the separation [them/us] has the effect of marginalising 'them' because 'they' have no place in 'our' world. It is therefore a device for deflating authority, but significantly, it is a means to designate and pinpoint those who are seen as a threat to the separation. (Gregg, 2006: 38)

Hoggart's interplay of cultural and material relations might at first seem a stretch too far for the project at hand, the application of his thinking to the (digital) media ecosystem. To restate, our field's characterisation of 'us' for this project describes a less agentive relationship with media than Hoggart implies—either an inability or a lack of desire to look beyond immediate circumstance and detachment (on both sides) from the normative systemworld literacy as framed by formal education. The group must also be understood as an 'othering' device for the lower-middle classes who see social mobility in their own experience and intersectionally; in this sense, there are many 'us', and they converge as one 'us' for us, here, in some ways but not others. This is quite different to the more obvious acknowledgement that 'You are bound to be close to people with whom you share a lavatory in a common yard' *(Hoggart, p60)*. And yet several writers who offer accounts of working-class life today, and evoke Hoggart in different ways, would appear to resist such a narrative of then and now:

> Had the social changes he documented been deeper and more effective at erasing class distinctions, I wouldn't have spent the last fifteen years or so repeatedly looking to his work for its continuing relevance to my life. I am, in his words, one of the 'uprooted and anxious': at one socially mobile and psychologically stuck, or at least divided, somewhere between our place of origin and the place we inhabit in order to 'get on'. (Hanley, 2017: xii)

12.3 Precarity: The (Ongoing) Age of Anxiety

Selina Todd (2014) deconstructs enduring myths about social mobility: its representation as purely statistical, entrepreneurship as the route to advancement, the success of selective education and low aspiration as an obstruction, the necessity of imitation of those higher up the ladder, the framing of social mobility as a social good and its status as an essential lever for policy with the objective of empowering people with control of their situations. The sum of these discursive parts gives us a sobering antidote to the idea that Hoggart was then and media literacy is now:

> Policy debate has been fixated on the minority who experienced upward social mobility in the last century, and has suggested that their gains—uneven and ambivalent as they were—

---

[1] This and related arguments in this chapter are based, with permission, on work which first appeared in McDougall et al. (2020).

outweigh all the injustices perpetrated by a hierarchal capitalist society on the majority. (Todd, 2014: 19)

The role of literacy education in both offering a route to 'mobility' and creating a nomadic anxiety was described by Hoggart himself, many times, and echoed by Hanley. This paradox remains at the heart of the discussion of social class, precarity and literacy in the United Kingdom and is a context for media literacy here, in a way which is, perhaps, less pervasive elsewhere.

In *Respectable* (2017), a personal story of crossing class divides, for example, Lynsey Hanley makes over a hundred references to media texts—including in her title—and cites Hoggart on 33 pages of 227. Those mediated reference points are sometimes environmental/incidental (*The Mirror*, *Titbits*, Motown), the popular culture that was in the house or on the screen, sometimes 'played out' at school, so curated socially (Adam and the Ants); sometimes they are bound up with her more personal curation of class identity (*NME*, Frankie Goes to Hollywood, New Order, *Billy Elliot*); sometimes they speak directly to habitus and anxiety (Private Eye, Shakespeare refusal); sometimes they anchor her writing to moments in history (Oasis and the 'third way'); and sometimes they seem to be put to work as a play on Hoggart: 'I must stress that I wasn't reading sociology books whilst working at a mass circulation magazine (Heat) to annoy people, it was more the case that I liked both' (p. 163).

In *Lowborn* (2020), an exploration of poverty in contemporary Britain, Kerry Hudson is restricted to environmental descriptions of texts that were 'around'; in her account of material lack, the privilege of mediated curation is absent. But like Hanley, Hudson describes the *use* of popular culture as both social container (Richards, 2017) and form of escape in the playground (routines from *Dirty Dancing*, Kylie and Bros, *Footloose* and *Grease*). At college, *Melody Maker* provides the same signifier as NME does for Hanley, but for Hudson, culture is less a matter of choice. The most striking resonance with *The Uses of Literacy* describes her mother's curtailed mobility:

> She enrolled in an OU course in English, read Dickens and spent hours in an armchair with a cheap notepad and biro trying to write her essays, but gave up after the first one saying her tutor 'didn't get it'. (2018: 124)

A 'vivid' analysis of the uses of *media* literacy, then, demands another 'us', partly for the reasons addressed in the opening chapter, new ways of seeing 'the working class', not to refute the evidence cited in surveys and the arguments above but partly also to decentre and decolonialise 'the group'. If the media literacy researcher and/or educator is 'positioned as a human agent within a dynamic process' (Jones, 2018: 23) and is thus to bear witness to the ways in which people in everyday literacy practices use digital media to interact with wider sites of social struggle—as opposed to acquiring them as competences or lacking them as deficient—then they must capture as 'core behaviour', as opposed to radical exception, techno-social repertoires that challenge a rudimentary updating through Hoggart's line of sight:

When we examine black feminist use of social media, we see that they are constructing 'publics' that are both individual and communal, local and global, cathartic and revolutionary. Networking allows them a pluralism that is antithetical to essentialism and demands an interactive collectivism that is both a model for and product of contemporary black feminism. (Matthews, 2019: 391)

This view of the construction of digital media assemblages as *model for and product of* is, we argue, *media* literacy's dynamic variation on Hoggart's anecdotal ethnography of conservation. If the group has been hitherto obstructed from constructing its public sphere, then the mass culture will enable a very different kind of transition, a much closer focus through Jones' reframing social justice lens on 'abject' communities—resonating with our working definition from the field. Hanley accepts as enduring Hoggart's 'distinction between a cynical mass culture and the kind of culture we can produce if we're encouraged to do it for ourselves'. (p. 214). So, in looking for disruptive uses of social media, for example, either for new modes of civic engagement (Mihaildis, 2018), identity work in conflict and crisis zones (Melki, 2018) or 'woke' intersectional reading such as Matthews describes, we move beyond and above models of deficit and competence or the banality of 'screen time' discourse—perhaps this would be the easiest updating of 'the mass persuaders'—to really claim a 'vivid' assessment, decentring the white working class, in a dialogic relation with other 'abjects' to view the 'fundamental shakiness of the social escalator' (Hanley, 2017: 159) from other perspectives.

Clearly, what is being 'put up with' still, now, is *even* more unsettling, disruptive, intolerable even: a pandemic with savagely stratified impact on communities, austerity with no end in sight, and climate crisis, decreasing living standards and rendering mobility, to the extent that it can be a viable 'way out', even more unlikely. What would Hoggart offer as 'vivid and detached analysis' of the lived experience of the precariat class, the zero hours, 'gig economy' operatives comprising the new 'precariat' (Savage, 2015)?

To see Us differently also—indeed most urgently—requires an acceptance that *we* might be Them: 'In order to transform the institutional culture within academia to one that is culturally democratic and equitable, white students and staff need to become active participants in challenging whiteness' (Gabriel, 2017: 33). Just as (or rather even more than) we might have paid great attention to the kinds of nomadic anxieties or traversal of habitus clash that Hoggart articulated and Hanley reset, in the name of 'widening participation', Gabriel's necessary challenge is to see the intersectional marginalisation of the Black, female academic. As whiteness and maleness continue to trade with rich capital dividends, media literacy can only be inclusive for social justice if it starts out from a deconstruction of these 'interlocking systems of privilege and oppression' (Douglas, 2017: 1267). We might ask: Can the experience of the Black, female academic be seen to equate to that of Hoggart's 'scholarship boy', Hanley's 'joyless traipsing up the social ladder' (p. 147) or Hudson's 'vertiginous feeling' (p. 3)? Yet, clearly, our question resets the wrong order; it reduces, by proximal relation, the experience of the former to the vertical (white) discourse of the latter. Kwhali describes the lived experience of the 'accidental academic' without the means to trade whiteness:

I will never entirely reconcile the personal and political meaning of my race, class and gender within a higher education setting constructed around the epistemology of whiteness, maleness and class divisions... None of the institutions at which I have worked has attempted to understand how racial aloneness is experienced or how the knowledge that arises from my gender and race co-exists alongside the need to satisfy the white criteria of meaning. (Kwhali, 2017: 5,21)

As 'Why is my Curriculum White?' has cast its lens, we see that the experience of 'Us', described by Kwhali, is not only about being with Them and being in Their space but also about learning Their knowledge. The French Feminist Luce Irigaray complained that 'They never taught us nor allowed us to say our multiplicity. That would have been improper speech' (Irigaray, 1992: 207). Hoggart's scholarship boy is accepted into, but is then forever anxious in, an Enlightenment rhetoric—from the darkness of the Hunslet back street to the light of the academy *ex umbris in veritatem* (out of shadows into the truth). *The Uses of Literacy* does not seem to question this epistemology. Can media literacy education promote social justice, then, without directly challenging inequalities, without *Teaching to Trangress* (hooks, 1994)? Doesn't media literacy demand learning contexts that deconstruct power dynamics and oppression in both media and education itself?

Such work is underway, and it may be that our task is actually to move it from the margins of the field. Bali (2019) describes her situatedness:

As a postcolonial scholar teaching postcolonial students at a hybrid American/Egyptian institution, my approach to teaching digital literacies foregrounds reflections on identity and hybridity, a questioning of our own and others' biases while promoting empathy for 'the other', and an exploration of equity issues in real life and in the digital realm, before delving into digital literacies and topics such as fake news, privacy, data and algorithms. (2019: 70)

The UNESCO declaration on Media and Information Literacy includes an objective to 'enhance intercultural and interreligious dialogue, gender equality and a culture of peace and respect in the participative and democratic public sphere' (UNESCO, 2016). Clearly, this is more than a literacy competence. Rather, it's the *use* of literacy as social practice in everyday life. As we've stated, Hoggart's 'blind spot' was to the dynamic uses of literacy. Whilst media literacy is subject to static and narrow *educational* uses, not very different from in the 1950s, we see 'the masses' engaged, in the lifeworld, in much more agentive, dynamic literacy practices than did Hoggart, and we think this is not because those literacy practices, enabled by digital media, *are* necessarily more dynamic but rather that Hoggart's fixation on transition from 'good' working-class culture to the mass media rendered them passive and static. He did not view literacy as a set of lived practices. We *do* see media literacy that way. Nor do we see the digital as sovereign and approach media literacy from a sociology of the digital. Instead, we see media literacy as only the latest chapter in the ongoing project of renegotiating and better understanding what literacy means, how it is experienced, who is excluded from its educational framing and how that can change to include the people who are not silent but are not listened to. In this way, we are far more concerned, for media literacy, with 'drawing attention to the discursive frames that shape everyday lives and the literacy practices that are a part of them, and disrupting these frames through research and practice which challenges how they are set' (Jones, 2018: 14). This means that we are indebted to Hoggart for his attention to the duality of literacy and the lived experience of it in cultural transition, but we need to depart from his textual value hierarchies to bear witness to the more complex uses of *media* literacy.

12.4 Walking

Kate Pahl, in her deep ethnographies with families and communities around Rotherham, some 30 miles from Hunslet, accounted for the 'not yet' of digital literacies and the mediation of desires through media texts:

> This world of the home, of everyday cultures, is like the domestic embodied world that Hoggart also recalled and evoked in The Uses of Literacy. This space is full of sayings, practices, stories from the everyday, with oral cultures enmeshed with everyday practices and linked, through inscription, to writing. By seeing a space as constructed and a site of possibility, it is possible to imagine Rotherham as rich and alive with culture. It is this Rotherham I describe here, whilst recognising that the period Rotherham was currently going through as I was writing this book was intensely challenging, as services were cut back and benefits withdrawn from families. But the traces and echoes within this landscape, sites of previous industrial activity and stories circulating within communities challenge contemporary conceptualizations of culture. (Pahl, 2014: 16)

We can take Pahl's return to Hoggart together with Susan Jones' ethnographies of everyday literacies through a social justice lens and the intersectional, Black, feminist and postcolonial media literacy work in our field. That conceptual frame can further intersect with the emergence of posthuman ways of thinking about media, life and agency and the convergence of dynamic, third space media literacy with civic engagement and activism. These alliances and intersects can help us set out the 'uses of media literacy' as a richer, more nuanced set of lived experiences and objectives for change than competence models can account for.

Hoggart observed the longevity of hard conditions and analysed the battle between a resistant, internal culture and the powerful, strategic interests of commercial media from outside of the group, presented as inside, interpellated as 'us'— 'the gang's all here'. The resistance, in culture, was due to older, enduring values in and of the group rather than any coherent political movement. An epistemology of culture with a focus on transformation in social relations—as in the work of Kate Pahl and Susan Jones—seeks to articulate a different way of asking and answering questions. This assessment of the legacy of the original *The Uses of Literacy*, for Cultural Studies and, here, for media literacy, is about the importance of the enthusiasm of the discipline(s) to reinvent itself in the new problem space. This is our objective for the uses of media literacy.

This finessing of thinking on Cultural Studies and audience is available to later practitioners in a way that it was not at the time to Hoggart. He is, of course, endlessly reflexive in *The Uses of Literacy*, but not in the same way as the contemporary researcher. For a start, his trajectory is more or less unknown in a discipline which is just forming, and he is not seeking the ontological security of the modern, reflexive subject (Giddens, 1991). Hoggart's reflexivity is backward-looking, even as he is setting out the stall for much of what is to follow. At times he catches himself wandering into literary criticism, as in the long passage which links popular love songs back to the Elizabethan sonneteers, and yanks his own chain back towards the present popular cultural moment and the possible future foundation of Cultural Studies:

> It is true that this kind of assertion in love-poetry has a long history – the Elizabethan sonneteers, for example, employed this and many other conceits. But reminders of this kind do not really help much; we have to keep our points of comparison and development much more close and relevant. (Hoggart, 1957, p. 176)

Media Studies, Cultural Studies, literacies and media literacy, these 'problem space' unsettling projects, are, we would argue, often viewed in the same way still: not so much a 'curious coincidence' but part of the same excluding and self-perpetuating cultural power regimes that persist in both the academy and the media.

> As intersectionality has been increasingly taken up, discussions have focused on key questions, dilemmas and approaches to investigation. One is the challenge of making power visible. There is also the question of how to identify and work with categories, or vectors, of analysis, in coherent but sensitive ways. (Nichols & Stahl, 2019:3)

Intersectionality has been viewed as a political and theoretical lens, informed by critical race theory and legal studies, but is also subject to questions of method which are useful and applicable to media literacy (Springgay & Truman, 2019; Taylor & Ivinson, 2013; Hughes & Lury, 2013; Bhattacharya, 2009; Jones & Shackelford, 2013; Bhopal, 2017; Barad, 2006; Bell, 2012; Wargo, 2019). Sociomaterial developments in academic and educational literacy work posit an engagement with intersectional materiality as dynamic agency in social meaning. We thus need to understand 'working-class' uses of media literacy as more-than-human but also just as much stratified by inequality and power reproduction as 'just human' understandings. This amounts to decolonising the epistemologies of media literacy, as opposed to seeing it as in itself a decolonising project for literacy. However, this must be undertaken with the acceptance that it will not be a solution to power struggles and intersectional, automated inequalities, as Bhattacharya describes:

> Applying de/colonizing methodologies is akin to having pest control in my home. Even though my pest control man sprays once a month, I will never be completely free of pests. (2009: 1077)

Wargo writes about situated ethnography work with 'Gabe', who is observed performing the uses of media literacy as 'space-time-mattering'. This is media literacy *in use* as 'a constellation of unfolding and enveloping, a being/doing/knowing of the world' (2019:135). This kind of media literacy situates us as being always in the negotiation of knowledge about media and in mediation, returning to approaches we proposed in *After the Media* (Bennett et al., 2011), as we are 'part of what we study, not above or beyond what we observe' (Taylor & Ivinson, 2013: 128). In the intersectional and posthuman spaces of feminism, we can find valuable developments in the situated practices of 'patterning' literacy work. In this way, relations between people, media and literacy will always be transforming as they are learned and taught (see Bell, 2012: 17). This is a kind of 'doing text' (Bennett & McDougall, 2016): literacy is in movement and methods are walking, but they are always subject themselves to ethical and political challenge, as 'ethical and political domains of difference' (Springgay & Truman, 2019: 39).

Researching *dynamic* media literacies means employing approaches to engage social actors as researchers of their lived experience; it means reflecting on identity, to try to get to richer, more personal 'data', with all the ethical issues that are so often hidden 'below the line' in research; it means bearing witness to how 'people borrow and curate what is of interest to them in the "cultural stock" and then "mod" it and reflect their own interests and identities' (Cannon, 2018: 110).

Hoggart's original concerns were around the mechanisms behind the production and subsequent consumption of popular cultural texts for, and to an extent by, the working classes. He aimed to take the reader-observer through the complexity of cultural (re)production and representation in popular weekly magazines, weekly and daily newspapers and popular songs and to explore how these reached out to audiences, noting along the way that popular culture was, in some respects, breaking down divisions between lower and middle classes, even as the popular reading matter circulating was of low quality and 'holding people down', signalling Bourdieu's 'distinction' (1984, see also Grenfell & Pahl, 2018 and Lewis, 2021). In updating this to the present, we have to concern ourselves with the sites of cultural (re)production, how they have changed and how they are (at the very least) proposed as spaces for personal curation and co-production—the creation as well as the consumption of texts by all for all—within the promise of a converged culture. The focus, though, will initially have to be on the ways in which digital culture reaches *particular* audiences who remediate and produce cultural texts.

12.5   Coda: Springs of Action

Unbending. Adjective: not bending or curving; inflexible; rigid; refusing to yield or compromise; resolute; austere or formal; aloof.
Unhinge. Verb (used with object): to upset; unbalance; disorient; throw into confusion or turmoil; to dislocate or disrupt the normal operation of; unsettle.

Helpful ways of thinking awry from linearity and hierarchy which we can take from Deleuze and Guattari (2004) have informed feminism, intersectional literacies and posthumanism and are at work in the 'walking' approaches we want to apply to media literacy and its uses, to 'walk with Hoggart'. Whilst the field of media and cultural studies is increasingly rhizomatic (see Harper & Savat, 2016; Moores, 2018), the institutionalized educational framing of media *literacy* is yet to embrace these metaphors, as it also sidesteps the enduring issue of class. A foray in the media literacy field in this preferable direction is made by Fiona Scott's 'sociomaterial nexus analysis' of the media literacies of preschool children. Specifically pertinent for our focus is Scott's finding that:

> Middle-class parents of preschool children tend to engage in 'media practice schoolifica-tion', meaning that they engage with a child's interest in a media text and use it as the basis for engaging the child in 'school' or 'formal' literacies learning. In working-class families, the ways parents extend their children's engagements with media map onto operational, cultural and critical digital literacies and some traditional operational literacies, but in ways that tend not to overlap with the literacy practices common in formal educative settings. (2018: 341)

This is a kind of middle-class pedagogic 'rebending' of springs, but crucially, Scott's research does not support Hoggart's pessimism for the passivity of working-class engagement with mass media. Instead, we can see that the working-class family reception of media, their uses of media literacy, appears to be more of an assemblage; they 'plug in' to a wider repertoire than the restrictive schooled knowledge domain.

Whilst it may be merely coincidence, it is purposeful at this juncture to observe the use of 'unbending' in Deleuze and Guattari's work, as the order of 'arbolic' thinking they seek to disrupt with the rhizome. A feature of the arbolic system is, along with vertical, static and sedentary hierarchy, that it is unbending. The rhizome is an underground system of roots, connections, flows and assemblages, profoundly 'bending'. Hoggart was using the metaphor of bending/unbending differently; in his work, the springs of working-class cultural agency (his 'action') are straightened out in the gradual transition to an era of conformity to a passive media culture. But it is important to understand that 'rebending' those springs can only happen through media literacy, through a dislocation of their structural causality—in other words, thinking differently about the latent energy in the springs.

The media literacy project—through dynamic, 'walking' with texts—is surely more about *unhinging* than unbending, displacing the 'unifying object' as a situated practice of media literacy work as patterning. The act of unhinging presents an energy, so we might see the force of potential action in springs which branch out in unseen directions. People, things, texts and literacy are thus dislocated and deliberately unsettled (troubled) as we create new knowledge about them—thus moving the field out, sideways, underneath and across, to 'some useful action to improve things'.

Hoggart ends his own conclusion with the question of how freedom can remain meaningful as technology develops and makes us feel ever freer, when we may be less free.

There is much to disagree with in *The Uses of Literacy* and much to dispense with now, theoretically and politically, for the work of *media* literacy.

But this is still the question.

References

Bali. M. (2019). Reimagining digital literacies from a feminist perspective in a postcolonial context. *Media and Communication, 7*(2), 69–81.

Barad, K. (2006). Posthumanist performativity: Toward an understanding of how matter comes to matter. In D. Orr (Ed.), *Belief, bodies, and being: Feminist reflections on embodiment*. Rowman & Littlefield Publishers.

Bell, V. (2012). Declining performativity: Butler, whitehead and ecologies of concern. *Theory, Culture and Society, 29*(2), 107–123.

Bennett, P., & McDougall, J. (2016). *Doing text: Media after the subject*. Columbia University Press.

Bennett, P., Kendall, A., & McDougall, J. (2011). *After the media: Culture and identity in the 21st century*. Routledge.

Bhattacharya, K. (2009). Negotiating shuttling between transitional experiences: A De/Colonising approach to performance ethnography. *Qualitative Inquiry, 15*(6), 1061–1083.

Bhopal, K. (2017). Addressing racial inequalities in higher education: Equity, inclusion and social justice. *Ethnic and Racial Studies, 40*(13), 2293–2299.

Bourdieu, P. (1984). *Distinction: A social critique of the judgement of taste*. Routledge.

Buckingham, D. (2018). *The new left and youth culture*. www.davidbuckingham.net

Cannon, C. (2018). *Digital Media in Education: Teaching, learning and literacy*. Palgrave Macmillan.

Deleuze, G., & Guattari, F. (2004). *A thousand plateaus*. Continuum.

Douglas, J. (2017). The struggle to find a voice on Black Women's Health: From the personal to the political. In D. Gabriel & A. Tate (Eds.), *Inside the ivory tower: Narratives of women of colour surviving and thriving in British academia*. UCL Institute of Education Press.

Gabriel, D. (2017). Introduction. In D. Gabriel, & S.-A. Tate (Eds.), *Inside the Ivory tower: Narratives of women of colour surviving and thriving in British academia* (pp. 1–4). London, UK: Trentham Books / IoE Press.

Gee, J. P. (2015). *Literacy and education*. Routledge.

Giddens, A. (1991). *Modernity and self-identity: Self and society in the late modern age*. Cambridge.

Gregg, M. (2006). *Cultural studies' affective voices*. Palgrave.

Grenfell, M., & Pahl, K. (2018). *Bourdieu, language-based ethnographies and reflexivity*. Routledge.

Hanley, L. (2017). *Respectable: Crossing the class divide*. Penguin.

Harper, T., & Savat, D. (2016). *Media After Deleuze*. Bloomsbury.

Helsper, E. (2021). *The digital disconnect: The social causes and consequences of digital inequalities*. Sage.

Hoggart, R. (1957). *The uses of literacy*. Chatto & Windus.

hooks, b. (1994). *Teaching to transgress: Education as the practice of freedom*. Routledge.

Hughes, C., & Lury, C. (2013). Re-turning feminist methodologies: From a social to an ecological epistemology. *Gender and Education, 25*(6), 786–799.

Irigaray, L. (1992). *Elemental passions* (Collie, J., & Still, J., Trans.). Routledge.

Jones, S. (2018). *Portraits of everyday literacy for social justice: Reframing the debate for families and communities*. Palgrave.

Jones, S., & Shakelford, K. (2013). Emotional investments and crises of truth: Gender, class and literacies. In K. Hall, T. Cremin, B. Comber, & L. Moll (Eds.), *International handbook of research on Children's literacy, learning and culture*. Wiley-Blackwell.

Kress, G. (2003). *Literacy in the new media age*. Routledge.

Kwhali, J. (2017). The Accidental Academic. In D. Gabriel & A. Tate (Eds.), *Inside the Ivory Tower: Narratives of women of colour surviving and thriving in British academia*. UCL Institute of Education Press.

Lewis, M. (2021). *A critically-engaged syncretic language narrative of two building trades students and their families: Developing identity-resonance for self-actualising minorities' right to be, believe and belong.* Bournemouth University: Doctoral thesis: https://eprints.bournemouth. ac.uk/35201/

Littler, J. (2013). Meritocracy as plutocracy: The marketising of 'equality' within neoliberalism. *New Formations: A Journal of Culture/Theory/POLITICS, 80–81*, 52–72. https://doi. org/10.3898/NewF.80/81.03.2013

Livingstone, S., & Blum-Ross, A. (2020). *Parenting for a digital future: How hopes and fears about technology shape Children's lives.* Oxford University Press.

Matthews, C. (2019). 'Woke' and reading: Social media, reception, and contemporary Black Feminism. *Participations, 16*(1), 390–411.

McDougall, J., Bennett, P., & Potter, J. (2020). *The uses of media literacy.* Routledge.

Melki, J. (2018). Towards a media literacy of the oppressed. *The Media Education Research Journal, 8*(1), 5–14.

Mihailidis, P. (2018). *Civic media literacies: Reimagining human connection in an age of digital abundance.* Routledge.

Moores, S. (2018). *Digital orientations: Non-media-centric media studies and non-representational theories of practi.* New York: Peter Lang.

Nichols, S. & Stahl, G. (2019). *'Intersectionality in higher education research: a systematic literature review', Higher Education Research & Development,* https://doi.org/10.1080/ 07294360.2019.1638348

Pahl, K. (2014). *Materializing literacies in communities: The uses of literacy revisited.* Bloomsbury Academic.

Pahl, K., Rowsell, J., Collier, D., Pool, S., Rasool, Z., & Trzecak, T. (2020). *Living literacies: Re-thinking literacy research and practice through the everyday.* MIT Press.

Peim, N. (1993). *Critical theory and the English teacher.* Routledge.

Potter, J., & McDougall, J. (2017). *Digital media, culture and education: Theorising third space literacies.* Palgrave Macmillan/Springer.

Rancière, J. (2016). *The method of equality.* Polity Press.

Richards, B. (2017). *What holds us together: Popular culture and social cohesion.* Karnac Books.

Savage, M. (2015). *Social Class in the 21st Century.* London; Penguin.

Scott, F. (2018). *Young children's engagement with television and related media in the digital age.* University of Sheffield (PhD Thesis).

Springgay, S., & Truman, C. (2019). *Walking methodologies in a more than human world.* Routledge.

Street, B. (2003). What's "new" in new literacy studies? Critical approaches to literacy in theory and practice. *Current issues in comparative education, 5*, 77–91.

Taylor, C., & Ivinson, G. (Eds.). (2013). *Material feminisms; new directions for education.* Routledge.

Todd, S. (2014). *The people: The rise and fall of the working class.* John Murray.

UNESCO. (2016). *Riga Recommendations on media and information literacy*: http://www.unesco. org/new/fileadmin/MULTIMEDIA/HQ/CI/CI/pdf/Events/riga_recommendations_on_media_ and_information_literacy.pdf

Wargo, J. (2019). Lives, lines, and Spacetimemattering: An intra-active analysis of a 'once OK' adult writer. In C. Kuby, K. Spector, & J. Johnson Thiel (Eds.), *Posthumanism and literacy education: Knowing/becoming/doing literacies.* Routledge.

Williamson, B. (2016). Digital education governance: Data visualization, predictive analytics, and 'real-time' policy instruments. *Journal of Education Policy, 31*(2), 123–141.

Conclusion: Directions for Literacy Research in Precarious Times

Claire Lee ⓘ and Chris Bailey ⓘ

Mapping Trajectories

In Chap. 6 of this book, Chris Bailey presented us with a 'heat map' that was initially intended to visualise the routes he ran every day during the pandemic. Using this as a starting point, whilst drawing on Deligny's (2015) work on mapping, Chris implied that such visualisations can be useful in helping us to make meaning and extend our existing understandings of the world. Continuing to pursue this line of thinking, we suggest that it could be useful to think in terms of a similar 'heat map' in relation to literacy research and to consider how this would be expanded when populated by the terrain covered by the ideas in this book. Some of the metaphorical paths travelled by authors in this volume might overlay on existing thick, red lines—indicating established directions, albeit ones expanded on here in different ways or with a different emphasis. Other chapters might more likely be represented on our literacy heat map as thin, blue lines—indicating that these are newer, less well-trodden avenues. Whether the routes taken by the authors here are already established, or more tentative, in the places where the paths cross and intersect, it is possible to identify several key directions for literacy research that address the precarious nature of society's current challenges. In this conclusion, we do not intend to generate our own version of this heat map but invite the reader to visualise their own, perhaps thinking about how the directions taken across the chapters can help unsettle or extend their own personal literacy territories.

C. Lee (✉)
Children and Young People Network, Oxford Brookes University, Oxford, UK
e-mail: clairelee@brookes.ac.uk

C. Bailey
Sheffield Institute of Education, Sheffield Hallam University, Sheffield, UK

© The Author(s), under exclusive license to Springer Nature Singapore Pte Ltd. 2022
C. Lee et al. (eds.), *Unsettling Literacies*, Cultural Studies and Transdisciplinarity in Education 15, https://doi.org/10.1007/978-981-16-6944-6

Considering Context

This volume bears witness to a time of enormous precarity. When we started talking about this book in the spring of 2020, we recognised that we were living in a unique historical moment. We realised that with national lockdowns being enforced around the world, the COVID-19 pandemic would pose hitherto unimagined challenges to researchers, and it seemed important to understand how literacy researchers were responding to those challenges. However, we were also very aware of the intersecting precarities and inequalities that also defined the moment we were living in: systemic racism and the legacies of colonialism and slavery; climate disruption, collapsing biodiversity and pollution; disaster capitalism; economic instability and employment precarity; educational, health and digital inequities; increasing societal polarisation and rising extremism; and discrimination based on race, gender, class, sexuality, religion, age, disability or neurotype. For many, COVID-19 added an extra layer of marginalisation to lives which were already being lived on the margins. Understanding the roles that everyday literacies play both in maintaining those inequalities and injustices and, conversely, in foregrounding and disrupting them and reconfiguring power relations has, perhaps, never been more urgent and necessary.

Precarity, of course, is not confined to times of global pandemic, and all of the marginalisation, inequality and challenge listed above are ever-present in contemporary societies. In addition, precarity can be conceptualised in a broader and, perhaps, even more universal sense. Stewart's (2012) work in particular understands precarity as an ongoing, changeable and emergent state, positioning precarity as a mark of 'emergent phenomena', as a way of understanding events' 'plurality, movement, imperfection, immanence, incommensurateness, the way that they accrete, accrue and wear out' (p. 158). Understood in this way, a focus on precarity acknowledges that our lives on this planet are *always* lived in a state of precarity: unsettled, uncertain, delicate. We are, at any given moment, always on the verge of something else. Thus, our focus on precarity in this book has involved looking not only to the present and the past but also to the future. Stewart (2012) suggests that 'writing could be a way of thinking', a response or attunement to 'disparate and incommensurate things throwing themselves together in scenes, acts, encounters, performances, and situations' (p. 518). Each of the chapters presented here has been written, then, to help us, collectively, to think through and make connections between diverse issues around our various understandings of precarity in relation to literacies.

Whilst precarity is often deep-rooted and therefore often concealed, the very visible precarities that have defined experiences of the COVID-19 pandemic have also presented many with a call to action. In this way, far from being stories of despair, the chapters of this book are imbued with a sense not only of urgency but also of hope and possibility. Having seen the injustices and iniquities perpetrated by denial and apathy, our current generation is offered the opportunity to rethink society along kinder, more just and more sustainable lines. This opportunity challenges us as researchers to consider what kinds of literacies support people to live well with each other and the world. How can we think beyond the myths of social mobility, upward individual growth, hero narratives of human exceptionalism and the conquering of the planet? How can we support children to navigate the tensions between attaining the skills they require to succeed in precarious futures and the need to understand the interdependency between human and planetary survival? Part of this project is to imagine the kinds of literacy we need in a future we do not yet know. The troubling of what we know and the generative nature of not knowing, emergence and risk weave throughout this book in provocative ways.

In examining the paths being taken by literacies and literacy researchers, we are also challenged to consider the political and ethical dimensions of our research and the representation of our participants, which involves understanding our part in the production of knowledge and the ongoing colonising effects of that knowledge production. The thick red lines on the heat map are a helpful reminder that the paths we are travelling as researchers, educators, writers and editors are built not only on the achievements of those who have gone before but also on legacies of colonialism, marginalisation and oppression. Our focus on what is new in literacy research should not then occur 'at the expense of an understanding of the past in relationship with the present and future' (Gerrard et al., 2017, p. 388). And, looking to the future, we must ask how, as researchers, we are to avoid our research contributing to 'processes of closure and erasure: closed-off from the worlds and people being researched, whose histories and voices are obfuscated, displaced, and, at worst, erased' (Gerrard et al., 2017, p. 393).

Responding to the Chapters

We will begin our reflections by returning to this volume's final chapter, which will still be fresh in the mind of any reader who has worked chronologically through the book. 'Walking with Hoggart' by Julian McDougall, Pete Bennett and John Potter returns to Hoggart's (1957) influential text *The Uses of Literacy*. Here, the authors draw parallels between Hoggart's feeling of cultural 'uncertainty' and this volume's concern with 'precarity'. In this way, literacy research is described as an 'ongoing project of re-negotiating and better understanding what literacy means, how it is experienced, who is excluded from its educational framing and how that can change to include the people who are not silent but are not listened to'. By considering the relevance to the digital age of Hoggart's concerns with the lived literacy practices of working-class communities in the 1950s, McDougall, Bennett and Potter make the case for 'an intersectional, dynamic "take"' on Hoggart's sociomaterial approach. In many ways, by building on previous research and seeking to reframe and build on existing ideas in contemporary contexts, this chapter manages to distil the agenda set by the other chapters in this volume.

Running throughout this volume is attention to 'ordinary things that matter because they shimmer precariously' (Stewart, 2012, p. 519), a commitment to understanding the lived, everyday experiences of the unheard and hidden—and not as passive victims of oppression but as active and activist users of literacies who are disrupting mainstream narratives and authoring their own stories and futures. In Chap. 6, Chris Bailey writes about his experience of being diagnosed autistic during the pandemic lockdown in the UK. He makes a compelling argument for creative personal storying approaches that can illuminate lived experiences of those who have been misunderstood or misrepresented. He exemplifies how autoethnographic reflections on texts he encountered and created during that period not only offer an enriched understanding of the nature of neurodivergence but also shift normative perceptions of identity and worth.

It is these kinds of normative framings that pervade much schooled literacy experience. For example, as Cathy Burnett and Jennifer Rowsell have pointed out in the introduction to this volume, the UK primary school literacy curriculum focuses relentlessly on 'standard' English and grammatical terminology. This has led in many classrooms to the use of decontextualised grammar drills as test preparation and an emphasis on accuracy within prescribed norms over meaning-making (Lee, 2019; Safford, 2016). It is encouraging, then, to read Abigail Hackett, in Chap. 9, writing about children's literacies as they emerge in response to places and things rather than as steps towards a preknown, rational and controllable adult literacy. She argues that attending to young children's situated and entangled literacies opens possibilities for new understandings about what drives young children's language and literacy practices and how children can be in the world—not simply how they can progress rapidly towards the acquisition of certain skills. Similarly, in Chap. 7, Jana Boschee Ellefson and Kim Lenters write about children who, freed from the progress narratives and prescripted assignments of formal schooling, used spaces and materials to reach out to each other and their neighbourhood in spontaneous literacy events. The authors observe: 'youth and their assembled worlds are not *discussing* change, they are *doing*, *being*, and *living* it', in ways that are often invisible in traditional conceptualisations of schooled literacy practice. 'Their activism', write Boschee Ellefson and Lenters, 'speaks through their literacies.'

Another path taken in this volume is community research that blends activism and participatory inquiry in order to understand and foreground ways in which people take control of their own narratives, 'navigate dystopic structures' and imagine alternative futures. In their moving chapter on DIY media-making with 2SLGBTQ+ youth (Chap. 11), Casey Burkholder, Funké Aladejebi and Jennifer Thompson narrate how stencil production and drawing opened ethical and inclusive spaces in which young people could belong in their common resistance to reproductive injustice. They describe workshops in which the young people were supported in their activism at a local level, as well as ways in which they used social media platforms to reach a wider audience and call for much-needed reproductive justice and gender-inclusive health care. Central to this project was the need for attention to historical and ongoing intersectional injustices as well as for the researchers to be 'vulnerable with' the participants. These commitments are taken up by several of the authors throughout this volume.

Bethany Monea also describes supporting participants to story their own experiences; in this case, Latinx students create films about their transitions from high school to college. In Chap. 3, she reflects on the intricacies of digitally mediated participatory research in times of a pandemic, elaborating on ways in which the sociomaterial arrangements of screen sharing redistributed power within the group. She describes how students built a sense of community despite the fragmenting effects of their digital activity.

Michelle A. Honeyford, Shelley Warkentin and Karla Ferreira da Costa also narrate the unfolding of a community and process of inquiry in their discussion in Chap. 10 of a living process of curriculum design. Their work reflects Stewart's (2012) proposition that 'Writing culture through emergent forms means stepping outside the cold comfort zone of recognizing only self-identical objects' (p. 518). Shifting their emphasis away from the fixed notions of individual progress, expectations, outcomes and standards, they took a riskier, disruptive approach of collaboration, reimagining and agency. They reconceptualise curriculum as far more than a static, prescriptive framework; it is a living document, rooted in practice, about 'how we wish to live, act and be, individually and together in our local and global contexts'. They argue for openness to emergence, the new and the unexpected.

In Chap. 8, Linda-Dianne Willis and Beryl Exley also encourage us to remember that finding opportunities and methods to engage with stakeholders in research ultimately has the potential to reveal otherwise unforeseeable directions. They write about developing a collaborative 'metalogue' approach to reflect on the ethical and methodological challenges stemming from doing necessary but 'difficult' research. They explain how a desire to engage parents, community and students in inquiry around curriculum via social media led to challenges and tensions but also generated other opportunities for literacy teaching and research.

Similar themes are also taken up in Chap. 5, in which Amélie Lemieux, Kelly C. Johnston and Fiona Scott discuss the notion of 'diffractive reading'. Here, the authors explain how negotiating both the new conditions of working together via video call and the ever-changing identities they formed during the pandemic allowed them to develop what they term a methodology 'of the *other-wise*'. They exemplify a process of 'diff/reading' in which they read and responded to one another's data and came together to explore the alternative perspectives that emerged when data were read through different epistemologies, researchers' positions, situations, disciplines and embodied responses. Resonating with other work in this volume, this chapter reminds us again of the generative and generous nature of research that unsettles the certain and allows for risk, discomfort and openness to the 'what else'.

Reflexivity and attention to researchers' relationships with their research participants resonate throughout this volume. Sara Hawley and John Potter ask, in Chap. 2, whether research space can be rethought as a Third space. Addressing methodology and hierarchies in participatory literacy research, they talk of 'dwelling in possibilities' as a means by which to generate Third spaces in research practice. By drawing on their ethnographic work in playgrounds, the authors demonstrate how using methodological approaches involving media production, drawing on participants' existing skills, can help to flatten the hierarchies that exist between participants and researchers, helping us to consider how research practice can generate new meanings and productive new relationships.

In Chap. 4, Bronwyn T. Williams movingly describes how the shift to online research during the pandemic brought about different ways of being with research participants. Recalling the affective intensity of an interview he conducted during the pandemic, he considers how his affective experience of his conversation with Phillip—not simply as a researcher but as a fellow human—challenged him to rethink both the purpose and significance of his presence in the field and the ways in which the memories he was creating were shaping the self he was building as a researcher: 'Was I researcher as empathizer? Researcher as lifeline? Researcher as window to another world? Researcher as therapist?'

Unsettling our being and becoming as literacy researchers is also the focus of Chap. 1, in which Catherine Compton-Lilly writes reflectively and powerfully about the ways in which researchers have the power to decide which stories are told and which remain unheard. Compton-Lilly calls for us to 'unsettle' the field of literacy research, in part by reflecting on the field in which we, as researchers, operate within when conducting our work. Drawing on 'critical dimensions' of three students' trajectories from longitudinal data of studies relating to literacies and race, she reminds us that we need to acknowledge our limitations as researchers; she calls for us to 'peel back layers of analysis with an eye to the academic fields in which we operate, the social histories that define people's experiences and the humanity of participants'. How, she asks, have 'racism, colonization, inequity and cruelty… been part of our being and becoming as researchers'? She calls upon us to unsettle ourselves, to consider not simply 'how to *do* research, but how to *be* it'.

Final Thoughts

In this concluding chapter, we have sought to reflect on some of the strands that emerge, for us, following our readings of these chapters. Yet we are also acutely aware that the meanings we have made only skim the surface of the ideas on offer here whilst also being highly contextualised by our own individual relationships with precarity at this particular moment. Returning to our imagined literacy heat map, we believe that this volume serves to consolidate, complicate and extend the territories covered by the scope of literacy studies as a whole. However, we also suggest that these ideas will only take shape as part of this larger map if they are taken on by individuals. The most vital heat maps are *not* those that *we* have imagined but rather those that *you*, the reader, will ultimately make—individually and collaboratively—in relation to your own practice. Whether as researcher, educator or otherwise, we therefore encourage you to reflect deeply on your own readings of these chapters and to consider how the ideas presented here may help to guide you in developing your own trajectories as you navigate your particular pathways through precarity.

References

Deligny, F. (2015). *The Arachnean and other texts*. Univocal Publishing.

Gerrard, J., Rudolph, S., & Sriprakash, A. (2017). The politics of post-qualitative inquiry: History and power. *Qualitative Inquiry, 23*(5), 384–394. https://doi.org/10.1177/1077800416672694

Lee, C. (2019). 'I ain't no clue, but we learned it yesterday': Losing our way with the year 6 grammar, punctuation and spelling test. *Forum, 61*(3), 401–414. https://doi.org/10.15730/forum.2019.61.3.401

Safford, K. (2016). Teaching grammar and testing grammar in the English primary school: The impact on teachers and their teaching of the grammar element of the statutory test in Spelling, Punctuation and Grammar (SPaG). *Changing English, 23*(1), 3–21. https://doi.org/10.1080/1358684X.2015.1133766

Stewart, K. (2012). Precarity's forms. *Cultural Anthropology, 27*(3), 518–525.

© The Author(s), under exclusive license to Springer Nature Singapore Pte Ltd. 2022
C. Lee et al. (eds.), *Unsettling Literacies*, Cultural Studies and Transdisciplinarity in Education 15, https://doi.org/10.1007/978-981-16-6944-6

Index

© The Author(s), under exclusive license to Springer Nature Singapore Pte Ltd. 2022
C. Lee et al. (eds.), *Unsettling Literacies*, Cultural Studies and Transdisciplinarity in Education 15, https://doi.org/10.1007/978-981-16-6944-6

Lightning Source UK Ltd.
Milton Keynes UK
UKHW021832250522
403525UK00003B/217

9 789811 669439